A TRUE NUCLEAR
FAMILY

MARGARET WILLIAMS ASPREY

 www.trafford.com

North America & international
toll-free: 1 888 232 4444 (USA & Canada)
fax: 812 355 4082

This story of my life is dedicated to my beloved husband Larned Brown Asprey and to all my wonderful children: Pete, Betty, Barb, Bob, Peggy, Tom and Bill

Contents

Acknowledgments

I would like to acknowledge the help that was given to me in writing this book. I am grateful for many notes from and editing of the manuscript by my sister Kitty Kallal and many pictures from her husband Bob Kallal.

Also many thanks for finding time in their busy lives to edit sections of the book to my children Pete Asprey, Barb Asprey, Betty Strietelmeier, Peggy Asprey, Tom Asprey and Bill Asprey. I have used many of their suggestions and criticisms to good advantage.

Finally, I also owe a lot to Dee Davis who taught the class in writing that got me started and the reading sessions that kept me going.

Prologue

*Why are the girls in our family so different
from most women?*

An incident that happened on a "People-to-People Program" trip
to Mainland China with the American Nuclear Society in 1983,
induced me to start writing this story. In the early eighties when
the Chinese were first opening up to western societies, Larry and
I went on this trip for talks with the Chinese Nuclear Society. The
delegation consisted of nearly 50 men but only two women. (See
Chaps 19 and 25 for more on this trip) One of the wives who came
along asked me how I happened to get into such an unusual field for
a woman. I said that "'in our family, something like this just seemed
normal since two of my sisters are chemists, one has a degree in
physics, one was a statistician with math and physics degrees and
two of us are engineers." She then asked if there was something
about our family that led so many of us to enter such unusual fields
for women and I had to say that I really didn't know. Ever since then,
I have been trying to figure it out.

Our only brother, Grant, was a Navy jet pilot and aeronautical
engineer which is hardly unusual for a male. But somehow almost
all of the sisters one by one, gradually ended up in a technical field
even though some of them, such as Lydia (Economics) and Susie

(Dental Hygiene) tried to distance themselves from it. Once I tried to write up our parents' lives, thinking this might help me find some clues, but the notebook in which I was writing that was lost while we were building our current house. That left me very discouraged and nothing came of that effort. My sister Kitty gave me some notes about the family that she had written for her children and some family pictures for which I am grateful. I used some of her notes on the ancestors along with the family chart of our ancestors, which I made for our 50th anniversary in 1994 (Appendix A).

Seven Sisters: (bk l-r) Sally, Susie, Rosie
(fr l-r) Lydia, Kitty, Dottie, Margie

On NOVA, or a similar program, the other evening, I got one interesting clue as to why we might have taken these unusual paths. A man who has been studying the effects of testosterone on males and females came up with something noteworthy. It seems that testosterone is part of what makes the male brain develop differently from that of the female. He had observed that for most men the ring finger is longer than the pointer finger while the reverse is true in females. He concluded that this is also one of the results of testosterone. I looked at my hands and to my surprise, my finger lengths matched the male pattern rather than the female. We've also found that my twin daughters also have the male pattern in their hands. I hope to be able to compare hands with all of my sisters. For some time I've wondered if I got a greater amount of testosterone than usual since my interests are so different from most women. I'm larger than most and my voice is low for a woman. I can't tell you how many times I've been called 'Sir' over the phone, especially over the radio when I was learning to fly. I wonder if it's something in our genetic heritage that gave us more than the usual amounts of testosterone. Will try to check my sisters and daughters hands but haven't done it yet.

Long Range Background

A most interesting book that I have read recently is called "The Seven Daughters of Eve" written by Bryan Sykes, a professor of genetics at Oxford University in England. An example of the things that he has done was to prove through their genes that the polynesians came from SE Asia rather than South America which had been suggested because it was closer to Easter Island. He used the same methods that were used to identify a potential mitochondrial "Eve" in Africa of about 200,000 years ago. He has tracked the genes of Europeans using the female mitochondrial DNA and come up with seven potential 'mothers' of Europeans who must have existed at seven different locations over Europe and times when they would have lived, from about 5000 to 20000 years ago. He gave them all names and used what is known about life in the various periods to make them lively. The book offered for $200 to track a person's DNA to one of these seven 'daughters'. It was too expensive for me but several of my children heard about it, pooled their money and sent for me to have it done as a Mother's Day gift. Of course it will apply to all my children and to all my sisters too. The result was that our ancestress was determined to be the one that he called Katrine. She would have lived about 15000 years ago in northeastern Italy (above where Venice is now). And not surprisingly, the "ice man", recently found in the Alps, who lived about 5000 years ago, was also one of her descendants, making him also a very distant 'cousin'. To me that is exciting.

So there you have some ideas about our long range background. Certainly we mostly came fro Europe. Next we'll start off to look at what is known about our more recent ancestors over about the last 400 years. Maybe in time, we can even answer the question with which I started this introduction. What is there in our background or heritage that makes us females so different? Why are so many of the Williams' girls so interested and involved in scientific and technical fields? And that, despite the fact that stereo typically most successful technical women have small or no families, we almost all have large families, are enthusiastic about babies and have managed to stay married to the same men throughout our entire adult lives. In addition the seven girls have many Doctors, Scientists, Engineers, Computer Scientists, Architects and so forth among their children. So if this is in part a genetic heritage, it is continuing and is spread widely across the country.

Chapter 1

Ancestors, 1600-1957

Where Did We Come From?

Every child wonders about this. I know I did. My earliest memories are from Ferguson, a small town near St. Louis, MO. But how did we get there? According to family traditions, our background is mostly from the British Isles with additions from France and Germany. But given what has been learned from genetics, we're all originally from Africa and all people are descendants of those few ancestors. From what we are learning from genetics, all of humankind is more closely related than was originally realized. I've found it fascinating to read about the African mitochondrial Eve of about 200,000 years ago from whom all humans are descended. Not quite the Adam and Eve of the Bible or Koran but pretty close.

I've also been interested to read more recently, about the 'Seven Daughters of Eve' who as 'mothers' lived from about 5000 to 20000 years ago in different parts of Europe as was explained in the Prologue. I also took a genealogy course in July 2002 and learned how to look ancestors up on the internet. What I found there mostly confirmed our family traditions. Family legends ware quire correct about Atkinsons and Massons in Hamilton, Canada, and Russell's in New Bedford, Connecticut.

Mom's Side. Winers

One particularly fascinating ancestor was Dr. Andrew Winer who was a Surgeon with the German Hessians that the British 'hired' to help defeat those upstart Americans during the American Revolutionary War. Being a surgeon must have been extremely difficult during war in the days before anesthesia and knowledge of sepsis. I mentioned this ancestor to a friend when I was in Germany and his comment was "Yes I know about them. Their King 'sold' them to the British to fight their war for them."

Although he was on the losing side, when the Revolutionary War ended Dr. Winer decided to stay in the new world rather than returning to Europe. I found him in Philadelphia, Pennsylvania, in the first US Census of 1790. After this, he apparently married Phoebe Dickinson (by family tradition, the daughter of an American Captain who had served in the Revolutionary War) and they moved to Hamilton, Ontario, Canada. There he established a pharmaceutical company which may still be in existence today.[1] Our Grandmother, Sarah (born 1858), who lived with us as we were growing up, would probably have been his great granddaughter.

Captain Masson

Sarah's Mother, Maria Louisa Winer (born 1828), granddaughter of Dr. Winer, married a ship's captain, John Masson (born 1819), nearly ten years older than she. This marriage may have been doomed from the start since, in addition to the age difference, he

---

[1] Canadian biographical Dictionary, Ontario Volume, Pub 1880, Am. Biog. Publishing Co., Toronto, Chicago & New York

was away at sea a lot and she was apparently a party girl at heart as well as being a rather spoiled little rich girl. Not too much is known about John Masson's background, except that he was born in 1819, exactly where I don't know, but he was of Scotch descent. The name 'Masson' is by family tradition supposed to have come from the French word 'maison'. Also by family tradition, his ancestors were French Hugenots who fled to Scotland from southern France to escape religious persecution. Recently on the history channel it was mentioned that about 200,000 Hugenots fled from Southern France at that time, so this seems definitely a likely possibility. Interestingly enough, these same Hugenots refugees are also the tradition of my husband's family name, Asprey. On a map of Southern France, one time, I found a mountain range named Aspre, which may have been the source of his name.

Despite the lack of knowledge about his background, there are many interesting stories about Captain Masson. One of the family treasures is a beautiful silver coffee and tea service which was awarded by insurance companies to Captain Masson. This award was for a dramatic rescue that he made in 1853 of the wooden docks of Hamilton, Canada, from a burning ship, 'Queen of the West'. He tied a rope from his ship to the burning ship and towed it out into the middle of the bay where it could burn out harmlessly and no endanger the local docks. The inscription on the silver service reads:

Presented to

Captain John Masson
By Certain Insurance Companies and others
interested in Property endangered by the
conflagration of the Steamer "Queen of the West"
on the Ninth Day of July 1853 in testimony of his
systematic and zealous services on the occasion.

Captain Thomas Masson Silver Award

Captain Masson is also reported to have sailed between Canadian and American ports on the great lakes as well as to England and apparently to Charleston, South Carolina. One intriguing story that I've heard (but which may not be completely authentic) Maria Louisa with her daughter sailed on the ship, to Charleston, SC. Maria Louisa loved dancing and one night when she was at a ball in Charleston, her husband came to her and said: "We will be sailing at dawn, and you must be ready to leave. The tide is right and we can't wait." She said, "No, no, I am having too much fun. Surely you can wait another day." He replied, "No I can't. The northerners are coming to blockade the port. We're from Canada, a neutral country but if I'm caught in a blockade, I will almost certainly lose my ship." Since the American Civil War seemed about to begin (which it soon did), it is easy to understand and sympathize with his concern, but he did choose his ship over his wife and child. Or one could put it the other way, she chose her 'fun' over his ship which was his, and her, livelihood At any rate, she didn't believe him and when he sailed on the tide at dawn he left her behind with her toddler.

History does not tell how they got back to Canada, probably overland, or found another ship to take them back, but we know they must have gone back North. That would likely have been the end of the marriage. At any rate, after they got back to Canada and the marriage was broken, Maria and her only baby daughter Sarah were welcome to move back in with her well-to-do parents where Sarah now grew up to adulthood. Louisa was a convert to Catholicism from Episcopalianism and managed to arrange to send Sarah to a convent school run by French nuns so she learned to speak Parisian French. They even had one day a week on which they could speak only French. She also learned to play the piano and the harp. I always wished that I could have heard her play the harp which fascinated me, but it was long gone by the time she lived with us.

One of my sisters tells of a time when Sarah was an adult and her father wrote and asked to meet her. Sadly, her Mother had so poisoned her mind against him that she refused to even see him. Louisa's granddaughter, our mother Dorothy, once asked her grandmother Louisa what her grandfather had done that was so bad. She replied "Oh Dorothy, he had a violent temper. Once he became so angry that I saw him rip his glove!" Captain Masson is reported to have died in 1902 as a lighthouse keeper somewhere on the New England coast, never to see his daughter again.

The Atkinson Family

Sarah Masson married a man named, John Arthur Atkinson. Although he was born in Ireland (in 1854), he was descended from a long line of British lawyers who lived in White Haven, England. His parents, Isaac and Ellen Smythe Atkinson with most of their eight children, migrated in 1864 to Hamilton, Canada, and later to

Chicago where Isaac managed a very successful meat packing plant. Their third son (our Grandfather), John Arthur (also called Jack), stayed behind in England to finish his education but eventually joined them in Canada where he met his wife to be. After John Arthur and Sarah were married (1879) in Hamilton, Canada, a friend who owned a railroad, lent them his private railroad car to travel to Chicago via Niagara Falls on their honeymoon. John Arthur then worked with his father in the meat packing plant. In 1880, his father, Isaac, died of a heart attack when taking his usual morning swim in Lake Michigan and John Arthur took over managing the plant.

According to family oral tradition, there was malfeasance by the senior partner, Davis, in England. At any rate their meat packing business crashed in 1884. John Arthur continued to operate on the Chicago Board of Trade where he was the youngest member for many years. In later years he managed meat packing plants in Omaha, NB, Kansas City, and Hutchinson, KS. In 1895, the family returned to Chicago where John Arthur was Chicago manager for awhile for Sir Thomas Lipton's Tea Business. Eventually they again returned to Kansas where John Arthur died in 1913. Mom told about being fortunate to know him for a year or two after she graduated from high school and before he died. She quoted him as telling her that "if you learn to love reading you will be educated even if you do not have the opportunity of advanced education". She also quoted him as saying that "I cannot be insulted because, a gentlemen wouldn't and nobody else could". He sounds like a person who I would like to know.

Jack and Sarah had five children, four of whom lived to adulthood: Isabelle, Jack, Arthur and the youngest of whom was my Mother, Dorothy. When Sarah's husband Jack died in 1913, there was no insurance, social security or pension, to help her survive herself, or to educate or launch her two remaining children, Dorothy (19) and Arthur (20) The older children, Isabelle and Jack, were already grown and married and living back in Chicago. For Isabelle there had been an elaborate society wedding. For Dorothy there was no money even for education. Arthur was able to become an apprentice in an architect's office and went on to build hospitals and other large buildings in Tulsa, OK. Dorothy however was another story. Mom used to tell a lovely story or this period in her life. One day she and Arthur were moving some furniture down some stairs and wrangling over it the way siblings will. This got to be too much for Sarah. She called to them "Arthur, Dorothy, come down here." Then when they were down, she said "I will not have this arguing. You two must get along. I will do whatever I have to do to stop it. I am going to have a happy home if I have to make it a hell on earth to do it" Well this was too much for Arthur who burst out laughing. A hell on earth to have a happy home was just a joke to him.

Sarah had been raised in a wealthy family where she was not even allowed in the kitchen. As an adult, she was part of the financial aristocracy in Chicago, socializing with people like the Swifts, Armours, Potter Palmers, Sir Thomas Lipton and Thomas Edison. According to Sarah, Marshall Fields was just a tradesman and not part of society! Her education was not at all practical. She had musical training and played the piano and harp. She spoke French but did not know how to cook or clean. As the lady of the house, in the morning the cook would come to the morning room and Sarah would tell her what they wanted for dinner. The cook would then go away, buy what she needed, cook it and serve when ready. It sounds a lot like the household in the Masterpiece Theater Play, "Upstairs, Downstairs". But everything changed when the money was lost. She later told us of cooking a chicken without drawing it! and also of being left with 'only' two footmen and two 'ignorant' Irish girls for help. When her daughter wanted to find a job in 1913, she said flatly 'ladies don't work'. After much argument, Dorothy persuaded her mother that being a librarian was "ladylike" enough. So she took training classes at the public library and began work as a librarian. For most of the rest of her life, Sarah lived with us and we children loved her dearly.

Dad's Side, the Russells

As to my father's side, probably the most interesting ancestor, and one who can be traced back the farthest, was Joseph Russell, Sr, who was the founder of the town of New Bedford, CT. According to his family tradition, his ancestor Ralph Russell was one of a pair of twins who were younger sons of the Earl of Bedford. They came to the New World around 1600 to seek their fortunes, because by English primogeniture law, as younger sons, they would get nothing from their father's estate. In case you think this is so old fashioned and exaggerated that it has no relevance today, I recently heard a story from a German friend to the contrary. Before the beginning of the Second World War in Germany, her grandfather had been quite wealthy, owned a factory, with about 30 employees, and several large houses. After the war ended they were in the British sector of Germany when her grandfather died. Under British primogeniture law which was applied in their section of Germany, everything he had owned went to an older daughter, nothing even for the widow and nothing for the rest of the children. Everyone assumed she would be honorable and share but not so. She sold everything, and took off for another country leaving nothing for her Mother or her siblings! But under the law she had the right to do it and no one could stop her. At any rate the primogeniture law got our ancestor Ralph Russell, to this country.

Of the Russell family descended from Ralph, five generations remained in New Bedford but according to oral tradition, one of them, Seth Russell, fought at the battle of Lexington and Concord. Our great grandfather, Charles Butler Russell was born in New Bedford in 1836 to Alice Hathaway Butler and George Russell but he moved as a child with his family to Covington, KY. There, in 1866, he married Susannah John. Susannah (b 1842) was a descendant of Thomas and Sibiella John, her great, great grandparents, who immigrated to Chester County, PA. from Wales in 1745. Later they moved to Mononghela County, (now West) Virginia, then to Kentucky. Charles and Susannah had two daughters, Lydia (b 1867) and Susanna who was younger. Unfortunately their mother Susannah died in 1874 while they were still quite young. Their Grandmother John took over the care of the girls for a while. But, a few years later their father Charles, moved to Cincinnati, OH, and there married a second time.

His new wife was unwilling to take on a new family and insisted the girls be put in a boarding school and sent the grandmother packing. When he married this new wife, one of his friends told him that if he married her he would only be sorry once—and that would be always! But he married her anyway. She must have been quite something! So the two poor little girls were essentially raised without a mother and without even much attention from their father. The older one, Lydia Russell, was my Grandmother. My mom told a tale she had heard from Lydia about when she began menstruating and had no one to turn to. She was crying in the bathroom, thinking that she was dying. A kindly Jewish girl in the school found her and told her what it was all about and how to take care of herself. Things like this are bound to have an effect on a young girl. On the other hand I have a Gold Medal which she received for 'Elocution' in 1882. So she had some successes. I remember her as a quiet and rather withdrawn but competent person. In an early attempt to say "grandmother", I named her "GraGra", which she was called from then on. She and our grandfather, Grant Williams, were married in Cincinnati, OH in 1891.

Williams Family

Now we come to our family name, Williams. I find it very interesting how fast the female family names disappear leaving only the male names. Of my great, great grandparents, we don't have the last names of three out of 16 women and beyond that we have almost none. Grant Williams was descended from a long line of John Williams (I, II, III, IV) who lived in New England first in Connecticut and then in Darien, New York. Since Williams is such a common name, a trace is a little hard to sort out. John Williams, IV, in 1839 went from Darien, NY, to take up 'new land' in the Wisconsin Territory, leaving his wife, Anne Carter and his older boys to manage their old farm until he could send for them. In time they helped found Darien, WI. Later, a younger son, Orange Williams, married Mary Stone from Vermont. Their son, Grant Williams, born in Darien, WI, in 1865, was our grandfather.

As an adult, Grant moved to Chicago where he was an accountant with the Chicago, Milwaukee, St. Paul and Pacific Railroad. He was musically inclined and played classical music on the violin in a local quartet. He met and fell in love with a young lady, Lydia Russell, who was visiting from Ohio. She apparently had a beautiful voice and he heard her sing. They were married in her father's home in 1891 in Cincinnati, Ohio. They then built a house in Edgebrook across from a golf course on the far North side of Chicago. Here they raised two sons, Russell John and Grant Erwin (known to the family as Bob for some mysterious reason). My mother told about seeing Bob working on a car while Russell sat reading an Encyclopedia (one of his favorite activities). Every once in a while Bob would come in and tell his brother what the car was doing. "What should I do now?" After a bit of discussion, Bob would take off to try something suggested by Russell.

Differences Between Brothers

'Bob's' family was extremely different from Russell's. His wife, our Aunt Ella, insisted on having only one child, Barbara Jean, who was supposed to be raised 'perfectly'. Aunt Ella was very contemptuous of our mother for having so many children. Our cousin, Barbara Jean, was about a year younger than I and their house was completely different from our madhouse. Ella insisted on the house being neat at all times. If her Husband was reading the newspaper and got up to answer the phone, on his return he would find the paper neatly folded and put away. If he lay down on the couch to read, she would come and lift up his feet and put an old paper under them to keep the couch 'clean'.

We only played with Barbara Jean when we were visiting our Williams grandparent' s house since they lived about a block away in Edgebrook. Barbara Jean and her cousins (us) were only allowed in the kitchen and her bedroom. You had to clean your feet before you entered something we never bothered with at home. As she got older they were members of the Country Club and she had the most elegant gowns for the high school proms. We couldn't even go to proms let alone belong to a Country Club. When she got a little older, she married a man who apparently thought her parents were wealthy. When in her 20's she developed atherosclerosis and was in a wheel chair, he eventually found out the truth about the family finances and couldn't tolerate a cripple for a wife so left her. Her parents remodeled their house so they could handle her wheel chair and take care of her until she died, I think, in her late 20's, and they had no grandchildren. A very sad story but it just shows you never can know the future and it is not easy to know what is really important. So we were the only grandchildren Grant and Lydia had left, but fortunately there were lots of us.

Grandfather Grant Williams died early at the age of sixty in July of 1925. Although I was only four when he died, I vaguely remember him as a cheerful, happy-go-lucky, outgoing person. Apparently he particularly appreciated his granddaughters since he had no daughters of his own. He insisted on fencing our play yard in Ferguson to keep us safe. His widow, Lydia (Gragra), was a quiet and rather austere and withdrawn person very different from her husband. She was very active in the community, serving on many boards of charitable organizations. She was said to have gathered food to take into the inner city using her widow's pass on the train, so the children would have something to eat. She continued to be independent and worked as secretary to an organization of railroad veterans. My sister Sally tells me that according to our Mom, Gragra was 'practically the minister" of a local, nondenominational community church, teaching the children and preaching at services. One year she was named the Chicago, "Woman of the Year" (for what year and doing what I don't know, although it may have been for feeding poor children). She lived in the home that her husband built until she died at the age of 90 in June of 1957.

Finally, an interesting member of their household was Auntie Richards, which is, oddly enough, all the name that I know for her. She came to help when our Dad, Russell, was born and she never left until she died. There were always things to do of course and I guess she became the housekeeper when the boys were older. I remember 'helping' her make bread and the taste of the dough and the smell of it rising are still with me. She was always very good to me. What her background was and where she came from is something that I've never heard anything about. But she was usually in the kitchen as part of the family, had her own small room in the back of the house, and was always there until she died.

Chapter 2

Two Little Girls
Across the Generations,
1858-1998

There are two little girls that I wish I could introduce. I think they would enjoy playing together since both are only children and their Dads are away a lot. These two are important people in my genetic inheritance, one is the oldest person that I've known well and the other currently is the youngest member of my family. Under the circumstances of course, it isn't possible to actually introduce them, so I will tell you about them and introduce them in this story. Sarah was born in 1858 over 70 years before I was born and the other, Amelia, in 1998, over 70 years after I was born. Through knowing them I can reach across the generations to reach my past and my future.

Sarah Masson (Gaga) and Amelia Asprey (Mimi)

Sarah Elizabeth Masson—1858

The first little girl, my grandmother, Sarah Masson, was born on June 7, 1858 in Hamilton, Ontario, Canada. Her father, Captain John Masson, who has been described previously, was gone a great deal when she was small and before long her parents broke up and she never saw him again. Her mother, Maria Louisa Winer, was nine years younger than her husband and was the daughter of a wealthy businessman and pharmacist. When the marriage broke up, Maria Louisa, with her daughter Sarah, moved back to her parents home where Sarah was now raised in the lap of luxury but also, for a child, in a very restricted lifestyle. For example, she was never allowed in the kitchen where the servants were busy and did not want a small child in the way. She told of standing on a chair, with a friend, to peek over the top of the door into the kitchen to see what was going on. When she was a little older, she went to a convent boarding school where she learned to play the piano, the harp and to speak

Parisian French, all proper accomplishments for a young lady. But seldom was she allowed just to be a child and play.

When Sarah's first grandchild John, my oldest cousin, tried to say 'grandmother', he came up with 'Gaga'. Typically for her relaxed attitude about life, she cheerfully accepted being referred to by what was then generally regarded as meaning 'crazy'. And from then on she was never called anything else. When I was a child, next to my Mother, Gaga was the most important adult in my life and probably even the one to whom I felt closest. She was also the oldest member of my family that I ever knew. She bought children's books in French and read to us. I even remember the name of one of the books, "La Maison de Madame Souris". She set nursery rhymes to music and played the piano for us to sing along and dance. When I was in first grade, for the annual Christmas pageant, she played some of her creations on the piano while Kitty and Dottie (my next younger sisters) and I sang them. There was then no Sesame Street for us to watch. She bought children's music books and showed me how to read the notes and play the piano. To her I owe the pleasure of the several hours a day that I now play the piano.

She loved to play board and card games, such as bezique, cribbage, hearts and backgammon, and was always more than willing and eager to play with us. She and my mother both were chess addicts and would play whenever Mom had some free time. Gaga even taught me how to play chess, although I was never the addict they were. I remember them playing on the kitchen table while Mother was doing the ironing that was needed for so many girls. Gaga used to say that she would get up off her deathbed to play another game of chess.

When I was in high school and college, she had the only family radio and would let me do my homework in her room while listening to the radio and, I guess, keeping her company. I particularly remember studying Differential Calculus there. In the last years of her life, her eyes began to fail so she couldn't even read although she still could and did play card and board games. And of course she loved to listen to the radio. She particularly enjoyed listening to President Franklin D Roosevelt's Fireside Chats in the 1930's. She of course was a Democrat while my parents were both staunch Republicans who hated Roosevelt. I remember many arguments about this. I'm sorry that I don't have a picture of her as a child but only of her as a young woman. In the 1800's photos were not very common.

Amelia Marie Asprey

The other little girl, Amelia Marie Asprey (my youngest granddaughter, also called Milmi at her request when she was about two), was born August 11, 1998 in Spokane, Washington, USA. Her father, is my youngest son, William (Bill) Asprey. He has health problems and isn't always able to work and has often been away trying seeking help for his problems. Her mother, Susan (Susie) Henry is from Bloomington, IL, and is a high school science teacher. For many years she taught in Alamagordo, NM where they were only an hour away and often visited us so we saw much of Mimi when she was small. Now Sue is teaching science in Hoquiam, WA. where they now live.

The story of Mimi's birth is a very exciting if frightening one for her parents. She was due to be born in early October. So in August, thinking they had two months to wait, her parents went camping in Idaho, with their two big black Labrador dogs, Ruby and Lulu. Right after they set up camp and fixed dinner on the fire, unexpectedly Sue's water broke! As fast as possible they packed up their things and drove to the nearest small town for help. But there was nothing there but a small clinic with no doctor. And since the baby was coming this early, they felt they should drive immediately to the next largest town. On the way to this town, a large moose ran into the road and stopped in front of them. They chased him away and continued on their urgent way, but for a few years, they called Amelia "Moose" in memory of this incident.

In the next town, the available doctor also did not feel competent to handle such an early delivery so told them that the expectant mother should be airlifted to Spokane, WA, the closest big city. And of course, Bill wanted very much to go with her but what to do with Ruby and Lulu? Finally after much calling and searching they found a really good samaritan who had the courage to keep two strange dogs in an emergency! And off they flew to Spokane. There Amelia came into the world healthy, despite being nearly two months early. Still at four and a half pounds, she was amazingly close to a normal weight for one born so early. Being under five pounds, that was still considered premature so she had to stay in the hospital for a few weeks until she built up some weight. Her mother Susan was soon released but now unfortunately, they were far from their home in southern Washington. And their truck and the dogs were still back in Idaho where they had been camping. With no family in the area to help out, they found a cheap motel not too far away where they could be close by and could visit the hospital every day. Sue could nurse the baby and they could bond with their new born.

Bill now went back to Idaho to retrieve the truck and the dogs and bring them back up to Spokane where they were now staying. After a few weeks, they were able to convince the medical insurance company that if the baby were moved by ambulance to the small town hospital closer to their home, where she was supposed to have been born in the first place, it would cost them less, even with the cost of the ambulance, than if she stayed in the hospital in the much larger city of Spokane. And of course, the parents could then stay at home. After a few more weeks, they were finally able to bring their new baby home. We are all very pleased that she has grown rapidly and as far as is possible to tell, she has had no ill effects from her early entry into life. She is now a lively and happy grade schooler and is having the fun of learning to read. For a long time we were so fortunate to have them only about an hour's drive away so they could visit often and we could have the pleasure of watching her grow and develop into the delightful little person that she has become. Occasionally, we may still hear them l call her 'Moose' in memory of that wild night when the moose stopped in front of their truck.

Comparison

Sarah lived in what was an agrarian society when around 70% of the people were engaged in agriculture producing food. By the time I was born, the industrial society was well under way and only about 50% of the people were needed to produce food for all of us. Finally Amelia lives in what they call the information society and only about 10% of farmers furnish food for what is now a much larger population. The knowledge needed to make this transition has doubled many times over the period of a century and a half.

Chances are that Mimi is the last of our grandchildren and of course is currently the youngest. She is a very outgoing and friendly person and likes to have friends to play with. So now you have met the two little girls, the oldest and youngest members of my family that I have known well. Since they are both single children and their fathers weren't always available, they have many things in common. On the other hand, the 140 years between their births, mean that they have had astonishingly different lives. And of course they can only meet in my memory.

When Sarah was born, almost all transportation was via horses or on foot, except for the railroads that were beginning to be built. She told of her grandparents' horse drawn carriage being the finest in the town, so when Queen Victoria visited the area, their carriage was used for her transportation. When Sarah was to be married in August 1879, her Grandmother (Sarah Winer), took her to New York City to buy a trousseau and, I believe, a piano. They probably took the train part way but otherwise it would have been by horse drawn carriage or by boat to cross a lake. Overseas transport was only by sailing ships and that could take months so was only undertaken for extreme reasons.

The atom and chemistry were still alien concepts. Of course, there were no TV, movies, radio, phones or computers. Autos, buses, planes, any kind of motorized transport other than trains, were unknown. Electricity had not yet been put to practical use, certainly not in houses, although I'm sure they saw it flashing during thunder storms as we still do. The moon was not something you 'go to' but a ball of light up in the sky. In fact it was the principal light at night except for fireplaces and candles. There was no indoor plumbing and in Canada's cold winters, I'm sure it was no fun to go to the outhouse or do the laundry! At night one would use a chamber pot under the bed which would then have to be emptied in the morning. Cooking would have been done over a wood stove. Since they were lucky enough to have servants to do the work, she and her mom would not have done any of this. There were no canned goods to use in an emergency. All sewing was done by hand. Knitting would have been an important skill and Sarah became a very competent knitter and taught me to knit. A house would have been heated by wood burning fireplaces and so would mostly be pretty cold all the time particularly in winter. There were no gas furnaces, certainly none with temperature controls to turn them on and off as needed. So many things that we take for granted had yet to be invented or developed.

Halfway Between

Even in my childhood (halfway between their birth dates), many things, common today, still didn't exist. We thought that we were very modern because we had electricity and indoor plumbing. We had no refrigerator and only had ice cream if Dad made a special trip to get it at the drug store for Sunday dinner. We had one auto, of which I have no idea of make or year. An occasional small plane flew overhead. Such a plane could well have belonged to Charles Lindbergh who at one time lived up the street from us. Also we were not too far from the local airport. His flight across the Atlantic, in the Spirit of St. Louis, happened when I was about seven.

We had one telephone, firmly fastened to the wall and was used only for business or emergencies, of course. When I was a baby, my Dad had put together a crystal radio set just for fun but practically nothing was broadcast so it was little more than a toy to me. I remember an early joke on radio in the early 30's. One man said "Last night I got New York on the radio" another said "That's nothing I stuck my head outside and I got Chile". I don't remember whatever happened to Dad's 'toy' radio but I don't remember listening to it. Some of my younger sisters do remember listening it it later when there were enough stations to be worth while. Before 1930, when I was nine years old, I had rarely listened to a radio or been to a movie. I had ridden in a car and on a train once or twice but never in a plane.

The Rest of the Seventy Years

And what has happened since to make Mimi's life so different! The 2nd World War finally ended with the dropping of the Atom Bomb that my husband and I helped develop (See Chapters 8 and 9). Now atoms and chemistry did mean something very important! Now 20% of the electricity in our country is produced by the energy of the atom. Plastics have become omnipresent. Computers started during the Second World War, too and development continued to the point where at seven years of age, Mimi has frequently used one. Telephones are so ubiquitous that we all have one with us almost all the time. Being more a product of the previous age, I'm still not used to carrying a phone around all the time as the young people do. I can't use one as easily and efficiently as they do although I try. Copiers (xeroxes) and faxes are routine and taken for granted. Typewriters came and went during the period. While trains and ships have become less important, we think nothing of flying half way around the world on jet planes. I personally have flown to China, Australia, Africa and Europe several times

When Amelia was born, her mother-to-be was transported by helicopter to the hospital for her birth. The average home now has several cars. On the omnipresent TV, we have watched men walk on the moon. Now they are even talking about humans going to Mars. At the time this book is being written, they have robots exploring Mars under human control and sending back up close pictures.

In some ways Amelia is very different from Sarah in that she is a budding biologist, probably influenced by her scientist mother. I've watched her hold and stroke tenderly a dead lizard. I watched her let a snail crawl all over her hand and arm. One time Bill's dog found a dead mouse under a chair in the living room. When Mimi checked to see what the dog had found, she immediately got a paper towel and pulled it out for everyone to see, without the slightest sign of fear or loathing, before disposing of it. At six when she heard that her grandfather's body was being donated to a medical school and heard why, she wanted to go to the autopsy and watch it be dissected and studied. I can't imagine Sarah doing, or wanting to do, any of these things, while Amelia is eager to do them.

Our homes are completely different. We take it for granted that we will have electricity to run all sorts of appliances, such as lamps and other lights, toasters, refrigerators, freezers, dish washers, washing machines and dryers. We take indoor plumbing completely for granted and only use outhouses in parks or when camping. We do our sewing by machine and most of our clothes are readymade. Ironing of clothes, which used to be a major chore when I was a child, is almost never done because of the chemical changes in making materials. Zippers, velcro and other fasteners have mostly replaced buttons, hooks and ties. We cook with gas, electricity or microwaves. Microwaves, which only arrived in the 1970's, are so convenient that they are the major source of heating of food. Canned, dried, frozen and other preprocessed foods are usually available for emergencies. Most people don't wash dishes by hand but use an electric dishwasher. We take for granted that we will have gas, electric or oil furnaces to keep the house warm and usually under automatic temperature control.

Somehow, however, I am sure that the two little girls, Sarah (b 1858) and Amelia (b 1998) would enjoy playing together despite the fact that their worlds are so different materially. Babies are usually still born the same way from the love of a man and woman. Their parents, families and friends are still very important to them. They would still enjoy running, jumping and exploring. They would enjoy dolls, music, books and games. Those things change very little over the years.

Chapter 3

How Our Parents Met and Married, 1900-21

M y parents met while they were still in their teens. My mother's older sister Isabelle had married Fayette Soule, originally from Grande Haven, MI. At the time they lived next door to Grant and Lydia Williams, my father's parents, in Edgebrook on the north side of Chicago.

When our maternal grandmother, Sarah, with her younger children, Dorothy and Arthur, visited her older daughter's family, (probably around 1905), our mother-to-be first met our father-to-be. The three boys, Russell, Bob and brother Arthur, being all about the same age, hit it off right away However in the early teens, girls are usually regarded by boys as just a nuisance and not to be included in their games. Dorothy was furious at being left out and it was 'hate-at-first-sight' as she put it. She had no idea that one of them, Russell John Williams, was to be her husband many years later.

Russell was born in 1892 and grew up in Edgebrook, Chicago, IL. He started college (~1909) at the University of Illinois at Champaign-Urbana, IL, in Electrical Engineering but after a year and a half, he became ill with stomach problems and returned home. For a while he studied art at the Chicago Art Institute but decided that while competent at drawing he did not have the talent to be a serious artist. Also as became apparent later, he was much more interested in technical things. Since he apparently suffered from depression to some extent and his family home was quite comfortable with plenty of room, he remained at home for a few years. His Mom was apparently quite willing to have him and apparently bought things like shirts and shorts as she always had and just put them in his drawer. He also had a railroad pass and could ride it any time he liked.

Russell and Grant (called Bob) with their Edgebrook Home

Our Mom told about him sitting with a gun on the table in front of him and threatening to commit suicide, frightening his Mother half to death. Our mom also told about how he loved to argue with his Mother. He once declared that there was no God and being very religious herself, she would be very upset about her son's atheism and made her case for the divine. When he would seem to be getting the worst of the argument, he would say "Ok now Mom you take the bad side and I'll take the good side" Nothing like arguing just for the sake of arguing or to stir things up!

Some time before 1915, he and a friend who had a car, began a series of trips around the country. He told of being in Florida where the circus wintered and of carrying water for the elephants. They drove out to Los Angeles and along the way tried a lot of things. They laid railroad ties someplace, worked in the oil fields in New Mexico and Wyoming, looked into businesses in Los Angeles. Nothing seemed to work out on a permanent basis, so they returned to Chicago, sometime around 1915.

When our entry into World War I was imminent, he joined the army and was an aid to a veterinarian, Doc Haars, who cared for the horses of the cavalry. He told of being down on the Mexican border in Texas chasing Mexican bandits. He also told of shoeing a mule during some sort of a skirmish. Later, still in the army during World War I, he ended up back in Washington DC. Most of this he told me in 1966 at the time of my graduation. How I wish that I had been able to record more of what he had to say.

Mom's Background

As the youngest child of a prosperous family, Dorothy Atkinsons, earliest years were very comfortable. She told a story of the period when walking one day with her Mother. As they passed a low stone wall along the way, as most kids would, she climbed up and started to walk along it. Her mother declared "Ladies don't do that". Mom, as the independent person she was, responded "This Lady Does". So very typical of her. She was always a Lady but also very independent.

When the family money was lost and she graduated from high school and wanted to go to college, she was unable to because of lack of money. While she regretted it at the time, she later realized that it brought an unanticipated blessing in disguise. She really had a chance to get to know her father well for a year while she was still at home. And that year turned out to be the last year of his life as he died of a stroke before the age of sixty. After her Father's death, the family really fell on hard times as there was no insurance or means of financial support. Dorothy needed to get a job of some sort to earn some money. Having with difficulty convinced her Mother that being a librarian was ladylike enough, she was trained and worked in the Kansas City Public Library for a while. This library training turned out to be useful later in her life. When World War I came, Dorothy also ended up in Washington, DC. Her brother-in-law, Fay Soule, mentioned earlier, had been in Chicago planning to study law like his Dad who was a Judge. Apparently he spent too much time socializing to be a lawyer so went into some kind of construction work instead. When WW1 came along, he responded to the country's need for ships to transport troops to Europe by starting a shipbuilding company in Pensacola, FL, with headquarters in Washington, where contracts were to be had. Fay was spending much of his time at the Florida shipyard and needed someone to run the office so invited his young sister-in-law Dorothy Atkinson to work there as a manager-secretary. The company was also receiving plans for ships from France and as Dorothy was fluent in French, having learned it from her Mother and taken it in high school, she was able to translate the French on the plans for him as well as performing secretarial service. Here she also renewed her acquaintance with her former neighbor, Russell Williams, who was there in the army. In 1918 both of these young people ended up having the serious influenza (Spanish flu) that killed millions around the world. Dorothy's sister Isabelle Soule took both of the young people into her home to recover. Dorothy now decided that when she got to know him better, Russell was not so bad after all.

Russell J Williams & Dorothy A Atkinson

Marriage

After World War I ended, the Soules, Dorothy and Russell, all wound up back in Edgebrook in Chicago. The Soules eventually moved to Pensacola, so I assume the ship building company still existed although probably didn't have as much business with the end of the war. Meanwhile as the only two young people in the neighborhood, Russell and Dorothy were thrown together a lot in neighborhood gatherings. Since Russell wasn't much for talking, she finally asked him 'Well are we going to get married or not?' And he said 'Well I guess so if you want to'. But if they were to marry and have children, he needed to have a job. So she helped him write application letters and arrange interviews. And he finally was hired by a small specialty steel company, American Manganese Steel Co, (AMSCO) as what we would now call a sales engineer. He designed and sold steel castings, for dam gates, dipper teeth, and other parts to industrial operations such as factories, dam builders, mines and rock quarries.

Partly, I suspect, because his mother had been raised without a mother of her own, Dad had never been taught about the niceties of life. I can never remember him bringing gifts to us kids or helping with Christmas. Mom told about the Christmas before they were married. He brought home a package, stripped off the wrapping, pulled out a string of pearls, held it up and said to his fiancé, "Will this do?" Very unromantic but typical of him!

Both were now in their late twenties and they were married in January 1921 in the Rectory of the Cathedral of Chicago. They lived briefly on the South side until Dorothy became pregnant and then they moved to an apartment in Chicago Heights, IL, south of Chicago where AMSCO was located. There I, their first child, was born on December 21, 1921, followed 16 months later on April 24, 1923 by my sister Kitty (Catherine Louise). Many years later when we moved back to Chicago Heights and I was in 5th grade, the parochial school that we attended, was right across the street from the hospital where Kitty and I had been born. Now in one sense, I had finally found where I literally came from! This intersection where the school and hospital were located, was the intersection of what was then two of the most important highways crossing the country. Hardly highways as we know them, they were only two lane roads. One was locally called the 'Lincoln' highway which crossed the country from the East Coast to the West Coast. The other, was called the 'Dixie' highway, went from the Canadian border to the Florida Coast. We loved to imagine taking one of these in any direction to see the world! We were always eager adventurers. When Dad was assigned to the Southern part of the United States for his company (1923-1924), with Marge and Kitty and our grandmother, Gaga, the family moved to Ferguson, MO, near St. Louis and bought a small house.

Who They Are and Their Relationship

While I have shared an idea of my parents' physical backgrounds and how t hey came to meet and marry, there still remains the question of their psychological backgrounds and relationship. My Dad's view of himself as a child is transcribed in Appendix C. As a child growing up, who and what your parents are like and how they feel about each other is the very basis of your security so you need to be and usually are very aware of their interactions. What they say may be too much for you to understand but the tones they use are usually very clear. You know perfectly well when they are angry with you or with each other.

In this marriage, it was always very clear to all of us, that Dorothy was the dominant one who made the decisions. In a way when her father died when she was still in her late teens, she may have been forced into being head of the household but I think partly it was in her basic genetic makeup. Her Mother (Gaga), while lovable and intelligent, was to me clearly quite incompetent at management of a household. Russell on the other hand, was quite lacking in the social graces, not too surprising considering that his Mother didn't have them much either. Having lost her Mother at age seven and been essentially pushed out by her Father's new wife, so raised almost as an orphan, she didn't learn good social behavior either. Besides not bringing gifts, not celebrating holidays, he never played with us or took us anyplace much. To me when I was little, he wasn't threatening in any way. but just in general wasn't there. One thing I do remember about him very visibly is driving with Mother to the steel foundry where he worked to pick him up and watching the sparks flying in the mysterious plant as we waited.

But despite her dominance and pushing him, there were many little incidents that made clear to me that things were going on behind the scenes as to who was in charge. When it came to getting him employed, she clearly pushed him and got him started. But when he didn't want to do something, he didn't say much but somehow he did what he wanted to do. He was stronger than he seemed by being able to resist passively.

MouseTraps

One little incident that Mom told about many times was when she first brought me home from the hospital. After they had eaten dinner and she was nursing me, the baby, in the bedroom, her Mother, Gaga, was washing the dishes. Gaga noticed that the trash in the little pantry was overflowing and said "Russell would you put out the trash for me, please?" Well he was reading the paper and really didn't want to but did it grudgingly. There were many things on the floor in the pantry that belonged there but he said to Gaga, "Should I throw out all these things?" She had turned the job over to him and thought he should do it so said, "I don't know anything about it." Then he said "What about these mouse traps. Should I throw them out too?" She said "I don't know anything about it." Dorothy of course had been listening to all this from the other room so began to yell "I keep my mousetraps there". Well they didn't hear her and went on wrangling over what should be thrown out. So she kept yelling louder and louder, getting more and more hysterical. By the time they heard her she was quite upset, saying over and over "I keep my mousetraps there!" So for years she told this incident as a funny story and 'mousetraps' became a family code word for much ado about nothing. But to me, I now see the story as Dad's way of not doing what he didn't want to do. Not always successfully but he tried. Another point of view which has been suggested by a sister is that he really didn't know what was to be thrown out since he was so incompetent about everyday things and off in his own world.

Mom Throws a Frying Pan

Another incident that I remember was when I was in about seventh grade. They were arguing about something about which I was not paying much attention. Mom was washing the dishes, as usual sitting on her kitchen stool, and Dad was standing in the kitchen door not saying much. The tone of Mom's voice was getting more and more angry when finally in complete vexation, she grabbed a frying pan and threw it at him. Of course she missed and he left. You can't argue with someone who isn't there. I had no idea what it was all about, but I'm sure it was a major confrontation and I can still remember the shock and violence of the crashed frying pan.

In some ways while she pushed him about, she was very considerate of him. I remember her telling a cleaning lady "Don't touch the tools by his living room chair. That's his 'fancy work'. After all we let ladies keep their knitting or embroidery by their living room chair.

Why shouldn't men have the same privilege". And obviously from the number of children they had, they got along well enough in the bedroom. However, she confided in me once that she would just as soon not have so many children, but her religious beliefs would not let her practice birth control. On the other hand, if he had insisted that she practice it, to keep the marriage intact, she would be justified in doing it. But he would never do it on his own and she didn't feel it was morally right to tell him. Rather a catch-22 and did not seem very logical to me. Perhaps this was a key part in my own religious odyssey.

In a way this relationship may be one clue to the conundrum that I began this book with. We girls had a very vibrant example of a strong woman with her own ideas who was not bashful about saying what she thought and who almost always got her way. So we girls just thought that was the way women were supposed to behave, and acted accordingly. Obviously there is more to it than this because we could all have become lawyers or business executives rather than entering technical fields and we didn't. So some other factors must be at work as well.

Chapter 4

Childhood in the 1920's, Ferguson, MO

Ferguson

When I was born on December 21, 1921 in Chicago Heights, IL, my Mother named me Margaret for a friend of hers, Margaret Morley, from Kansas City, MO, but they called me Margie. My middle name, Elizabeth was the middle name of both of my grandmothers. My first sister Kitty (Catherine Louise), was born on April 25, 1923 also in Chicago Heights before we moved to Ferguson, MO. My earliest childhood memories then are of the small town, Ferguson, on the outskirts of St. Louis, MO. At the time it was right on the edge of open fields so it was somewhat countrified although none of our neighbors were actually full time farmers. For the first few years, one neighbor farmed a field next to us before selling it as a building lot. We had a big yard and Mom usually had a vegetable garden. I remember helping to pull weeds in the garden and in the lawn in the Spring. There was a big patch of violets on the edge of the woods next to our yard on one side and I loved to pick them. There were no restrictions on these. But Mom also raised a bed of Narcissus and these were off limits. Once as a special treat she even allowed me to pick some to take to school for some special feast day. My Grandmother, GaGa, lived with us most of the time as she had no home of her own after her husband Arthur had died. I particularly remember GaGa planting some beautiful ruffled double pansies one year which I was also not allowed to pick. I have tried but never found any like them since.

The House

Our house had been built for his family by a German carpenter without any architectural help and had not been well designed or laid out. The door from one bedroom opened into the living room and the other bedroom into the dining room. One had to go through the living and dining room to get to the bathroom from the bedrooms. One time Dad brought home a dinner guest early and Mom was trapped in the bedroom before she had been able to get into the bathroom and get cleaned up or dressed. Having to go out through the living and dining rooms in front of the guests to get to the bathroom was not nice. After this she insisted on some remodeling. I remember watching with great fascination when doors were cut through between the two bedrooms and into the bathroom.

In addition to the above on the first floor, there was a bedroom and bathroom upstairs which were Gaga's suite. The rest of the upstairs was unfinished and used as an attic for storage. Coming home from school one day, I found Mom in that attic, with dust in the air and everything moved out. At the time it just seemed strange and exciting to me, but later I realized that she must have been getting ready to add new bedrooms upstairs.

As our family had continued to grow and we were getting big enough not to need immediate supervision, it had apparently been decided to finish up that attic and turn it into three bedrooms, one big one for Gaga, and the other two small ones for us, and I mean small! Only a small cot would fit in one and a curtain closed off a small corner area for a closet. The old bedroom at the top of the stairs became a hall and playroom and eventually even had kids sleeping in it.

More Siblings and Frances Dies

After Dottie (Dorothy Jane) was born on October 16, 1924, shortly after we moved from Chicago Heights, other children came along rapidly. Frances was born April 27, 1927 and Lydia on August 14, 1928. Then came one of the most overwhelming events of this early part of my life. My sister Frances died on the day before her third birthday in 1930. She had double pneumonia one winter when she was two and recovered but the following year at almost three when she got it again, she couldn't make it. There were no antibiotics to help in those days. Mother came down from upstairs crying and when we asked her why she was crying, she told us "Francie died".

We had no idea what that meant. But later when Francie was laid out in a coffin in our Living Room for a wake surrounded by flowers and with candles at her head and foot we tried to figure it out. Not surprisingly after double pneumonia, she looked so pale and thin. The picture of her is still very vivid to me. I particularly felt badly because a few months earlier some neighbor woman saw the five of us in the car and said "Aren't you all cute. Can I have one of you? Which one can I have?" Meaning to joke I said, "Take Francie. She tears our paper dolls". And of course, I remembered that, when she died. Much later Lydia, the sister next younger than Francie, said to us 'Francie always likes to sleep'. She would have been less than two when Francie died so it's surprising that she remembered at all. The real irony was that Francie died the day before her birthday and three months later my parents finally had their boy, Grant Russell John (July 29, 1930)! Mom always said that she traded a girl for a boy. Which is one way to look at it if a bit ghoulish.

Having Fun

One afternoon, while lying on my back and watching the cloud formations, a small plane flew over. I was fascinated and right then I remember deciding that I wanted to fly a plane like that. Since the airport wasn't too far away and Charles Lindbergh lived up the street from us, it's possible that it was his plane, the Spirit of St. Louis. We didn't see too many planes however. Eventually, I did indeed learn to fly and owned my own plane. But that was a long way in the future.

Another of my earliest memories are of Mom playing chess with Gaga by the hour. Mom told me once that each of them, Sarah and Dorothy, when first married had played one time with their new husbands and beat them badly. After that, neither husband would play any more! I also remember both Mom and Gaga saying that they loved to play chess so much that they would get up from their deathbeds to play one more game. And Mom almost did that because she was playing a hard fought game when she had her stroke many years later!

Once in a while on Sunday, Dad would take us sightseeing in the car. With no movies, TV or radio, this was a great source of entertainment. One of the things that we loved to do while riding was to sing together. We of course, like most people then, had no car radio so our singing was the entertainment. When we would get a bit lost or come to a dead end and have to back up, sister Kitty would call it a 'mitsup' and we thought it was great fun to be in a 'mitsup'. Outdoors was always one of our best sources of entertainment. I remember getting up very early in the morning and walking barefoot in the dew which was sparkling with rainbows in the grass. Since there was no air conditioning at that time, in Summer on unusually hot and humid nights we were very excited to sometimes be able to sleep out on the grass and watch the moon rise. Other times we slept on the screened porches. Mostly if we could sleep at all, we just slept in the sweat drenched sheets in the house. On the other hand, Winters there, were not too severe but I can remember one time when there was a heavy ice storm, followed by several inches of snow. I remember Dad shoveling the several inches of snow off the ice on a small hill (maybe as much as three feet high) for us to slide down on our sleds. So he did do things for us but so quietly that we were hardly aware of him.

Dad was away a lot on business and besides my Mother and GaGa, my Mother had five girls in the first seven years. So we laughed and instead of the Williams Family, we called it the "women's" family, not counting one small boy born later just before we moved from Ferguson,. Mom was a very strong person and ran the household with a strong hand. She insisted that we behave and do what we were supposed to do. She was clearly in charge and we knew better than to challenge her authority, at least until we reached the late teens.

The Threesome

During the early years in Ferguson, we three oldest girls, Margie, Kitty and Dottie, were always very close and did everything together. I remember Mom putting out a big washtub which we filled with a hose for us to paddle in. That was the only 'swimming' I ever did until I was in High School. One little incident that I remember with amusement and shows the differences in our three personalities. One morning, Kitty said with great distaste, "There are specks in my oatmeal and I don't like them". Like a good big sister, I said, "When I find specks, I just put them to one side". And Dottie said "When I find specks, I eat 'em". She was always the relaxed one about everything.

One of our favorites of the nursery rhymes that Gaga set to music for us in those early days about the threesome, was:

Rub-a-dub, three girls in a tub
And who do you think they be?
They're Margie, and Kitty and Dorothy Jane,
Turn 'em out queens all three!

The Daring Threesome: (l-r) Margie, Dottie, Kitty

Exploring

One time we three got really daring and climbed the fence at the back of the lot where there was a big field bordered by a stream with a broken up small cement dam. There was a rumor that the field on the other side of the stream had been slave quarters before the Civil War, and that people had died there, which made it even more exciting to us. We wondered if there were any ghosts of dead slaves over there. At any rate, we had a great time climbing around the broken cement until we suddenly noticed a large bovine animal in the field approaching us. Knowing nothing about animals, we assumed it was a bull and was after us! I had a red sweater on and having heard that red colors enraged bulls, I ripped it off and threw it over the fence. As fast as possible we climbed back over the fence and never went there again. In hindsight, I suspect that it was simply a curious cow but we didn't stay to find out. Who would have believed that these three little girls would have ended up being a nuclear engineer, a physicist and a chemist while also having produced 7, 11 and 5 children respectively?

Mother told of GraGra (my father's mother) taking me shopping one time when she was visiting from Chicago. We came back with strangely (to Mom) colored dresses—green, red, purple—not Mom's taste at all. She liked blues and whites! But it was mine and GraGra's. She said it made her realize that we were not just her descendants but had other inheritance as well. I don't think she learned the lesson very well because as long as she lived she was still trying to make me over into her model. I think this is a very common problem with new parents and many people never get over it. One thinks the babies are just extensions of oneself and they are not. They are completely themselves and they will go their own way, not the way the parents expect them to go at all. Mixing those genes produces very different combinations. I certainly learned it from my children although probably not well enough either.

Grandfather Dies

While we may have visited more than once in Edgebrook (on the North Side of Chicago) with our Williams grandparents, it was different when grandfather Grant Williams died in 1925. I remember Mom talking about Dad insisting on her taking the three of us babies up to visit GraGra after this. Mom thought that three babies underfoot was not what she needed but he insisted, so she took us. That may have been the time that I remember taking a sleeper on the train from St. Louis to Chicago, something that certainly didn't happen often. I remember the negro pullman porter making up our berth. He was very friendly and to me seemed to have huge hands. He took the pillow by two corners in one hand, stuffed it into the pillowcase with one motion. Strangely enough, I don't remember much about getting to Chicago or about the funeral of my grandfather Grant. And the memories of that house all run together so I don't know which are of that time and which are from much later after we moved back up to Chicago.

An English Visitor

One time one of Mom's father's sisters, Aunt Nettie, visited from England. I remember three things about her. First when she came, some of the big news stories of the day were about Al Capone and all the shooting, such as the Valentine Day Massacre, that he and his gang were guilty of in Chicago. So she flatly refused to change trains in Chicago coming from the East Coast because she might get shot. Later in the thirties when we lived in Chicago as teenagers, and rode streetcars and busses all over the city, we thought this very funny! Second, she, like many Brits was a great walker and just had to walk every day no matter where she was or what the weather was like. So she set out to explore Ferguson. Well, this was new to us kids but we thought it a great idea so set out with her. In the week or so she was there, I saw more of Ferguson and the surrounding areas than I ever did before or since.

Finally, Mom told of a conversation they had. Nettie asked Mom, "if there should ever be trouble between England and America, where would your sympathies lie?" Mom replied, "Well I am an American so of course they would be with America". And Nettie said, "Well I realized that you had married an American but I thought . . . ." And Mom said "What did you think? That I was just a little English girl who had never been home?" And I guess she laughed and they left it there. It was really not too illogical, since some British went to India for many years but never thought of themselves as 'Indian' even if they took wives and had children there. Gave me a different point of view of a different mind set.

I also vaguely remember a visit to Pensacola to visit Aunt Isabelle but don't know who else went besides Mom (or Gaga) and me. I remember Aunt Isabelle as a grand motherly sort of person, since she was 13 years older than Mom. I also remember a cousin, Betty Merritt, as a teenager who was old enough to drive. One time, she drove me in a convertible out a long causeway over the ocean to an island in the gulf. I particularly remember the wind blowing her skirt up so that her garters showed. I guess that I was a bit of prude and was shocked that she didn't pull it down but let it blow!

Gaga Playing the Piano

Of those early years, some of my most powerful memories are of the piano in our living room. My grandmother, GaGa, played it well and we loved to dance to her playing. She also wrote music for many of the nursery rhymes such as, Mistress Mary, Rub a Dub (three 'girls' in a tub), Little Jack Horner, Blow, Wind, Blow, and so forth for us to sing. When I was in first grade, Kitty, Dottie & I sang some of these while she accompanied us on the piano as part of the usual Christmas Pageant at school. Later she wrote music to some of Robert Louis Stevenson's 'A Child's Garden of Verses', such as The River, The Friendly Cow, The Swing, Wind and others. I still remember and like to sing them. It's too bad they have never been written down, because they'll probably be lost when I die because no one else plays or sings them.

Learning to Play the Piano Myself

When I was about six, GaGa started teaching me to play the piano myself. There was nothing formal about it. She got a child's music book, showed me how the notes worked and turned me loose. She never made me practice, memorize or perform. It was entirely up to me and I enjoyed it thoroughly. If I had questions, she would answer them but that was about it. She would correct me if she heard me play something wrong. Otherwise, I continued by myself as I found things I liked and finally by about fifth grade, reached the level of Chopin and Beethoven. One of my most vivid memories happened at the end of 7th grade, when I was playing, ending with Beethoven's 'Moonlight' Sonata, one of my favorites, as I finished I was startled to hear applause at the front door from two neighbor girls. I had not known anyone was listening and still remember the real jolt of adrenaline that I received from the unexpected applause.

Since Mother had so many children so fast, she usually did not let us have neighbor children over to play much nor were we often allowed to go to their houses. So while we were small, I remember a few neighbors, but mostly we played with our sisters. We always welcomed new babies with great enthusiasm. To us they were much better than dolls to play with! Also, since there were so many of us, our clothing and hair styles were kept as simple as possible. All of us were given what was then called 'Dutch Boy Bobs', cut straight across the back and bangs cut straight above our eyes. My hair was never curled at all until I graduated from 8th grade and was given my first permanent wave. For clothes, we wore an invention of Mom's, which she called 'sandbags'. These were little sacks with holes for the legs and no sleeves, but with two buttons at the shoulder. So they had to be taken all the way off for the bathroom. Of course when we went to school we wore little dresses and long cotton stockings but our hair style didn't change at all.

Starting School

When I started school, I was very shy and didn't interact much with the other children. The first day, as I walked to school, I turned around and came back home. Mom said: "Margie what happened?" I said "'A big dog looked at me". Well school was serious business and this wouldn't be allowed, so I was marched back to school and never tried that again. It was a small school with only four classrooms, two grades to a room. My first and second grade teacher was a young nun named Sister Ida. Outside there was a merry-go-round that was pushed by the kids and a pole with ropes attached and hand holders that one could hold and swing around a little. Mostly the bigger kids used these but I only used the merry-go-round occasionally but the pole swing never because I was too afraid.

School was all right but rather boring. I remember the excitement of numbers and learning to read and became an avid reader. Mom having been a librarian before marriage, early introduced us to the local library which I remember with great affection although it seemed small even to me as a little girl. It still smelled of fresh cut lumber so must have been very new. I remember the thrill of discovering the Bobbsey Twins Books and read every one of them that I could find. Then I found the Oz books and devoured them. In fact the most wonderful gift I every got was "Ozma of OZ" which GaGa gave me for my birthday or Christmas. I'm not sure which because birthdays never meant much to me, because being born on Dec. 21, so close to Christmas it got rather mixed up with the big holiday. I never had a real child's birthday party and many of my gifts were combined. I guess none of my siblings ever had anything but a family birthday celebration either. Still, I remember feeling a bit neglected and one time Gaga told me that I could use hers on June 7th because she didn't use it much any more. I actually tried it for a year or two but couldn't decide how old I was so stopped doing it.

There were other 'books' that I remember very vividly but can't exactly remember where I came across them. I think that it was in Ferguson after the upstairs was remodeled. I think that they belonged to Gaga and I also think that I was probably not supposed to be looking at them because they contained a lot of nudity. They were mainly etching of scenes from Dante's 'Paradise Lost'. They were beautifully executed but obviously fantasies of the Inferno, where souls were being tortured; purgatory, and the seven circles of paradise. In addition there were pictures of the Alhambra in Granada, Spain. All of them have haunted my dreams ever since. Finally I even managed to visit the Alhambra and it wasn't as exciting as the pictures.

Christmas

Christmas was an extremely important day to us. There was not the big preparation that there is now and there were no decorations until the day itself arrived. The four weeks before were 'Advent' which meant like 'Lent' a time of prayer, penance and fasting. We children sang for all the Masses on Christmas morning, with the younger one's singing the earliest. We would get up early, dress and walk in the dark to sing the five o'clock Mass. Also part of the tradition was a large and beautiful manger scene in the back of the church which appeared only on Christmas morning. We had to spend a few minutes praying there before we went home. When we returned, the living room curtains would be closed, with colored lights showing below them. Breakfast would be ready and despite our excitement, we had to eat our cereal before the curtains would be opened.

Then the curtains would open to show the gorgeous and surprising tree and the gift's laid out (not wrapped) below it. The gifts were simple from a current view point but impressive to us. Each child's space was marked by crepe paper strips radiating out from the tree. I remember getting books of paper dolls, crayons, coloring books, harmonicas, and a very special gift would be a small doll, doll dishes or a tray which held shaped blocks in a pattern (a great favorite). The commercial paper doll books were special because normally we were given old Sears, Roebuck catalogs to cut up for paper dolls.

As an adult, I wonder how my Mom did it all after we had gone to bed. Dad never did anything about any celebrations, this was all Mom's department. Putting up the tree and laying out the gifts she did all by herself. When we were older, Mom finally let us older kids help put up and decorate the tree. The gifts became jump ropes and ball and jacks as well as books. There was never anything as elaborate as bikes because Dad had seen a child killed on a bike and wouldn't let us have one. Also they probably couldn't afford them. I did finally get a pair of roller skates which was a great thrill. And as we got older and began to exchange gifts among ourselves, we began to wrap them which eventually became the tradition for everything but only later when I had my own family.

Chapter 5

Moving to Chicago, Depression, 1930-1934

Chicago Heights

For me, the end of fourth grade was a time of great change, because we moved back to Chicago Heights, IL. Kitty and I had been born there, but were too young when we left to remember anything about it. When we were getting ready to move, Mom encouraged us to get rid of our 'junk'. As she put it "Are you gypsies or squirrels? Gypsies keep things to a minimum so they are always ready to see the world and have adventures. Squirrels save and store everything away and so they never get to go anyplace". And of course we all wanted to be gypsies and see the world, So we tried to keep as little as possible like gypsies, although I'm sure we kept quite a lot of junk like all kids do.

After two years in Chicago Heights, we moved briefly back down to Ferguson for about two months in order to repair and get our house ready for renting. It seems the people who had rented it before not only didn't take good care of it but didn't pay the rent. Mother told of talking to the local druggist who had been a friend of hers. She said, "I feel a bit sorry for them (the tenants) because I understand they had quite a bit of illness". The druggist snorted and said "Well the only thing they bought at my drug store was white soda and you don't drink that by itself". In other words they didn't pay the rent because they had to pay their bootlegger, since this was during the time of prohibition. Well in those few months that we were there, they found good tenants and had no further trouble with them so we moved back up to the far south side of Chicago.

Chicago Heights: (bk l-r) Kitty, Margie, Sally, Dottie, (fr l-r) Lyd, Grant

These two periods, in the Chicago Heights and Beverly Hills areas,were very similar. They covered 5th through 8th grades for me so my memories of the two rather blend together and are difficult to sort out. Mom and Dad added two more girls to the family, Sally (Sarah Isabelle, November 13, 1931, Chicago Heights) and Rosie (Rose Anne, March 6, 1935, Chicago) in this time period. We also had a great deal of illness including Influenza, Diphtheria, Measles, and at the very end, Scarlet Fever. With the last three diseases, the whole family would be quarantined for long periods. When any of us didn't get too sick, which was usually the case, we thought it was wonderful because school was rather boring to us. Being quarantined and avid readers, as long as books were available, we could read to our hearts content. I remember particularly in Beverly Hills, we would all go to the library every two weeks (in the Spring, Summer and Fall on our roller skates) and take out as many as we were allowed to (it varied by the grade you were in school—five for Junior High, two before that) and then we all three older girls would read all twelve of them—nearly a book a day. As for school books, as soon as we would get a text book at the beginning of the school year, we would each read the whole thing in the first week and then go on to other library books.

Our move to Chicago resulted from the Great Depression which began with the stock market crash of October 1929 and really got going in1930. Mom told of going to the bank with Dad's paycheck in hand to deposit it, to find the bank closed up tight. In a way she was lucky because the check could be cashed elsewhere and then we had cash that we used to buy food. Dad lost his job about this time because the son of a member of the board of directors of the company where he worked had lost his job and they just arbitrarily gave him Dad's job. Just like that! Mom fought back and pointed out that the family had moved to St. Louis because the company wanted him to cover the Southern territory and they had promised to move the family back to Chicago later. They agreed to that and paid for the moving expenses of the family back to Chicago Heights. However, I'm not sure why my parents would rather have been in Chicago except that they came from there.

Aborted Vacation, Whooping cough

One summer while we lived in Chicago Heights, Mom decided to take the older kids and drive up to Grand Haven on the far side of Lake Michigan for a short vacation. There were two cottages there which belonged to Mom's relatives that we could use cheaply. The relatives were the family of the man, Fayette Soule, who had married Mother's sister Isabelle. One cottage, the "River Cottage", which was small and was on the Grand Haven River was used by Aunt Julie. The other was much larger and was directly on Lake Michigan, called "Windy Dune". Gaga was staying home to take care of the two babies, Grant and Sally. It was about a half day drive and we got there close to noon. We kids jumped into our bathing suits and excitedly ran down to the gorgeous beach for about an hour. Then Mom came down to tell us the sad news that we had to go back home. Grant, the two year old toddler, had managed to fall out of a second floor window and, while according to Gaga, he seemed to be all right, Mom thought she should go back right away. So we got dressed and sadly took off. I remember riding after dark through wild areas and the kids saying it would be fun to stop and camp out. Mom said we couldn't because we didn't have tents or sleeping bags and of course she was right. We weren't realistic enough to worry about details like tents and such.

Windydune, Our Aborted Vacation

The next day when the Doctor came to check Grant, he heard baby sister Sally upstairs coughing in a suspicious way. He checked and sure enough she had Whooping Cough, so once again we were quarantined. At that time, they did have some kind of shots which could mitigated the severity of the disease. So for six weeks each of us six kids had a weekly shot.

Imagine the crying children! That was the end of our summer vacation. Oh yes!

Grant was completely unharmed as he had pushed the screen out ahead of him and rode it down to land on some bushes! Years later as the big tease he was, Grant told Sally that it was all her fault, that she had pushed him out the window! She was sucker enough to believe him and feel guilty. Since she was only about nine months old, not even walking, and in a crib. it's laughable to think she could have pushed a two year old out the window.

However she's a lot like me, a very gullible person, and I'm sure Grant thought it great fun to tease her and have her fall for it.

Beverly Hills

Sometime later in this period, probably in Beverly Hills in South Chicago, we had a wonderful experience. Uncle Arthur, Mom's beloved brother, a year or so older, came to visit. He was the one who had become an architect in Tulsa, Oklahoma and was a tremendous favorite with all of us children. For one thing, he played the piano. In addition to very difficult classical music, he played songs that had been used in burlesque, knew all the words and sang them with great enthusiasm. Two of our favorites were "Abdul the Bulbul Amir" and "Willie the Weeper". The first is about a battle between Abdul, a son of the 'prophet' and Ivan Zkovinski Scovar, a son of the Czar. Willie is about a drug induced dream. A line that has stuck with me over all the years is: 'I had a million dollars all in nickels and in dimes. I know it cause I counted them a thousand times", and more such nonsense, but we loved it. The other thing our Uncle did was magic tricks. He was always pulling coins out of people's ears. I remember that often Gaga would not get his jokes and he used to say that she would have a happy old age laughing at all the jokes she missed. She was a very literal person so maybe that's where Sally and I got this trait. At any rate we all thought him great fun.

During this period, Mom had several miscarriages and one time I can remember her being carried down from upstairs to an ambulance. We of course did not know what was wrong or why she was being taken away, but I remember feeling very apprehensive and wondering if she would ever come back or if I would ever see her again. She did come back of course, so I was worrying more than necessary. Sally tells about this time, as a very small child, she tried to go into Mom's room and was steered away by Gaga who said "You can't see her now because she has lost her baby and is quite sick". Sally took this very literally and spent several days looking in all the closets and cupboards in the house for the 'baby' that her Mom had 'lost'. It's always surprising the way small children see the world and interpret things they hear.

1933 World's Fair

In 1933, there was a Worlds Fair in Chicago. I first remember finding out about it when we went to Gragra's house for a visit. She had an advertising sticker about it on her front door. When we finally got to go to the World's Fair only one time, the three things that I mainly remember about it were what they called, the Magic Mountain, a big screen on which they showed designs generated by matching classical music to colors and a futurama display. The Magic Mountain was actually only an enclosed slide that was higher than most and had all sorts of decorations on the outside. I only went down once and it really wasn't as much fun as I had expected. However I do remember sitting on a bench watching the large screen with the shifting colors and listening to the classical music for a long time. I don't know how the color matching was done but the colors and music were lovely and made me feel very happy. Finally,I remember the 'futurama' where they predicted what would happen in the future. Boy were they wrong on so many things but I don't remember any details!

I remember a couple of other incidents from this period while we lived in Beverly Hills. Apparently when I took an admission IQ test that was offered in 7th grade, I got the highest mark that anyone in the school ever had. I must have had a good day and it caused quite a commotion, but they never told me what the result was they just told Mom about my high score. Another thing that I remember, one day, my teacher in 8th grade, Sister Winifred, spoke to my Mother about me. She said "I'm worried about Margie. I know she knows the material but when I ask her a question, she can't answer it. What do you suppose is wrong?". Mom asked me about it and I said, "Mom, I get so bored with hearing the same thing over and over, that I start thinking about something else and when she asks me, I don't have any idea where they are or what they are doing" She passed that on to the nun, who burst into laughter and said, "I guess I can understand that. I get bored too!"

One of my favorite activities in the summer was to sit on the porch with crossword puzzles and a dictionary. I would spend hours looking up words to solve the puzzle. When I finished one puzzle, I would start the next. The main thing I enjoyed was the fun of looking words up in the dictionary and one word would lead to another. Perhaps it's the same idea that leads me to love the game "UpWords" so much now that I'm retired.

Theater in the Basement

One of the most memorable things that we did in the summer between my 7th and 8th grades. We became friends with two girls down the street, unusual to have friends outside the family. One, Anne Schwinn, was a year older than I and the other, Evelyn Young, was in the same grade and they were lively and imaginative and fitted into our family very well. Along with my younger siblings, we put on plays in our basement. It was filthy because we used the space where the coal pile was kept in the winter for the furnace. And if you have ever been around coal, you know how black the dust is.

Our biggest and most successful production, was "Little Women" by Louisa May Alcott. We essentially made up the play from the book which we all knew by heart. We cut up and painted old cardboard cartons to make scenery. We used two bed sheets hung on clotheslines for curtains and when we needed an outdoor scene, we cut the grass in the yard and spread it on newspapers. Then we found some branch cuttings to spread around the back of the 'stage' to simulate trees. When we were ready, we made signs to post around the neighborhood and charged a few cents apiece admission. Probably a dozen neighbor kids came and sat on trunks, boxes, or the floor. When we were spreading the grass on newspapers, some small boys reached under the curtains, tried to grab the grass and said 'My but grass grows fast in these days'. One of my younger sisters, Dottie, stepped on the boys hands and kept spreading the grass. Despite our amateurish efforts, everyone seemed to enjoy it as much as we did. You have to realize there were no TVs at the time, radios were limited and movies expensive so we tried to make our own entertainment. At least it was something to do in the crowded outskirts of a big city. At the end of the Summer, we were busy memorizing and planning how to set up a production of Shakespeare's Macbeth for the next Summer, but this was never to be.

Scarlet Fever

In the last half of 8th grade, the following year, the most serious disease of all struck. Scarlet Fever had become an epidemic and was so serious that in some cases it could damage the heart like strep throat does. From what I have read, no one really knows why it seems to have disappeared or at least become less serious. It could be something like the change from the killer flu of 1918. Since it was extremely contagious, when each child was diagnosed with the disease, they were immediately carted off in an ambulance to the Cook County Hospital in Chicago, where you were not allowed out of bed for three weeks not even to go to the bathroom. One got used to using a bedpan.

The walls of the rooms were all of glass so that the nurses could watch you all the time to be sure you stayed in bed. There were two sizes of room that I heard about: Eight bed wards and two bed rooms but other than that I couldn't see any difference in the two type of accommodations. TV had not been invented yet and radio was much too expensive for such a poor county hospital. There were no games or toys of any kind. Not even books were allowed because ot the possibility of transfer of infection. If your parents paid for it, you could have a subscription to the daily newspaper, the Chicago

Tribune, which could then be burnt to prevent infection transfer. So to say the least, it was a pretty boring experience for all of us kids.

My sisters, Dottie and Lydia, caught it first in mid February, Lydia on the 14th and Dot on the 21st. Mom was expecting the next baby (Rose) in early March, so before the first two came home from their three weeks in the hospital, she went to stay with Grandmother Williams so she and the new baby wouldn't be exposed. When Dad brought Dot and Lyd home that first week in March, the written instructions for the parent said "They are still very contagious. Keep away from other children". Unfortunately, Dad was so overwhelmed by taking care of the household and all those kids, that he didn't read the instructions until everyone had a big hug feast first. So,not surprisingly, Kitty, Grant and Sally were also infected and carted off to the hospital.

Kitty was in an eight bed room with baby sister Sally who was just past three and couldn't understand what was going on at all. She thought that she had been completely abandoned by her family and would be there forever. When your parents came to visit you, there was a central hall where they stood behind large glass windows behind the glass walls of the patient's rooms. They would hold up printed signs in front of the glass and if you were old enough to read that was the method of communication. At three, Sally could see Mom and Dad and got all excited thinking they had come for her and when they left, she would curl up in a ball in the corner of her bed and cry. Kitty felt so unhappy that she couldn't hold Sally and help soothe and reassure her when she cried almost continuously. Sally told me recently that she just couldn't eat the cold, lumpy oatmeal and the nurses told her she couldn't go home until she did. One day when she sat looking at it sadly, one of the older girls in the room who was apparently partly retarded, but knew enough to be sympathetic and defiant of the orders not to get out of bed, came to her and said, "Give . . . it . . . to . . . me." She took the bowl into the bathroom, Sal heard the toilet flush and the girl brought back the empty bowl. I'm surprised that the nurse didn't catch on but she told Sally what a good girl she was and that now she could go home! Apparently the girl who helped Sal out, just ignored the rules and got away with it.

It Finally Catches Me

I was the last to get Scarlet Fever and we had all hoped that I might be immune. Just in case, I had been sent to my grandmother's house for several weeks at the end of March. This was a great treat for me because I loved her house. It was always so calm, clean and orderly, with all sorts of interesting books, (not at all like our madhouse). Furthermore, when Auntie Richards was baking bread (something Mom never did), it smelled delightful. However, a few days after I returned home in mid April, the other three kids were brought home and, of course, it got me. I was all set to sing in the choir for Easter Week services, when I woke up covered with the red rash and I too was carted off to Cook County Hospital.

I was in a two person room with a year old baby in a crib who also cried the whole time. I also felt very unhappy for the baby but couldn't do anything for her. As a thirteen year old, because there was no one to talk to and we couldn't have any books, games or toys, it was terribly boring. The daily paper to which my parents subscribed for me was my only salvation. I appreciated it very much and read it from first page to the last page even about sports which I purely hate and the want ads but it was something to read. The food was also anything but good. Breakfast was lumpy cold oatmeal with tepid skim milk. Lunch was mostly peanut butter sandwiches. I cant even remember dinner but the one good food of the day was our night time snack. We had graham crackers and really cold skim milk! It's still a favorite food for me.

While I was there for my three weeks in bed, the time (May 1) came for the family to move to the Volk House on the west side of

Chicago. Details of that house are given in the next chapter. After I came home from the hospital, in order to finish up and graduate from 8th grade, I took a two hour street car ride from the west side of the city to the far south side and then about a mile walk to get to and from school. I did this two or three times a week and despite all the time out for quarantine and my three weeks in the hospital, I still managed to pass all the tests and graduate from 8th grade with no problem.

Trip to Cincinnati

Also that summer, my Williams grandmother, GraGra, paid for my first permanent wave as a graduation-from-8th-grade gift. It was an unusual experience because the curlers were hung from the ceiling but after they were attached to your hair they rested on your head and were very heavy and hot being heated by electricity. The resulting permanent was awful! It was frizzy and I couldn't comb it for weeks. At least it wasn't straight which I had always hated. Also that summer, GraGra took me with her to Cincinnati to visit her wealthy sister Susie. I had a bright green dress, with a high gold braid collar, that made me feel very grown up and everyone said made me look pretty (which I didn't believe for a minute).

Just why I always thought that I was so ugly is hard to say although I always felt that way through my teen years. Partly I suppose it was because I had to wear heavy glasses all the time. When I was in 7th grade, it was discovered that I was very nearsighted and couldn't see the blackboard at school at all. I was taken to an eye doctor who gave me prescription glasses which I always hated. However, once I found out that with them, I could see the blackboard in class and that it was even possible to see separate leaves on trees not just a green blur, I wore them all the time and even learned to tolerate them. I also suppose that part of my feeling ugly resulted from being taller and larger than any of the other girls in my class so that I felt awkward and clumsy. I also wore some of my Mom's old dresses, which didn't help. I believed my hair was unattractive because it was completely straight and I didn't know how to curl it or take care of it at all. Finally, since I had only one very small brother, I didn't know anything about boys. They were intriguing but I was really afraid of them. My husband told me later that I was too smart and the boys were probably afraid of me. All possibilities but hard to know which was the true reason.

Chapter 6

Entering The Teen Years, 1935-38

T he teen years really began for me at thirteen with the bout of Scarlet Fever described above. While I was surviving that long intolerably boring session, my family moved from the South Side of Chicago near 103rd street where I had gone to 7th and 8th grade. The 'new' (or rather different house) was at 2228 Neva Avenue, on the far west side of Chicago. It was one block inside the East edge of the city, Harlem Avenue, and somewhat north of Oak Park and River Forest. My Mother, who was normally very law abiding, avoided the last days of quarantine on the South side by hiding the quarantine sign in the bushes until they got moved out. The quarantine was really pretty useless at this point, since I was the last of the children to get the disease and then was immune. Adults didn't seem to get it at all. When they took me home from the hospital, 'home' now was this magnificent, if a bit seedy and rundown 'haunted' house. When I had gone into the hospital, it was still winter (mid-April) but now it was spring (mid-May), and everything was green and the house was surrounded by a very large yard including many lilac bushes. I never did go back to that old house, so it was for me an amazing transition!

At 13, Do I Look Like the Mother of 6?

The Volk House

This 'new' house was clapboard on the outside and as I remember had at one time been painted white, but now looked gray to me, probably from the Chicago dirt. A big wide porch, approached by half a dozen wide steps, was wrapped around three sides of the front of the house. Entry from the porch was on the right through a vestibule between two pairs of large, heavy carved mahogany double doors. The entry hall beyond included a very large flight of carpeted stairs with a mahogany railing, with the usual coat closet and storage space underneath. An electric organ sat in the corner beside the doors on the left; with a gigantic grandfather's clock across from it. Between them, there were two doors, a double door leading into a music room with a piano along with stacks of music. Since Gaga also had a piano (in the living room), for someone like me who loved to play, with three instruments, an organ and two pianos to choose from, I was in heaven! Another door to the right of the grandfather clock, led from the entry hall, into a reception room, where Mom kept her desk and there were two chairs with a radio in between for Dad. Between the music and reception rooms was a large living room with four very tall windows covered with what had once been beautiful lace curtains. These curtains are a way to begin the story of why the house was considered haunted.

Volk (Haunted) House

What Made it a Haunted House

The Volk family had consisted of parents and three sons. They had been very wealthy before the stock market crash of 1929. That they had been wealthy was obvious in many of the things around the entire house. When the crash occurred, they lost all their money and it was too much for Mr. Volk. He and his two older sons went down into the basement and hung themselves. Not surprisingly, we were always a little afraid of that basement. After that disaster, Mrs. Volk moved into an apartment and the house stood empty for several years with all the possessions and furniture still there. While empty, at least one time (possibly several), what we then called 'bums', rather than what we now call 'homeless', broke in and there was a fire. It was put out fairly promptly, but there was fire and smoke damage to the living room curtains. I know about those curtains because I helped mom cut off some ot the damage, patch, wash, and starch them. She got an adjustable curtain stretcher frame, which we put them on one by one, let them dry and then rehung them in the living room. They were probably twelve feet tall originally and reached the floor and were probably about ten feet tall when we were ready to hang them and reached only to he window sills. After the suicides, the fires and the house being empty for so long, It is easy to understand why the neighborhood children were convinced that the house was haunted.

How Did We Get Such a Big House?

Despite being the depths of the depression, Dad had found a source of income. He went back to the company he had worked for before he was fired, American Manganese Steel Co. He convinced them to let him work on commission. So by working with some of his old customers, he had been able to get enough money to keep us alive. My Mother also had managed our money well in the past so had good enough credit that we were able to live partly by charging things which wasn't usual in those days. The big job that finally made the difference was the Fort Peck Dam on the Upper Missouri River, out in Montana. Dad was able to design and sell steel control gates to the government for this dam and we lived for quite a while on the commission on those gates. They are undoubtedly still in place after all these years.

However, he mostly would get nothing until the completion of the job. So how were we able to afford what had once been such a magnificent place? It seems that Mrs. Volk had been a good friend of our Grandmother, Lydia Williams (Gragra). So when Dad was looking desperately for a house, big enough to hold his still growing brood, he remembered Carl Volk, the surviving youngest son, who dealt in neighborhood real estate and talked to him. I guess he was looking after the old house and came up with the idea of having our parents, (partly as friends), rent his Mother's house. For a reasonably small rent we would move into the house, move some of the Volk furniture to the servant's rooms or attic, and otherwise take good care of the rest of their property. Since Mrs. Volk had worried about the house sitting alone and unattended and she felt that we were trustworthy or at the very least people she knew, she agreed that this was a happy solution for everybody. Later when talking to Mrs. Volk, Mom said something about how sorry she was about Mr. Volk and her sons, but "sometimes tragedy brings out the best in people" (meaning Mrs. Volk). She replied somewhat bitterly, "It brings out 'what's' in people".

So we had moved in and Mom said afterwards that, for the four years that we lived there, she felt like "the keeper of a zoo (us kids) and curator of a museum". Since I had been in the hospital during the move, I missed all the move in and merging of the two sets of furniture that the rest of the family had done. The house was always very crowded and, not surprisingly cluttered, but we kids loved the place and enjoyed exploring it. I rather wonder how my Mother survived the ordeal of keeping it reasonably clean that. I guess we always had chores to do but we took that for so much for granted as just part of life, that I don't even remember them.

The Rest of the House

Beyond the entry rooms described above, the dining room was huge. It extended the full width of the house, including a twelve-foot-long dining table, with space at each end of the dining room for two large, comfortable chairs. There were tall windows behind each of the chairs which made perfect places for us to read. There was a triangular buffet on the west wall, with mirrors above it, cupboards below and undoubtedly a great chimney in the center. In one of the cupboards, we found a package from the downtown store, Marshall Fields, that had been delivered before the tragedy and never opened. Of course, in accord with Mom's promise, it was not ours and we were not allowed to open it. I suspect she delivered it to Mrs. Volk. It was one of those details that made the tragedy of the house very real for us. On the north end of the house, in the center of the dining room wall, an outside door led to another porch similar to the one in front but much smaller.

One door from the dining room, to the left of the buffet, led into a library with shelves on three sides loaded with books. There were complete sets of the works of Dickens, Thackery, Walter Scott and many others. As you can imagine, we teenagers had many delightful days reading through that library. Again from the dining room, to the right of the buffet, another door led to a large kitchen with a six burner gas stove and very large sink. I've been told there was a pass-thru behind the ice box which we had brought in. I've even been told, sister Dottie even crawled through the pass-thru but I never saw it. But this was before I came from the hospital and by then it was covered by the ice box (no refrigerators then). The ice man regularly delivered a large chunk of ice to keep food at least cool. One of our favorite 'snacks' was a chunk of that ice, wrapped in a clean rag, which we would suck on. We could never afford the ice cream bars from the Good Humor Man who came by the house. I craved them then and still do.

From the kitchen one door on the left, led to a flight of stairs leading up to two servants rooms on the second floor in the back. Another door, straight across the kitchen, led to outside stairs in the back down to the basement. We rarely went down to the basement except to carry laundry outside to be hung out to dry. Besides the tragedy that occurred there, the luxury of two large oil furnaces freed all of us from the need to shovel coal as we had in all the other houses we had lived in. It may have cost a lot to heat with oil but it was very nice for us.

Upstairs

Upstairs, in addition to the two servants rooms out back reached from the kitchen, there were four family bedrooms, three of them large, plus one small one off the master bedroom, either for babies or for a dressing room. There was one bathroom at the front of the house for the whole family! Our grandmother Gaga, who always lived with us and was still part of the family, had one large room in the front next to the bathroom. Our parents shared the next large one in the center, off the babies' room. At first we four girls shared the third room which also had a door into the babies room. Through the closet in the girls room, and down a few steps, there were the two servants' bedrooms which were also accessed from the kitchen. The larger servant's room was stuffed with extra Volk furniture so one couldn't even get into it. The smaller one was, ultimately, cleaned up, papered and painted by my Dad for me. It was only large enough for a cot and one small chiffonier (large mirror with two small drawers on either side). The ceiling went down to one foot high at the back. There was one window and no heat. In the winter, if I had that window open, I was quite likely to wake up to a bed covered with snow! Servants weren't given much luxury in those days, but to me it was great to have my own place instead of having to share many to a room as my sisters did.

The Scary Attic

From the front hall on this second level, another set of stairs went up to a large attic. Part of it had been finished off for a 'game room' but we had made it into a bedroom with a couple of double beds. At least I slept up there during the summer. Being alone up there was a bit scary but I wasn't about to admit it. Since it was unheated, it could not be used in Chicago winters but in summer we could spread out. I've been told that our one brother, Grant, slept up there later on.

The rest of the attic was also stuffed with extra Volk furniture. It also included many artifacts from Mrs. Volks wealthy time of life. There were dozens and dozens of hats and shoes, all much too small for big kids like us, even if we had been allowed to try them on, which we were not. Most intriguing of all, were boxes of slides of photos which Mrs. Volk had taken on many of her the trips around the world that she took in their affluent days. Again we were not supposed to touch them although my curiosity was enough that I thought it harmless to peek at them a bit. Since only black and white photography was available at the time, she had hand painted them and gave travel talks to women's clubs around Chicago of all the trips she had taken. Perhaps talks at women's clubs is where she and our Williams grandmother had become acquainted.

Finally, from the attic, there was another set of very narrow and steep stairs leading up to a tower with windows on all sides, from which one could see around the entire neighborhood. The whole area of this tower was very dusty and covered with cobwebs, but to us it was exciting. The windows were all small and sealed shut so we didn't go up there very often. After you looked out the windows once or twice, there was really nothing to do, so it was pretty boring.

The Yard and Tennis Court

The house having been empty and uncared for during several years, the yard was quite a mess. One of my sisters remembers Dad trying to cut foot high grass with a pair of hand clippers, although I never actually saw him doing it! Eventually he gave up and acquired a push mower. All working together, at whatever level we were capable of for our age, we eventually got the yard into reasonable shape.

The most memorable part of the yard, toward the back was what had once been a tennis court during the wealthy Volk years. During the years the house was empty, it had been used as a handy dump by the people of the neighborhood. The posts for the net were still in place and we found the required net in a closet inside the house, so there was nothing for it but to put it back into shape for tennis which we proceeded to do. We cleaned off the piles of debris and piled it to one side (or sent it off to the dump, I don't remember which). We raked the court as level as we could and, with a rented roller filled with water, rolled it as smooth as possible. Dad rigged up a gadget, from an old handle and a tin can with holes punched in it to spread lime to make lines. Using string and Dad's gadget, we lined the court according to the dimensions we found in the Encyclopedia and put up the net. Rackets and balls were fairly cheap at the neighborhood dime store.[2]

Of course this made us the center of the neighborhood, and, along with all the kids from the neighborhood, we spent many

---

[2]   Dime Stores: In the thirties, large department stores were only found in the downtown sections of big cities, such as Chicago. Locally there were only small stores for groceries, drugs and clothes. But then a new type of store appeared in the neighborhood, Woolworth and Kresges 5 and 10 cents' stores. At first everything was to be 10 cents or under so they were called 'dime' stores. Of course it wasn't long before some things cost more than 10 cents but the name was convenient and it stuck for a long time.

happy hours playing tennis. EVentually after spending many hours chasing balls across the street and in the bushes we even rigged up some chicken wire around the back ends of the court so we didn't have to chase quite as many balls. I even got good enough to beat my athletic friend Molly (See below) and to win a school trophy one year. Aside from tennis, we loved to roller skate around the neighborhood although we thought that we were getting a little too old for skating. In summer, we played hide and seek with all the kids from the neighborhood. I remember a fair coming to the neighborhood a few blocks away and we were each allowed a few rides. Along with a few rides on the merry-go-round, I had one ride on the ferris wheel which was great but not exciting enough to be very upset much about not having anymore.

First and only Halloween Party

When Halloween came, we held the first party we ever had and invited all the neighborhood kids. We talked Dad into being the 'Welcoming Committee'. We covered him with a sheet and put a pumpkin on his head. Since he was almost 6' 4" tall anyway, this made him seem gigantic. Then he held out a glove filled with water or wet sand to shake hands. Some of the kids were so spooked by him that they wouldn't come in through the front doors, so we had to bring them around through the side door into the dining room. The rest of the party was pretty traditional with games and bobbing for apples. It was fun but the neighborhood kids were more convinced than ever that the house was haunted.

Trinity High School

The Fall after my 8th grade graduation, I started my freshman year in a Catholic girl's school called Trinity High School. It was run by Dominican nuns, was located in River Forest, just outside of

Chicago and north of Oak Park. Mostly I didn't fit in or relate well to the other students. I never felt that I belonged but was always an outsider. Possibly it was partly because I was mature for my age and always wore glasses. There was a picture taken of me and my five younger siblings. My Dad showed it to friends at work and one said 'How young your wife looks!' meaning me at 13!

I had no interest in the clothes, hair styles, jewelry, dates and dances that most of the other girls spent time talking about. The only girl that I became friends with, Mary Margaret Molitor (called Molly), was from our immediate neighborhood,. She went to the same school but was a year ahead of me. We had become friends over the summer playing tennis and rode the public bus to school together. Along with some of the other kids, we loved to sing loud songs at the top of our voices, such as: "There is a Tavern in the Town" and the "Man on the Flying Trapeze". I'm sure the other passengers didn't like it too well but they tolerated it. We enjoyed it as a way to pass a lot of boring time. The school was about two miles away, so sometimes, when the weather was nice we would even walk home from school.

In addition to playing tennis in our yard, Molly was into any and all sports so, like me, she was also somewhat of an outsider at school but for a different reason. She liked basketball, volley ball, baseball and any other sport around. She was always trying to get me to play them on Saturday and of course we had to play some in Gym class. But I really only liked tennis and played the others only when forced. The newspaper, the Chicago Tribune, even offered free baseball tickets for ladies day, Wednesday, at Cubs Park. Molly would send in for these free tickets and insist that I ride the streetcar with her to the games downtown. I went a few times, but I can't say that I enjoyed them very much because the games seemed long and boring to me. One sport I did try, was golf but I didn't think too much of that either. Free golf lessons were offered for this and Dad had clubs that we could borrow from his youth living across the street from a golf course. We couldn't even consider anything unless it was cheap (7 cents for streetcars) or free.

Some of the things that I really did enjoy were the trips that my sisters and I took by riding the streetcars to downtown. We particularly liked museums such as the Field Museum of Natural History. There were also free Chicago Symphony concerts in Grant Park on the Lake front. The program was given in the daily paper so we knew if a given concert would be things we liked. On Saturday mornings, we also attended CISCA, (Chicago, Inter Student, Catholic Action) an organization for Catholic high school and college students to encourage them to take part in community activities. All of those I enjoyed but Molly didn't, so our friendship was somewhat limited by our different interests.

The only other neighbor friend that I had was Jean Tarbox who lived across the street. She was a year younger than I was, in 8th grade, and went to a different, probably a public school She was the victim of a strange tragedy that occurred one autumn afternoon. She was dismissed early from school and came home alone. One would think she would be safe enough at home in a quiet neighborhood like ours. Her mother was off playing cards with some friends. They had a large swing attached to the branch of a very large tree in their back yard. Like all of us, she liked to twist around and then let the swing untwist. But somehow, no one knows how, she got her neck caught between the twisted ropes and hung herself. She had a younger brother who came home sometime later and found her dead. He ran the several blocks to where his Mother was playing cards to give her the awful news. To me it was a terrible shock because it was so unexpected in one so young. Going to her funeral is probably one of the most powerful memories of my teenage years. It gave me a strong realization of how fragile life is.

While my mother and I didn't get along very well, I did respect her very much. (I guess she was too controlling for my taste). She was an amazingly educated, competent and independent lady. After dinner particularly on winter evenings, she would get out a big old brown poetry book and read to us. Many of the things she read she almost knew by heart. One great favorite of hers was James Russell Lowell's "The Vision of Sir Launfal". It's a story told in poetry about a crusader who sets out to find the Holy Grail (the cup Christ is supposed to have used at the Last Supper). He ends up coming back home to find that the Grail is really at home in the cup of cold water one gives to the poor. But it is told in beautiful poetic imagery and I set out to memorize it myself although I only learned about half. The following are samples:

> *What is so rare as a day in June.*
> *Then if ever come perfect days.*
> *Heaven tries earth if it be in tune,*
> *And over it softly her warm ear lays.*

* * *

> *Down swept the wind from the mountain peak,*
> *From the snow five thousand summers old.*
> *It carried a shiver everywhere*
> *From the unleafed boughs and the pastures bare.*

Mom also loved to tell stories and I always enjoyed them. One of my favorites was about the absent-minded professor from the days when babies were born at home. His wife upstairs was in labor and when the baby arrived, the nurse came down to tell the new father about the new arrival. She knocked and said "Professor, it's a little boy" and he responded "Eh! What's that?" And she repeated "Professor, it's a little boy". And he said "Well ask him what he wants". This story was told at an English dinner party by an American Newsman. After the punch line, there was an embarrassed silence. An elderly duchess leaned over and tapped him on the arm with her fan and said, "Oh do go on, I love naughty stories. What did the little boy want?" That became a family saying, 'What did the little boy want?'

I remember two other little poems from this period that had a strong effect on me. The first was from a teacher at school:

> *The gum chewing girl and the cud-chewing cow*
> *Are alike and yet different somehow*
> *Ah yes, I remember it now*
> *The intelligent look on the face of the cow!*

I definitely did not want to look like a stupid cow. The second came from my Grandmother Gaga, who used to say it to us:.

> *Lost somewhere between sunrise and sunset*
> *Two golden hours each set with sixty diamond minutes.*
> *No reward is offered because they are lost forever*

This made me think about how important our time is, and how we can't afford to waste any of it because once gone, it never returns.

Uniforms for School

One of the things about school that was most irritating to me was that we had to wear heavy woolen uniforms to school. They were navy blue with long sleeves, high necked with detachable washable white collars. We wore underarm pads underneath, which could be washed more often, since the uniforms were only dry cleaned once in a while. Under the uniform we had to wear a long, one-piece girdle attached to long cotton stockings. In the middle of winter, we must have been quite stinky. After one winter in this miserable uniform, when spring arrived, I took it off with great delight and put on summer clothes (skirt and shirt, no shorts for girls in those days) and dashed out to play. To my horror, things had changed inside me over the winter, and I had bouncy breasts that were a great nuisance when I tried to play any running games, especially my favorite, tennis! So it was back to a bra in place of the girdle to my great disgust. Mom had told me some details of the facts of life in 8th grade and my periods had started, so this was not a problem but I had not expected these structural changes.

One night while I was still 14, Molly's older brother, Ralph, offered to take me to the local drug store for an ice cream treat. While not too fond of Ralph, I sort of wanted to go on the 'date'. However, Mom vetoed it as she thought, probably rightly, that I was much too young to 'date'. Males in general were very fascinating to me but also very frightening. Since Dad was away a lot, and my one little brother was just a baby, I had no experience with males in the family. Perhaps had I had older brothers I would have been more comfortable with them. Aside from that brief experience, I had no offer of dates until I was in my twenties. It didn't surprise me because, frankly, I still thought that I was very ugly and no man would ever be interested in me. Part of the trouble, of course, was that, since I went to a girls school, I didn't meet many boys.

The things that did interest me in my teens, aside from reading, the piano and tennis, were flying, Mathematics, and Astronomy. Flying had been a particular fascination for me since I saw that first small plane over Ferguson in my early years. I read everything about flying that I could get my hands on. I never could go to the airport or fly myself, but I made up my mind that someday, somehow I would learn to fly. Eventually in my fifties I finally did! But more of that much later. My mathematical interests came at school from a very good teacher, Sister Raymond. She taught geometry, plane and solid, and also ran the bookstore. We loved to help her there. I guess that I was always good at math but she solidified and confirmed it.

Finally, I became fascinated by Astronomy in General Science and the books I came across in the library on the subject. The more that I read, the more intrigued I became. It is a fascination that I have never lost and now it extends to Physics and Cosmology, the history of the Universe.

Family in my Teen Years (Volk House in Back)

Finally, one opportunity that I really felt fortunate to have, was a chance to take a three to four day class trip to Washington, DC. I went with my sister Kitty, at the end of my Junior year and her Sophomore year in high school. We, of course, rode the train with our classmates. It was an overnight trip and to us it was a great treat. One of the things I particularly remember was the smell of gardenias, which were sold very cheaply on the street corners outside the hotel in Washington. Of course we each had to buy one and wore it with great enthusiasm. On the last day of the trip, we were taken on a bus to visit the Naval Academy at Annapolis. We were so fascinated with the place that Kitty and I got lost and couldn't find the bus. And were we chastised and teased! I probably felt closest to Kitty, of all my sisters, partly because being so close in age we did many things like this together. But also because we share an interest in Chemistry and eventually I married a Chemist and she a Chemical Engineer.

Chapter 7

Growing Up and Becoming Independent, 1939-42

High School Was Boring

In high school, I found most of the courses, such as History, English, Latin and Religion, completely boring. The only courses which held any interest for me were Mathematics, General Science, and to some extent, French and Biology. Chemistry and Physics were held only in alternate years and were for Juniors and Seniors only—not the one year when I was there as a Junior. I approached Mom to let me transfer to the public school, so I could take more interesting courses, but she wouldn't hear of it, and what she said is what happened in our house. One thing she did do is decide to speed up my classes so I could go early to the all-girl's Catholic College (Rosary) down the street (also run by Domincan nuns). She thought that I could get an extra year of college for the cost of a high school year. I didn't argue with her because I just wanted out. My sophomore year in high school I took two extra courses, skipping the required Latin. Then the third year, I took the second half of the second year of Latin, along with six other courses. At the end of those three years, I was just one hour short (4th year English) of enough hours to graduate from high school, but did have enough to start College at Rosary (Only three years of English required). So with an NYA job (National Youth Administration, administered by the schools as part of President Roosevelt's program to help college students pay their way) and some help from my Great Aunt Susie, who shared my Mom's religious enthusiasms, I started college.

Rosary College

Rosary College, while a bit more elegant and the classes somewhat more challenging, was really to me nothing more than a continuation of High School. In the first year, I did enjoy the Math, French, Glee Club and the Dramatics Guild, GREX. The best part was the Drama Guild. I was involved with four different plays over the first year. One was a medieval mystery play originally written in French (we read it in French Class in the original) but it was performed in English. The play was "The Tydings Brought to Mary" (L'Anonce Fetes a Marie). It was about a woman who gets Small Pox and everyone assumes she got it as a sexually transmitted disease. We put on one of Moliere's plays, "Medecin Malgre Lui", actually in French. In between there was a revue for the Sophomore class for which I worked on scenery and props. It was a light fluffy piece of nonsense but the kids liked it. Finally, each of us had to direct and act in a play put on for local kids. I had the fun of directing and being the 'Beast' in 'Beauty and the Beast'. The little kids seemed to enjoy it. Except for this last play, I was never in the cast, but only on the crew that built scenery, managed props and ran the lights.

In the Spring, at the end of the year, a very beautiful ceremony called 'Rose & Candle' was held for the graduating seniors, who were moving on, and the juniors, who remained behind. It was held outside at night by candlelight. The juniors gave a rose to each senior who passed a candle to each junior. Passing the light of learning I guess was the idea. The lower classes normally didn't take part in this. However the Glee Club dressed in dark red robes sang a number of selections for the ceremony so as a member, I was able to attend.

Best Math Course Ever

At the end of my freshman year in college, during the summer, Mom let me take Differential Calculus in a local Public Junior College. It was then, and still is, the most enjoyable class that I have ever had. The setting was very unusual because seven different levels of math were taught by one elderly professor all in one large room. Most of the students were freshmen or sophomores at various levels who had flunked out during the year. My class was the exception because although there were only four of us, two boys and two girls, all from different schools not one of us had ever had less than an A in a math course. The professor gave us text books, put us in the back of the room, assigned chapters to read and problems to work and turned us loose. Then he went back to his delinquents up front. We had a ball, competing to see who could work the problems fastest. Once in a while, he would bring us up front for a brief lecture, or an occasional test, and then send us back to our own devices. It was delightful and I learned more calculus than before or since!

Early that fall, the family moved to the near South side of Chicago, about two miles from the University of Chicago. This meant that I would have to become a boarding student to continue at Rosary college. I still had my NYA job and GraGra's sister, Aunt Susie, was helping to support me, so I could just manage it, but I did not like being committed to so much expense. It seemed grossly unfair that the family should be paying out so much for something that I really didn't want. However, I was still under Mom's control so did what I was told.

World War II Begins in Europe, 1939

Just before school started that September, while visiting a friend, Agnes Morley, we were listening to their radio and it was reported that Hitler was moving into Chezkoslovakia and taking it over. I had never paid very much attention to what went on in the wider world (partly because we had no radio) but this caught my attention like nothing had before. I was appalled at what was happening over there, and felt sure that the world would have to do something about this sooner or later.

That Fall, there was no math for me to take at Rosary, since I had taken Differential Calculus during the Summer, Also, I was beyond the level at which I was interested in taking more French. History, English, Religion, Psychology and such were all that was available and all completely boring to me. Since I was a boarding student, I couldn't do much with dramatics. I stuck it out for one semester and then absolutely refused to continue. So back I went to the family's new home out near the University of Chicago.

Hyde Park

The first years in Hyde Park (4901 Dorchester) were rough ones. It was still deep depression and money was very tight. The house was really an old dump in an area that was going down hill very fast. Although like the Volk house, it had been very nice at one time, the Dorchester house had not been cared for during many years. Two elderly sisters, with little money, had lived in it after their parents had died, and essentially no maintenance had been done on it during those years. Even though at one time it had been a beautiful house it had not been constructed or insulated very well. The entry way through a vestibule and carved doors, similar to the ones on the Volk house, was impressive. Once inside, a heavy sliding door on the left led into a large ornate living room. To save money and conserve heat this was kept closed up in winter. Carved folding doors on the right led into a library. Beyond the library, a heavy sliding door led into a large dining room with an elaborate mirrored buffet between two windows. A butler's pantry with many glass fronted cupboards, separated the dining room from the kitchen and contained our very first refrigerator with real ice cubes! Off the kitchen was a room that we used a little for sewing, but was mostly just for storage. Later when Mother's older brother Uncle Jack was having marital and financial problems, he stayed with us and used it as a bedroom. Also off the kitchen was a pantry for food storage. Cockroaches were a constant and ongoing battle, mainly in the kitchen, but the mice were everywhere. Again we had to cope with a coal-fired furnace and it was a real struggle in winter to combat the cold leaking in through the cracks in the uninsulated walls. The basement was accessed by enclosed stairs between the library and kitchen, which connected all levels of the house from the basement to the attic. The laundry was also done in the basement and in the cold winters the clothes were hung in the basement. So the basement was for laundry and shoveling coal.

Up the broad, elegant front staircase, there were four large bedrooms and two smaller ones. While there was only one bathroom for that many bedrooms, four out of the six bedrooms had mirrored sinks for face and hand washing which took the pressure off the bathroom to some extent. This was fortunate because, at one time there were as many as fourteen of us living there. At the front were Mom & Dad's room and one for older girls. Next across from the stairs coming up was GaGa's room. The younger girls had a large room to the left and another small one to the back. The very smallest bedroom with no windows, beyond the bathroom, was assigned to Grant, the only boy. I don't think that it was actually meant to be a bedroom but only for storage.

Pearl Harbor Brings us Into the War

When the war began in earnest in 1941, after the attack on Pearl Harbor, shortages of food, shoes and gasoline began to be felt. We had to deal with rationing coupons. We saved grease and fats; flattened cans for recycling the metal in them; and ragmen came around collecting old rags and metal, mainly cans and iron.

There are a couple of little incidents that stick in my mind about this period. One time a couple moved into the house next door and they had two boys, about the same age, each from a previous marriage, and a new baby from the current marriage. The woman was having a great deal of trouble controlling the two boys and asked one of them how Mrs. Williams (my Mom) made Grant, about the same age, behave so well. His response was "i don't really know. She looks at him hard and he gets read in the face and then does what she says". The woman reported this to my mother, who really couldn't answer her either. It just never occurred to most of us, even when we argued with her, not to eventually do what she said.

One amusing incident occurred when some Psychology students from the University of Chicago, who lived down the street from us, had been assigned to give IQ tests to some neighborhood kids for a Sociology class. The Williams clan was handy so they gave tests to several of the middle children, probably Lydia, Grant, Sally and Rosie. Well the tests were all above 130 and Lydia's was 180. When they turned in these results, the Professor said something about these can't be right, so throw them away and find another group. But from what I've seen of our family, I suspect they were quite correct, but who knows. The Professor just didn't know our family!

There were many good things about the neighborhood, such as the Blackstone Branch of the Public Library, just a block away, which was very large and had a magnificent collection of books. The Jackson Park Museum of Science and Industry with a live Van de Graaf generator, a working coal mine and many other exciting exhibits was a few miles away. Also, it was only about a half hour streetcar ride down to the Field Museum of Natural History, a great favorite, and the beloved free concerts by the Chicago Symphony in Grant Park down on the lake front. On the other hand, the neighborhood was going down hill and one time a small child was found dead nearby and the killer was never found. Sally, then in grade school, tells of being 'kidnapped' by a gang of rough teenagers from the neighborhood who she called 'children of the Mafia'. They snatched her and Grant on their way to school. They told Grant to go get money to ransom her. He went home and the only money he could find was what we called the 'Penny Box' where Mom and Dad emptied out their change for lunch money and such things. The amount was never very much, but he took all he could find. He also took Dad's gun, but with no bullets. In the meantime the thugs didn't watch too closely and Sally broke loose but at the expense of having her shoulder damaged. She went on to school where Grant eventually joined her but both of them were late. Grant managed to slip in but Sally got in trouble with her teacher and was kept after school. Well Mom's approach was that 'if 'you are in trouble with sister, you're in trouble with me' so also punished poor Sally. She didn't dare tell about her kidnapping for fear she would get punished again by Mom for 'lying or that the Mafia would kill her and the family as they threatened! She was traumatized enough to believe them so never told. She is finally having the shoulder repaired after not being able to write well for all these years. Grant did get in some trouble for taking the money from the 'Penny Box'. He apparently managed to straighten that out without telling about the kidnapping. I don't know what he said because I didn't know anything about it at the time but only what Sally has told me since.

Another thing that I remember from this period is that Mom began to play in the Chess Clubs around town, of which there were quite a few, to find some real challenges for her chess. I had learned to play early and even finally got good enough that I occasionally would win a game from Mom and sometimes even fought her to a draw. However I was never very good and didn't like to play anywhere near as much as she and Gaga did. Since she liked company, she talked me into going with her quite a few times. The principal clubs where we played were, the Hyde Park Chess Club in our neighborhood, one at the University of Chicago, and one downtown, the Chicago Chess Club. She became very well known for her playing and eventually became the Illinois Woman's State Champion. In her later years, she was even invited to go to Russia for a tournament, but would have to pay her own way and didn't have the money. She was always bringing stray male players home and I remember many of them much younger than she playing with her on our kitchen table late in the evening.

Business College

Mom's rule was that, once we were out of high school, she would give us a bed and feed us but any money for clothes, transportation, further education or other expenses, we had to earn. We also had to pay 20% of anything we did earn for what she called 'taxes' as rent and general household support. I always thought it was a very fair approach and never understood those kids who felt they had a right to keep living at home for free as long as they liked. So after leaving Rosary, I tried to find jobs in the local and downtown stores but the minute I said that I had no high school diploma, they were not interested in hiring me. I found jobs baby sitting and working in a corner dress shop as an alterations girl (turning up hems, taking in and letting out seams, etc.), but that was it. And that only paid 10-20 cents/hour. There were ads in the paper for local business colleges which guaranteed you a job at the end of a ten month course. If you couldn't find one, you could come back to the 'college' indefinitely and improve your skills until you got one. So I borrowed some money from my grandmother (Gaga) and in January 1941 went to a different kind of school.

To get to the Business College, I rode the Illinois Central which ran past the Midway at the University of Chicago. I can remember during that long gloomy Spring, looking down the Midway as the train went by, and wanting so desperately to go to school there. At the school I attended, I worked as many hours as they were open taking typing, shorthand, bookkeeping and office machines. In four months I had essentially completed the ten month course. My short hand at only 90 words/min was not quite up to the required 120 words/min but everything else was. So in May they sent me off for job interviews and within a week I was keeping records and books in the office of a General Electric appliance dealer, R Cooper Jr., twelve blocks south of the Chicago Loop. With my business college diploma, they didn't ask about high school. I stayed there from May to September of 1941.

University of Chicago and Marshall Fields

At the end of the Summer, I had saved all the money that I possibly could, as well as paid back my grandmother. I still wanted desperately to get back to 'real' school at the University of Chicago which was only about two miles away but very expensive. So I took a day off and went to talk to the school. Of course, I couldn't leave my job and register for school unless I had a part time job lined up. However, at first, the school would not help me with job possibilities, unless I was already a registered student. So it seemed to be an impasse and I started to walk the two miles home. On the way, I kept thinking this doesn't make sense, there should be a way. So I turned around and went back. This time I got a different answer and was taken into an office to talk to someone. It seems that they had just signed an agreement with the big downtown store, Marshall

Fields, to hire students part time while they still went to school. I was to be one of the first participants in the program! I couldn't believe my good luck and I am sure that turning around that day was one of the turning points in my life. What I learned is that It takes a lot of determination to get anywhere.

On the first of October 1941, I started my first Chemistry course along with Math and Biology Survey courses and started working in the downtown Loop for 30 hours a week for the princely sum of 40 cents an hour compared to the 10-20 cents before. I started in the Furniture Department as a file clerk.

Marshall Fields

A few days after starting my new job, at a nearby unattended desk there was a phone which rang and rang and rang. One of the other girls told me to answer it but I really didn't want to. (At home, when I was small, we were not allowed to touch a phone because it was for Dad's business so I guess I was afraid of it). But since I was told to do it, I picked it up. A man who had apparently been on hold for a long time, said in a very frustrated voice "What is your name?" I told him and he responded "'I ordered some furniture last week. It was to have been delivered yesterday and it has not come. If it does not arrive by 5:00 PM today, I will have you fired.'" Of course this completely panicked me. I guess I had the presence of mind to get his name and number so I could call him back. At any rate, I started asking around the office about how I could find out about this required furniture. I found the responsible salesperson who said that she would take care of it. Apparently it was delivered on time as I never heard anything more about it and I was not fired. It seems that the desk where the phone rang was the furniture complaint desk and the person responsible was off for the day. Eventually, I ended up in charge of the complaint desk and had my own office. The job wasn't so bad but that 'baptism by fire' almost did me in.

The University of Chicago

The most interesting of the classes that I was taking, introduced me to the world of the Chemist and was completely and endlessly fascinating to me. As I first entered that great big lecture hall as one of around three hundred students, the first thing I saw was a huge chart of the elements. It was on the wall behind the lab bench where the lectures were given and experiments performed. Atoms? Elements? What were they? In those days most people, like me, didn't know much chemistry in particular or science in general and I was one of those who knew very little.

Looking back over the centuries, as I have learned later, the Greeks were the first to even develop the idea of an atom. If you take a piece of material, such as iron, and cut it in half, each half is still iron. Take half and cut it again and again each half is still the same. Now suppose you continue this process as the pieces get smaller and smaller. How far can you go before cutting one more time will produce pieces that are not iron? Of course this is only a 'thought experiment' because the pieces get too small to see. This last tiny 'piece' the Greeks thought of as an 'atom'. As to elements, the Greeks thought they had solved this too. There were four of them, earth, air, fire and water, and they thought that everything in the world could somehow be made of some combination of these four. Air and water weren't too far away—air, mostly a mix of two elements which we know as oxygen and nitrogen; water, a molecule made of the elements hydrogen and oxygen. However they missed on fire which is a form of energy and not an 'element' at all. And earth is such a mix that it's impossible in general to say what it is. Oddly enough they actually knew about two elements, silver and gold, but didn't recognize them as such.

Chemistry, a Great Fascination

But this doesn't answer the question, where did that chart of the elements come from? Gradually, over the centuries, mankind sorted out many materials that they couldn't divide into smaller 'atoms'. They figured out how to measure the 'weight' of an atom of each of some of these 'elements' by how much of one joins another element. During the 1800's one man, a Russian Chemist named Mendeleef, set out to try to organize and understand the relations among the 'elements which had been gradually identified over the years. He wrote the name of each that was known at the time on a card along with the weight of an atom and then moved them around and tried to order them by weight. He also considered how they were related and began to see patterns of behavior. Of course, there were big gaps but the patterns began to be clear and eventually the overall outline of the chart took place. It worked so well that as time went on other elements were discovered to fill in most of the gaps, such as Germanium, Scandium, Gallium and so forth, to give the chart that we were using in 1941. However, at that time, the chart ended very abruptly with the heaviest element then known, Uranium. Of course the questions immediately arise. Are there heavier ones that we don't know about yet? If not, why not? Within a very few years these questions would be answered resoundingly.

For the rest of that year and the next years,1941 and 1942, I continued to take as many courses in Chemistry and Math as I could possibly afford and fit in while working down at Marshall Fields. Generally I loved every minute of it. Of course, I had to ride the train to downtown for my job but otherwise, I walked. The days were long and I was always tired, but I kept going. Sometimes when the weather was very nasty, It was a bit difficult but rather than spend seven cents to ride the street car, I would walk the two miles to school.

Riding the Streetcars

The mechanics of the Chicago street cars of those days which we rode so much, were clumsy but effective. They ran on rails embedded in the pavement. They were driven by overhead electric wires which were attached to the cars by spring-loaded straight rods, with a small wheel on the end that ran on the wires. Depending on which direction the car was to run, there was one of the rods at each end of the car. Since the car was symmetric, it did not have to be turned around. The conductor pulled down the rod which had been at the back and fastened it down. He then released the one which had been at the front and let it rise up until it reached the power wire. Then he took his control from the former front and moved it to what had been the rear and now was the front. Then he was ready to let the passengers board. The floor was made of two-by-fours on edge to let water and snow run off. The seats were simple benches covered by woven straw with pipes for arms to hang onto. There were also overhead pipes and straps to hold onto when it was too crowded for all to sit. The cars were unheated, clumsy, noisy and rattled as they ran, but we rode them a great deal because they were cheap (7 cents per ride with unlimited transfers all over the city of Chicago), frequent (usually every ten minutes or so during the daytime), convenient and went to all the places we needed to go in the city.

Chapter 8

Attack on Pearl Harbor, Manhattan Project, 1941-45

I n December of 1941 after the unexpected Japanese attack on Pearl Harbor, we finally went to war with Japan and by default with Germany when they declared war on us. It was a Sunday afternoon when the news came and I was studying as usual, so didn't hear about this life changing event for a while. Since there were no boys of the appropriate ages in our family, we didn't have to worry about the draft. So it really didn't have much immediate effect on us. All eight of the children in the family were still living at home at 4901 Dorchester Avenue.

My sisters Kitty and Dottie after finishing high school, then went on to St. Xavier's College run by the Sisters of Mercy. It was much cheaper than the University of Chicago so they could go through faster and not have to work so many hours. Had I been sensible, I would have gone there too but my experiences with Rosary made it completely unappealing. Kitty eventually completed her degree in Chemistry and then went on to the University of Illinois at Champaign-Urbana where she got her Masters degree in

Chemistry and met and married her husband, Bob Kallal. Dottie while taking Physics at St. Xavier's, found an ad about a wartime job in electronics with RCA (Radio Corporation of America). She was first sent to Purdue University in Indiana, for some classes in Electronics and then on to New Jersey where she spent the rest of the war years working for RCA. So the war was beginning to have some effect on us.

In the Fall of 1942, while I was going to school at the University of Chicago, there began to appear troops of Navy personnel marching between classes. They had set up a Navy Signal School with the sailors sleeping in bunks in the mostly unused gym[3]. It was a big change for what had been a very quiet school with a few quiet students wandering around. The buildings were all medieval in style and ivy-covered with many huge old trees. I particularly loved the melodious chimes that marked the passing hours.

In the winter of 1942-1943, I took the toughest schedule yet, two upper level Chemistry courses with long attached labs in addition to working 30 hours a week downtown in the loop at Marshall Fields. The weather was particularly bad and the walking harder than ever. I can remember being particularly miserable when walking the two

---

[3]   The reason that the gym at the University of Chicago was not used was that back in the middle 1930's, a new President of the University, Robert M. Hutchins, had decided that organized sports was taking too important a role for a University. He had immediately withdrawn from all intercollegiate sports, such as football, baseball and basketball, with only intra mural sports allowed. He had also instituted a new program of studies to help impoverished or motivated students go through faster. There were four basic courses of study, (humanities, sociology, biology and physical science) with published reading lists available that one could cover on one's own without going to classes. One could then take a comprehensive exam at minimal cost to get complete credit for the course. This really appealed to me. The year was divided into four quarters rather than semesters as was customary in the past. It really shook up the educational world at the time although not many other universities followed his lead.

miles home at 7:00 PM in the evening with the temperature down below zero and the wind blowing violently off Lake Michigan. And then in the evening, I had mounds of homework to do and experiments to write up for as long as I could possibly stay awake. As that quarter ended at the beginning of March 1943, I decided that I had had enough for a while and was, as usual, running out of money. I decided that I was going to try once again to get a regular full time job rather than this hectic double life with which I was living.

Changing Course

Walking home one day shortly after I had made that decision, I decided to take a different route home. There I met a girl that I had seen at church, where we sang in the choir together (although I never did know her name then or now). I was telling her about my change of plan, and that I was going job hunting. To my surprise she said "I think I know where you can get a job. I'm a secretary there. Go to the Physics Building'" and she gave me the room number. So the next day, I went where she had told me and sure enough, I was immediately sent for an interview back in the Chemistry Building where I had been taking all my classes! And she was right, I was hired on the spot as a chemical technician by the group leader, Roselle Curtis! So not only was I going to work on my beloved campus, but I would even be using my hard earned expertise and in the very building in which I had taken most of my classes! To my surprise, since I had noticed people going in and out of locked doors with keys on an attached chain, I was to join them immediately. A lot less attention was paid to security in those days. Despite this lack of security, it was the best kept secret of the war, except for what the Russians learned through the people sent to Los Alamos from (and cleared by) England.

Manhattan Project, What a Surprise!

At first, we were not told what it was all about, but only that it had to do with Uranium, the last element on Mendeleef's chart of the elements, described in Chapter 7. About six weeks later, those in charge of the project decided that, while it was all top secret, and we were to tell no one what we were doing, they believed that we should know what was going on, rather than gossiping and guessing. So we were all called in for a meeting. Now came some of the answers to the questions asked earlier about why the chemical chart of the elements ended with Uranium at #92.

In the early 1930's, the neutron, a particle about the size of a Hydrogen atom but with no charge on it, had been discovered by James Chadwick in England. It was then discovered that the nucleus of each element contained a number of protons, each with a plus charge, equal to the number of it's place in the periodic table. This number of protons determines the chemical behavior of each element. The nucleus of each element also contains at least an equal number but usually a greater number of neutral neutrons. These probably act partly as buffers, keeping the positively charged protons from repelling each other so much. However the number of neutrons varies to some extent. These nuclear particles generate the isotopes—same number of positive protons in the nucleus, matched by an equal numbers of negative electrons outside the nucleus, but variable numbers of neutrons in the nucleus. The variable number of neutrons results in a slight change in the atomic mass for each isotope. The mass that is given in the periodic table was an average of the masses of the different isotopes, depending on how many of each isotope exists, which is different for each element. This all may sound very esoteric but understanding it became the basis of the Manhattan Project.

Finding Fission

Later in the middle of the 1930's, Otto Hahn and Lise Meitner in Germany had discovered that certain isotopes of Uranium when exposed to a source of neutrons would undergo fission, or break apart, and produce several neutrons for each atom fissioned along with large amounts of energy. Enrico Fermi in italy had also been working on the problem of what was producing unexpected smaller elements in Uranium samples although he had not recognized that they resulted from fission. He and his wife had left Europe and gone to Sweden where he received a Nobel Prize in Physics. Because his wife was Jewish, they had not gone back but had come over to the United States. and now was one of the principle operators on the Project. When Leo Szilard, also a refugee from Hitler's Germany, heard of the discovery of fission, he was immediately convinced that a bomb could be made from these particular fissioning isotopes of Uranium. At the time, German Universities were scientifically the best in the world, so he and others were convinced that if anyone could do it, the German's could. They were also convinced that Hitler was working on it as part of his attempt to conquer the world. Given these circumstances, they had drafted the famous letter to President Roosevelt pointing out this possibility. Being world famous for his work on Relativity, they believed Einstein would be more likely to be believed. This letter convinced Roosevelt to initiate the Manhattan Project on which we were now going to be working.

In addition, J Robert Oppenheimer, who ended up in charge of the project, had also discovered when he was at Berkeley, CA, that if a certain isotope (238) of Uranium was also exposed to neutrons, it would absorb a neutron and emit a beta particle[4].

---

[4]   A Beta Particle is the same as a negative electron, which circles the nucleus, but comes from the nucleus. This turns a neutron into a proton thus increasing the atomic number of the element by one.

This turned Uranium-238 into an isotope of Element 93 (since named Neptunium-239) which shortly thereafter, underwent the same beta particle reaction and turned into an isotope of element 94 (now named Plutonium-239) which also, from what they understood about fission, should be capable of fissioning. Now we are really past Uranium at element #92. They thought Plutonium-239 could probably also be made into an atomic bomb, using an even smaller amount than needed of Uranium. And they turned out to be very right.

Just Theory?

This, of course, was all only theory, because no one had ever done it before. In the talk that day, they told us that if some day we heard that a large part of the US had been blown up, the Germans had succeeded in building a bomb before us. At any rate we were part of the project that was trying to beat Hitler to this theoretical atomic bomb. Not knowing which, if either, would work, they decided to try all possibilities. And the answer to the question of why the atomic chart ended at 92 was that it indeed did not have to! But any element heavier became more unstable (radioactive) and the still heavier ones were even more unstable and did not last very long at all. Much later, I heard that tiny amounts of Plutonium have actually been found in nature, although it is extremely rare. And over the years since, higher and higher elements up to 100 and more have been discovered but they are all very radioactive and short lived.

Whether I heard then or later, I'm not sure, but three months earlier (December 1942), while I was still taking Chemistry courses, the Italian, Enrico Fermi, Walter Zinn and others had actually successfully built the first 'nuclear reactor', which they called an 'atomic pile' under the West Stands of he Athletic Stadium across the street from where I was taking classes. It was called Pile I, and consisted of a structure of Uranium and Graphite blocks with Boron rods inserted. The Uranium blocks, of course, contained atoms of the fissioning material; the Graphite, called a "moderator", served to slow down the neutrons and make them more liable to be absorbed by the Uranium atoms; and finally, the Boron was the control material. The Boron in the form of rods, had an unusually strong ability to absorb neutrons thus it kept the fission reaction under control until the rods of it were withdrawn.

The Chain Reaction Begins

Early in December, they reached the stage where it was decided that the pile was large enough to carry out a chain reaction. From all reports, it was a very exciting moment as the boron rods were slowly withdrawn, criticality approached and the geiger counters measuring the neutrons clicked faster and faster. One man with an ax, was poised above the 'pile' with a bucket of Cadmium (also a good neutron absorber) tied to the ceiling. If the reaction happened too fast he was to cut the rope and everyone was to run like hell. The reactor became critical and the chain reaction occurred exactly as predicted. Of course this was done in the middle of the big city of Chicago, but apparently Fermi felt absolutely certain that they could approach it slowly enough not to cause any damage. And it turned out he was quite right. The Cadmium was 'just in case'. This was the first confirmation of the possibility of making nuclear reactors which would produce the Plutonium for more bombs.

To explain what is meant by 'criticality', Uranium has a number of isotopes, 233, 234, 235, 236, 237, 238, and 239, resulting from the varying numbers of neutrons in the nucleus as explained before. Most of it is isotope 238 which does not fission but which does make Plutonium when it absorbs a neutron to become isotope 239. The principle fissionable isotopes are U235, usually about .07% of natural Uranium, and tiny amounts of U233. The fissioning of an atom of

U235 results in a 'chain reaction' which can be used to set off an atom bomb or to make a reactor go critical depending on how it is used. As an atom fissions it produces two or more neutrons, each of which goes on to cause two (or more) fissions, now producing four neutrons, four fissions and so forth. This can occur only if the Uranium is in a reasonably compact form like the pile so the excess neutrons don't escape or become absorbed uselessly by nearby non fissioning atoms. Since the fission occurs so fast the resulting chain reaction occurs very rapidly and must be carefully controlled. The difference between a nuclear reactor and the atom bomb is like that between coal fired, energy producing plants and explosives. The first in each case is controlled to produce useful electrical energy and the other is uncontrolled so used as weapons of war.

Working Conditions on the Project

At first the conditions where we worked were quite primitive because Kent Hall, the old Chemistry building was about 100 years old and had not been upgraded in many years. Also we were crowded in, with a dozen of us in a room designed for three or four. Frequently, we did things on an open bench top that were normally done only in a vented hood. One time someone was recycling some ether and it caught fire and exploded. There was only one door to the room, right next to the fire, so we could only watch and hope for the best, while others put it out. The man next to me said quietly 'That's what it feels like when your ship is torpedoed.' I had not known that before he came to the project, he had several merchant marine ships sunk under him by German torpedoes, but was one of the few lucky survivors. After the explosion and fire, they shut down the room to air it out and clean it up.

After several days, when painters came to clean it up and paint it, the smell was still so bad they complained bitterly. Of course, we had been working there for weeks and hardly noticed the smell of the chemicals. The rumor was that, with all the radioactivity around, we would probably all be sterile and never be able to have children (obviously from my personal experience, very wrong) and that if we did, they would probably be abnormal. Our family laughs about this and teases each other about being "children of the atom bomb".

As time went on, they were sending chemists to Chicago from DuPont to be trained with what we had learned about the chemical behavior of Uranium and Plutonium so it became more crowded than ever. Plants were being built in Oak Ridge, TN, (others by Union Carbide in Ohio) to make the concentrated Uranium and by Du Pont in Hanford, WA, to build reactors to make Plutonium. Since they didn't know what would work at all, they were trying every possibility. Of course all this was top secret and we couldn't tell anyone about it.

Joined the Shotgun Group

My second job on the project was in what was known as "The Shotgun Group", from the fact that a 'shotgun' of neutrons was applied to material samples to find out about their reactivity and effect on neutrons. While Fermi had proved that a pile of Uranium and graphite blocks with Boron rods which soaked up neutrons for control could be made to go critical, not much was really known about the details of the interaction of most materials with neutrons in what later were called 'Nuclear Reactors'. And if Plutonium was to be produced in quantity to make atom bombs, much needed to be learned and fast.

So, after the first reactors out at Hanford, WA had been run for a while, material was taken out and samples sent to us. We used a Radium-Beryllium source on the end of a long rod to generate the neutrons which were then slowed by a large block of paraffin. We put, usually uranium, samples in a small round bin in a drawer containing the bottom half of the paraffin, then taped an Indium foil over the sample, closed the bottom drawer, inserted the source and waited a carefully measured amount of time. The Indium foil would become activated more or less depending on how many neutrons were absorbed by the sample and how long it was left in. After removing the source, the Indium foil was removed and taken into another room and wrapped around a detector tube attached to a geiger counter. The tube was then covered by a large moveable lead shield on tracks to prevent counting irrelevant cosmic rays, and the number of disintegrations from the foil were counted. We would plot these results and report them back to those who sent us the samples. One of the things we learned was to be very careful about keeping our hands clean. If even a tiny amount of radioactive material from the lab got on the Indium foils by mistake, they would add to the count which would then make our experiments meaningless.

Guessing How Long the War Would Last

One of the things that I particularly remember from that period is some of the discussions we had in the 'Shotgun Group' while waiting for the samples to be counted. We talked about how the war seemed to go on and on. With the awful news that kept coming from Europe and the South Pacific, we wondered how long the war was likely to go on. At one point several of us made our best guess as to the ending date of the war. Most of us thought that it would last into the fifties, the earliest date that anyone picked at that time was 1947. We wrote our names and the dates we picked on a piece of paper and each put in a quarter and wrapped it up and put it in my safe. Then I forgot about it until much later after I had stopped working. I no longer had a badge so could not go back and check on it. I've often wondered if anyone found it and who actually won for the earliest guess. Certainly, at that point in time, if someone had told me that in 40 years I would be working in Los Alamos and Germany with

Germans and Japanese on reactors, I would have told them they were crazy. But that is what actually happened many years later.

Keeping Things Secret

For me, as a 21 year old girl, a very strange thing happened that first summer on the Project. One evening, I was sitting on the porch, talking to my father who was always so knowledgeable about everything, and, as a child, I believed knew everything. Since he sold steel castings of various kinds throughout the South, he talked about having observed an amazing place down in Tennessee (Oak Ridge) where they were building this huge plant and nobody knew what it was for. One theory that he had heard was that they were building submarines for the Navy and were going to dig an underground tunnel to send them to the Atlantic coast. But to me, the shocking thing was that I knew what they were doing and why but I couldn't tell him! I've wondered since if he ever guessed what it was all about. If so I never heard him make any guesses that implied that he did. My sister Kitty who was also studying Chemistry in college at the time, now tells me that she and Mom did guess but they never said anything. I wonder how I would have reacted if they had said something.

Moving to New Chem

As the year 1943 went on, a new building a few blocks away from the campus was built for us to work in, and it was called 'New Chem'. Now they had more room for workers and began to actually send army personnel to help out. Since most young men had been drafted and in those days not too many young women like me went into scientific fields, they couldn't find anywhere near enough people to do the work that needed to be done. Our family was rather unusual in that in addition to me, my sister Kitty was also majoring in

Chemistry and as a side job was working in a bread Chemistry lab. About this time she had a bad lab accident when boiling wax was spilled over both her hands. For months they were bandaged up and she was not able to work. Eventually she recovered and continued with her degree. Our next sister, Dottie, as described before, spent the war years doing electronics work for RCA. It was quite clear why I had been hired so fast. Also one of the young army personnel being sent to the Project by the Army, held the key to my future.

Chapter 9

Meeting my Husband
and Marriage,
1944

Setting the Scene

O ne of the secretaries on the project where I was working, was married to a Divinity Student at the University of Chicago. As a side job to support himself, he managed a nearby men's club, the Dorchester Club, which had an indoor swimming pool, along with a large, pleasant meeting room. At 53rd and Dorchester Avenue, it was only four blocks from our house at 49th & Dorchester Ave. As part of his 'pay', he had the option of using the facilities for private parties which he and his wife did for people from the project. The girls were asked to bring cookies for refreshments in addition to the punch which was furnished by someone. Since there weren't too many girls on the Project, we were always encouraged to bring along extra girls, Since I had two sisters, Kitty and Dotty, of an appropriate age who were going to St. Xavier's College nearby, I was able to bring them along when they were around.

Because the club was only four blocks from our home it was an easy walk. The indoor pool in winter was a particularly great treat, so we loved to go. It was also especially nice for the army personnel, who were being sent to the Project by the US Army. They had been taken out of uniform to help keep secret the fact that the Army was involved, so they couldn't go to the USO (United Service Organization) dances and other places available to the service men who were in uniform. So my sister Kitty and I went all during the Winter of '43-'44 to the parties which were held on Saturday night every other week. By February, Dotty had gone off to Purdue to be trained in electronics, Kitty had established a fairly stable friendship while I as usual hadn't developed such a relationship.

On this particular night, February 12th, I had decided that since I never seemed to get any dates, maybe it was because my glasses frightened men off, so I decided to leave them at home. It was a very crucial decision, since I was blind as a bat without them, but because it was only a four block walk from home and the streets were well lighted, I didn't think that I would need them. At the party, I had been swimming mostly by myself, and when I got dressed and came out about 10:00 PM, it was apparent that there was an unusually large proportion of men (it varied every time depending on who decided to come). At one table, playing penny ante poker were three guys, one of whom, Walter Beard, I knew fairly well from the lab. As I was by myself, Walter waved me over and introduced me to the other two, one of whom, Larry Asprey was brand new a couple of weeks previous. The poker wasn't too much fun, so they took turns dancing with me to the record player, particularly this new guy. Since it was run by the Divinity student, no liquor was served and after a while (about 1:00 AM), the three guys decided that they wanted to go some place to get something stronger to drink than the punch which was being served and I was willing. My sister Kitty had met her current friend so I was on my own and the three guys agreed to see me home.

Leaving the Party

So off we went, walking a few blocks east along 53rd Street, through a foot of snow to a local bar on Stoney Island Avenue. The guys had several drinks and somebody bought one for me. Well at 3:00 AM the bar closed and we had to leave. Now what to do. The four of us started walking rather aimlessly in the direction where the two other guys lived but South, in the wrong direction for me. Wherever we went, Larry would of course have to take a streetcar to his room. They talked vaguely about finding something to eat, but everything was closed up tight since this was really a family neighborhood. I tried ineffectually to get them to tell me what the sign said on the street car stopped across the intersection on 55th Street, because without my glasses, I couldn't read it, and was too embarrassed to admit that I couldn't read a simple sign. They didn't pay any attention to me, not surprising because they did not realize that I wasn't able to see. Then the streetcar took off and went North in the direction that I needed to take! Now there wouldn't be another for about an hour and it was so cold! About then, the other two guys decided that they lived not too far from where we were, so they would go on home if Larry would take me home which he agreed to do.

Being new in town, Larry had no idea where we were or how to get me home. All sensible people were home in bed and there were no taxis or telephones around. About now a streetcar came along on 55th Street but heading in the wrong direction (west instead of north), I decided that we should take it, because at least for a few minutes, we would be out of the cold and there was someplace to sit down. When it came to Cottage Grove Ave, it was going even farther off west in the wrong direction, so we got off and again started to walk. Again we walked through snow drifts, until we got to 47th Street and once again were only about a mile from my home, with a street car parked at the intersection. And again ineptly, I tried to find out what it said, without any luck just as it took off! Again in the direction East that I needed to go! We had traveled around two sides of a square a mile on a side. By this time it was about 4:00 AM, so again we started to walk to keep from freezing to death. In a few blocks, we found another bar open on 47th Street but it was a real dump, full of loud and argumentative drunks. However, we were so cold we decided to go in anyway and Larry had a drink. Many years later he didn't even remember that bar but I do, very vividly, since I had never been in any place like that before.

At 5:00 AM this bar also finally closed, so again we had to get out, and again, started wading through the snow. Finally we reached my home after walking about another mile and, to try to warm him up, I invited Larry into the sleeping household. I can still remember looking at him as he stood on the register in our library, trying to warm up a little. It didn't do him a lot of good, because we had a coal fired furnace and it hadn't been 'loaded' since the night before but it was somewhat warmer than outside. I thought to myself 'he seems like a nice guy but after this wild goose chase, I'll probably never see him again'. By now it was nearly 6:00 AM and the day streetcars were starting to come somewhat more frequently. So I pointed him in the right direction and he took off for his room. At the time I thought that everyone was sound asleep enough not to be aware of our very late arrival, but my sister Kitty recently told me that she had been awake enough in the night to worry about me, but she didn't say anything at the time.

After that wild night, it still seems strange to me that Larry didn't run and keep running. But the following Monday morning at work (February 14, some valentine!), he had Walter Beard bring him down to show him where Marge worked and he asked me for a date. And I was so socially inept that I made him ask me in front of my colleagues, (which after 60 years, he still complained about). And, of course, I had my glasses on, so that cat was out of the bag, but that didn't seem to bother Larry very much. So I guess, the glasses weren't the problem after all. I just had to find the right person.

Larned (Larry) Asprey

By this time, the beginning of 1944, World War II had been underway for over two years. Larry had been in the army for most of those years. He had been born and grew up in Sioux City, IA. He had an older sister Winifred, called Tim, and a younger brother, Robert, called Bob. He had attended Morningside Junior College in Sioux City (even having a summer German class there with Dear Abby and Ann Landers, the Friedman twins). He then finished his BS in Chemical Technology at Iowa State College in Ames, IA in 1939. After graduation, he had felt lucky enough to find a job as a chemist, making the magnificent sum of $29 per week with Campbell's Soup Co. It was in Chicago near Oak Park, not very far from where I had lived at the time!

When first drafted into the Army in 1941, after basic training, he was sent for over a year to Fort Warren near Laramie, Wyoming,. There he had been assigned to the office and told to set up files for the 'Fort'. When he told them he didn't know anything about filing, and asked 'did they have some books on the subject'? 'No, just make it up', was the response. So he did! And, I've often thought, what fun they must have had trying to find anything when later he left suddenly which he did. Since he was thoroughly bored with filing, when he heard about the ASTP[5] program, he immediately applied. He was then sent to Ohio State University in the Summer of 1943 for

---

[5]   ASTP was the Army Specialized Training Program, which was being set up by the US Army to bring some of the soldiers up to the skills needed for the technical equipment that the army was now acquiring including the Manhattan Project.

some more courses in Chemistry. It could well have been with the Manhattan Project in mind although he didn't know it at the time.

In January 1944, along with some other friends in the same program, he was given orders to report to a Sergeant Bidlack at a phone number in Chicago. The phone number was for a small hotel on 63rd Street. When Sgt. Bidlack came out, he was in civilian clothes and hastily told them to call him Mr. Bidlack not Sergeant. Then they were told that if they lived within 200 miles of Chicago, they were to go home and bring back their civilian clothes because they were to go to work on a secret project at the University of Chicago. Larry told him that he lived 210 miles away, could he go home to get his clothes? And when Bidlack said 'yes', Larry said that he knew that he was probably essentially out of the Army, because the Army mindset would have insisted on the exact distance and not let him go! He was told that it was even "Top Secret" that the Army was involved with the project, which was the reason for the civilian clothes.

On the project, he was put to work with Walter Beard and Marty Studier on the chemistry of Plutonium. We were finally beginning to receive samples big enough to see, from Hanford, WA. I remember the first one coming in early 1943 which was too small to see. Walter Beard talked Larry into going to the fateful party on that Saturday night where we met. Although we probably would have met eventually anyway, since we were working just down the hall from each other. But it was more astonishing and memorable to meet the way that we did on that 'Enchanted Evening'.

Proposal? Sort of

On our second date, about ten days after we met, he kissed me hard and I said partly in jest, "You shouldn't kiss like that unless you're serious" and he said "I think I am". I said "You mean you might be serious and want to get married?". (I still didn't believe I was attractive enough to have any man be interested). How did I know this was it and that I was really in love? I don't know, but I did know that there was never any question in my mind that he was the nicest, most wonderful man that I had ever met, and I still felt that way to the day he died. Also after a few evenings of talking about everything, we felt sure that we had a great number of interests in common, to say nothing of a joint interest in Science. He soon found a rental room close enough to our house that we could walk to work together which we did every morning from then on. My Mom let me invite Larry to Sunday dinner a time or two in February. He has recently told me that the friendly, cheerful family was one of the things that attracted him to me. (And here, all this time I thought it was just my overwhelming physical attraction!)

As he was meeting my sisters, for the first time, he said to me 'more and more beautiful women keep turning up'. When Larry and I met, he had been introduced to me as 'Larry', so I assumed that his name was Lawrence and introduced him to some of my sisters that way. He laughed and corrected me by saying that his name was actually Larned but he liked Larry better and used that name at work. Strangely enough his family never called him that but only used Larned. The only other name they had for him was 'Bobe', which his older sister had come up with when she tried to say 'brother'. They thought it very strange that I called him Larry. Who was that? On meeting him, my Mom was very impressed and liked him very much. When someone said something about 'sticking a knife in to see if the cake was done', he came back with 'If the knife comes out clean, stick them all in'. Mom thought this hilarious. I've recently thought that perhaps he may have reminded Mom of her brother Arthur Atkinson.

After a few weeks or so having decided that there were no real reasons to wait, in early March, we went to my parents and told them that we wanted to get married. (Dad never said much about anything, but certainly made no objections). So, they were agreeable to having him in the family. As plans for the wedding continued, another problem arose. Larry was now out of uniform and everyone in our family and neighborhood thought he was a civilian. However, everyone back in Sioux City, knew he was in the Army. So what were we to put on the announcements (we didn't have invitations)—Mr. Asprey or Sergeant Asprey? Mom compromised and put nothing— just "Larned Brown Asprey" much to the disapproval of the woman who was taking the order for the announcements. She didn't think it proper not to have a 'title'. As usual, Mom was running things, and the announcements had no title for Larned Brown Asprey.

Meeting His Family

In late March, to introduce me to his Mother and older sister, Winifred (Tim), we took the train out to the University of Iowa, in Iowa City, IA, where Tim was in graduate school in Mathematics. His Mother, Gladys, came down from Sioux City and they stayed with Tim, while I stayed in the apartment of a friend of Tim's. Interestingly, as in my family, his Mother was the dominant person and made most of the decisions. In a time when few women went to college, her family had a tradition of sending their girls to Vassar College. Tim, her Mother and Grandmother were all Vassar graduates. On the other hand, his father, Peter, had never gone beyond 8th grade, because his family was large and quite poor, so he had to go to work to help support them.

Gladys was, however, extremely prejudiced against Catholics, which I was at the time, but she decided that I was presentable enough for her son. Larry was quite independent of his family and I don't think she could have stopped him from marrying me even if she wanted to. However whether because of illness (which they said) or because of prejudice, neither she nor his father (whom I didn't meet until much later) came to Chicago for the wedding, although his sister Tim did. It's true it was a long distance, but in a way, it was sad, because he was the only child of theirs ever to marry and have children. His younger brother Bob also did not come to the wedding but he was in the Marines and unable to come because of the war. He did come for a brief visit on his way through Chicago later, after we were married, on the way to the South Pacific where he eventually ended up for the rest of the war. Later, he was in the first wave during the invasion of Iwo Jima and, after the war he was stationed in mainland Japan.

Larry's Father, Peter Asprey, however, did arrange an engagement ring for me. Because Larry didn't have much money and I cared little for jewelry, I had told Larry that he needn't bother getting me an engagement ring. But, his Father had been a manufacturing jeweler before he was married and still bought and sold diamonds for friends to make a little money on the side. In fact that was how Larry's parents met in the first place over some jewelry that he made for her. When Larry was in high school, his Dad had given him a ruby ring which Larry never wore. (He wasn't fond of jewelry either) So when Peter, his Dad, had a chance to sell the ring at a nice profit, he promised that when Larned got engaged, he would get a ring for him. So when he heard that we were engaged, he immediately got a diamond ring and sent it to Larry in Chicago. Being a tease, when I asked Larry to pick up a spool of white thread for me in the local dimestore, he put the ring in the bag with the thread. When we met he handed the bag to me and said, "Aren't you going to check that it's right?". When I looked inside and saw the ring, he said "Now you can tell everyone that you got it in the Dime Store. Typical Larry! He always made jokes of everything, but I never could do that.

Marriage

When Larry and I had decided to get married, we rented an apartment in the neighborhood and Larry moved into it in advance. Kitty helped me move my clothes over there, also in advance. The wedding was to be held at the Williams home at 4901 Dorchester Ave, on the evening of Wednesday, May 3, 1944. In those days, since Larry wasn't a Catholic, to express their disapproval, the Church's rule was that we couldn't be married in the church but were to be married in the rectory, the Priest's residence.[6] Mom however made special arrangements to have it in our house instead which was much nicer. She was always good at that sort of arranging and this time I really appreciated it. We decorated the fireplace in the living room with flowers and greens as sort of an 'altar' or a background for the priest during the ceremony.

At 5:00 PM supper was served for the Williams family, most of whom lived there, but our Williams grandmother, Gragra, and Dad's brother Bob Williams and wife Ella were also included. Unfortunately most of Mom's Atkinson family were not able to come because of the difficulty of wartime travel. At 7:00 PM the Priest, Larry, Marty Studier, his best man and friend from the lab, and his sister Tim arrived. Tim was to be my attendant. I did not have, and really did not want, a long white wedding gown but wore a simple short blue dress with white polka dots and a little white hat. My Atkinson grandmother, GaGa, played the Mendelssohn Wedding March on the piano while Dad escorted the first of his many daughters to be married down the stairs. I didn't feel nervous, just happy, but Larry told me later that his knees were shaking. The ceremony in the living room was short but very traditional. Afterwards. we signed all the required papers and then some of our friends from the laboratory arrived for cake, punch, champagne and a few toasts. After this, we took a taxi for the few blocks to the apartment where we spent a long wonderful, weekend before going

---

6   To discourage Catholics from marrying non-Catholics, what the Catholic Church called a 'mixed' marriage like ours was not to be completely solemnized. It was not allowed to be held in the church. Normally it was to be held in the Priest's house which was called the 'rectory'.

back to work on Monday. What happened at the house after we left, I have no idea, nor did I care.

The Way We Looked in June '44

Above is what we looked like at the time. No one in the family had a camera nor could we afford a professional photographer for the wedding, but this was taken a few months later and the dress is similar to what I wore for the wedding. Larry was not in uniform for the marriage but one month later the US Army decided that secrecy or not, they couldn't figure out any way to pay for the civilian clothes that the soldiers were wearing so they just had to put them back into uniform. It seemed very sad to Larry. He said that he would gladly pay for his own clothes for the privilege of being out of uniform. But the silly Army could not be convinced that the secrecy was that important. Our landlady looked really shocked when the civilian turned overnight into an Army Sergeant. Nothing like keeping things secret by making them conspicuous!

Chapter 10

First Years of Marriage and Parenting, 1944-49

First Quarrel

In getting better acquainted with my new husband, those were important first months. One morning I put a rather messy butter plate on the breakfast table. Things like that were standard in my parent's household as everyone there was always in a hurry, and there were so many of us that we didn't worry about such details. Dad didn't care about such details and kids never do. But Larry had been raised with household help did not approve and let me know it. I told him 'too bad, I'm in a hurry since I also have to get ready for work'. So we had angry words and yelled at each other for the first time. But we managed to resolve the problem as we always have over the years. Eventually, I agreed to be neater and he to try not to be so fussy. I did clean up the butter plate!

A Honeymoon

The following June, we took the train from Chicago to Sioux City to visit his parents. I finally got to meet my new Father-in-Law and also more of Larry's aunts and uncles. Larry's Uncle, Dr. Harold Brown (better known in the family as 'Uncle Doctor'), offered us the use of a lakeside cottage in Northern Iowa for a belated honeymoon. We had not taken been able to take a honeymoon trip at the time of our marriage in May. Since he also offered use of a car to drive up, we happily took him up on it. Spirit Lake was small and the water muddy but the air near it was cool and made a delightful change from the heat and noise of Chicago. There was a swing on a small porch overlooking the lake. It was very private so we could enjoy a little lovemaking there even though it embarrassed me somewhat to Larry's great amusement.

In the field around the cottage, there were many noisy frogs, and as a boy Larry had always enjoyed catching them. So he used his skills to catch a bunch and we had frog's legs for dinner the second night. This was a new and very startling experience for me, because they jump around in the pan while frying. However they tasted surprisingly good, something like a cross between chicken and fish. It was the last vacation that we were able to enjoy without children for a long time.

From my earliest memories I was crazy about babies. When my first sister, Kitty, was born, I was 16 months old and she was 'my baby'. Who needed dolls when you had a baby sister? My Mother told me later that when the baby would cry, I would call out "Don't you cry Katsy baby. I'se a comin'". I felt that way about each of my eight younger siblings as they came along. Not that I did too much baby sitting because, Mom thought that Kitty was such a klutz in the kitchen, (with which I did not agree), she should baby sit and I should work in the kitchen, doing boring things like washing dishes. I thought this was very unjust but I didn't have a choice.

As a teenager, when I became fascinated by science and wanted to be a scientist, I used to say to myself, "It isn't fair. Men don't have to choose between science and marriage. Why should I have to choose?" But I thought that was the way it was. I also thought that no man would want to marry me anyway because I was so ugly. So I concentrated on my studies and aimed at being a scientist.

A First Baby

As told above, to my complete surprise, a wonderful man did want to marry me. Now I could hope for babies. And three months after we were married, while still working of course, I was indeed pregnant with my first baby. I continued to work on the project ignoring the posssibility of radioactivity for about six months more. Then I thought that I had to stop because my cultural, family and religious traditions all said it wasn't right for a mother to work when she had small children. My grandmother had told my mother 'Ladies don't work'. So I had already violated her precepts by working at all. According to the Catholic Church, children were the primary purpose and reason for marriage. They are certainly one of the most important things in life. Finally, I personally believed that babies when small were better off having their mom's full time and attention. So I stayed at home in our little apartment near the University of Chicago from January until April.

People have asked me why I believed that one shouldn't work after having children. I was not alone in believing that and many still do today. Many even go so far as to say that married women shouldn't work either. Certainly many men would rather that their wives stay at home and not work. Recently I read a comment by Dr Jocelyn Bell Burrnell, an astronomer who discovered pulsars, that makes clear that it's still a live attitude. In 1969 when she was working on her PhD in Astronomy at Cambridge, she went on vacation and returned wearing an engagement ring. She said "that was the stupidest thing I ever did, in those days married women did not work". Work for a little while but "everybody knew that if mothers worked, the children would become delinquents. Her engagement ring was her signal that her professional life was over." More people congratulated her on the engagement than on the major astrophysical discovery. It was right for her to get engaged but not to discover pulsars. This was quoted in the magazine "Radiations", Fall 2004. So I was not alone in my beliefs even if they were somewhat incomplete.

As the due date for the baby approached, we had to make a decision. Larry was told at this time that he would soon be ordered to work at Los Alamos. Civilian scientists were able to bring spouses and children but Army personnel were not. Since Larry was in the Army, the baby and I would not be able to go. The lease on our apartment ended on May 1, a few weeks after the due date and we were either going to have to sign for another year or move out. With Larry gone to Los Alamos and me no longer working, we probably couldn't afford the apartment. So we asked Mom if there was room enough for us to move back into my old home since Larry expected to be gone soon. It was a very large house and two of the other girls were away at work and college. We would pay rent and I would be available to help Mom with the housework. Mom agreed and so after Pete was born, we moved back home.

Moving Back Home

I really was not eager for this move. Having gotten away from Mom's dictatorial regime, I really didn't want to go back. Fortunately, Larry got along with her so well that he served as a buffer between us to some extent. And there were huge amounts of work to be done. It wasn't as easy as it had been in the apartment. In addition to the usual cooking and dishwashing for so many, keeping the house clean was a continuing battle with the mice, cockroaches and spiders as well as the usual Chicago dirt. I also remember cleaning out cupboards for Mom, something that she rarely had time to do. Laundry for a large family meant carrying mounds of laundry down two flights of narrow stairs to a dirty basement. There we were fortunate to have a washing machine with an attached wringer. After filling the washer with hot water from a hose, white things were put in and the agitator turned on. You might shovel some coal while you waited since that had to be done every few hours. Or maybe go back upstairs for some more dirty clothes. The agitator of the washer was then turned off and the clothes fed by hand through the wringer into the first rinse sink. The next load was put in to agitate, meanwhile the first load was put through the wringer into the second rinse and finally into the laundry basket. Now it had to be hung up, outside in the summer and in the basement in the winter. And don't drop anything or it will have to be washed again because the floor was filthy and it wasn't much better outside. Then repeat the procedure for the second, third and as many loads as you had. The second load would be light colored clothes and the third load would be the dark things. By this time the water would be dirty enough that the washer would have to be emptied and refilled and the process started again.

I hope that I was really able to be of some help to Mom with the huge burden she always carried in addition to the extra work we made and I certainly tried. My younger sisters also seemed to enjoy having a new little baby to play with. At the time, it never even occurred to me to go back to work. One of my sisters Sally thought that I did go back to work, because she said later that "Mom let her play with Pete". Not so! Mom may have let her play with him rather than do housework but Pete was my baby and I can't remember Mom even picking him up. However things were moving so fast on the Manhattan Project that Larry never was sent to Los Alamos. We stayed on at 4901 until Larry was released from the Army in February 1946.

First Baby, Pete, April 1945

When that first baby (7 lb. 3 oz) arrived on April 23, 1945, we called him Peter Larned, for his grandfather, Peter, and his father, Larned. When I woke up the morning after he was born, there were a dozen beautiful red roses on the table by my bed. To my amazement, my beloved husband had sent them to me. I didn't know men did things like that since my Dad never did. When we brought Pete home from the hospital and Larry carried him into the house, his comment was "He feels just like a little puppy". What a wonderful Daddy he was then and always!

That Fall while living at 4901, there was an accident at the lab and they did not realize that Larry got radioactivity all over his hair. When it was realized, they sent technicians out with Geiger Counters to check the house in general and our bedroom in particular. The radioactivity was all over our bed and the baby's crib. Everything had to be scrubbed down and all linens washed in that miserable laundry system. My grandmother who had the room across the hall was very curious to know what it was going on. We tried to tell her it was unimportant and to get her to stay in her room but she kept coming out and asking questions. Not too surprising, because several strange men carrying Geiger Counters running around the house, were quite unusual and she wasn't willing to accept our assurances that it was 'nothing important'. Of course secrecy applied here and we couldn't tell her the truth even if we wanted to.

Baby Pete, was very healthy despite both parents having worked with radioactivity and all the warnings we had received about the dire possibilities. I was able to nurse him with no solid food for ten months. I had so much milk that he tripled his birth weight in three months rather than the usual six or more months. Since my family had eight girls and only one boy, It was a great treat to have a baby boy in the family. With a great-grandmother, grandmother, six aunts of various ages and one uncle to say nothing of a fun loving Daddy, he was played with so much that he never really learned to crawl. He went straight to walking at a year, but that was faraway in California and another story.

World War II Ends

In the summer of 1945, World War II came to a crashing end when the atom bombs were dropped on Hiroshima and Nagasaki. It was much sooner than we had expected as a result of the stunning success of the Manhattan Project to which Larry and I had contributed, We heard about the bombs being dropped in August of 1945 when Pete was four months old while we were on vacation. We had taken him out to introduce him to his Asprey grandparents in Sioux City. When the paper came in the afternoon, Grandfather Asprey was reading it on the porch and left it there in the swing saying nothing about it. Larry came out and picked up the paper. There was the huge headline about the bombing of Hiroshima. Since it had been the best kept secret of the war, and Grandfather didn't understand it at all, it certainly did not mean to him what it did to us. We had not been told that we were free to say anything and Larry soon received a telegram telling him that he was not to say anything. Before it came he had already told his sister Tim that it was partly a result of our efforts during the war. We both felt very unhappy that it had to be used on people, but recognized that it was probably necessary. Chapter 8 describes our work on the bomb.

The Family Before We Went West

Larry had signed the petition by the Manhattan Project Scientists which they tried to send to President Truman asking that the bomb not be used until the Japanese had been given a chance to surrender before it was used. Because I was now home with the baby, I did not have the opportunity to sign it but would have if I had been still working. From what I have read since, an attempt was made to get the Emperor of Japan to surrender but the Japanese military would have none of it. Also what we heard later from Larry's brother Bob who was in Japan after the surrender, a huge number of lives were actually probably saved by it. He saw an example of the awful slaughter during the island landings when he was in the first wave landing on Iwo Jima. He also saw the powerful defenses and booby traps that had been set up on all the beaches of Japan itself and during an attack, our men would have died like flies. Also, I'm sure most people have heard of the early suicide bombers called 'The Divine Wind". It consisted of squadrons of light planes flown by volunteer suicide pilots who dove directly into the American warships and so could not be stopped. Suicide bombers are not new. The conventional fire bombing of Tokyo had killed more than a single atom bomb did. In sum, I feel strongly that when the Japanese attacked Pearl Harbor without warning, killing so many Americans and destroying so many ships, they opened the door to whatever happened later. War is just hell! No matter what weapons are used.

Heading West

Larry, lwhile working in Glenn Seaborg's group at New Chem, had worked directly for Burris Cunningham, who had become a good friend and respected mentor. He had been a Professor of Chemistry at the University of California (UC) at Berkeley before the war. So after the war, Larry decided to go back to school for his doctoral degree in Chemistry, working for Burris. He had also been offered a part time job in a research lab at UC Berkeley

In February, 1946, after Larry was officially discharged from the US Army, we headed first by train to Sioux City, IA, to visit his parents on our way to California. Since WW II was just over and no new cars had been made for about six years, all productivity for those years, had been directed to military tanks, jeeps and war related hardware. So all that we could find in Sioux City and could afford, was an old clunker, a 1936 four-door Studebaker. What little furniture and other property we had was shipped to the west coast.

Bidding Larry's parents good-bye, with Pete not quite a year old and not walking, we set out to drive to California. Along the way, we first kept getting flat tires but couldn't find new ones to buy. So we would have the old ones patched up and keep going. Because I had never learned to drive, Larry had to do all the driving and I got to hold restless Pete the whole time. I would have given a lot to have a change and drive for a while.

Our Auto Fails Us

Finally, just as we entered Colorado, the motor threw a rod. An ancient hay truck pulled us into the nearest small town, whose name I don't remember. The men in the garage there, couldn't do anything for us but they called around and found a garage, about 30 miles away in Sterling, CO, where they had a rebuilt motor that could be put in. The car was towed there with us riding in it. We moved into a motel for several days and wired his parents to borrow some money since we had very little, certainly not enough for a motor.

At about 11 months old, Pete was dying to try to walk but everything was so dirty in the garage (and the motel wasn't much better), that he couldn't spend much time down on the floor. Furthermore there was no tub in the motel room but only a tiny washbasin and a shower which frightened him so much that I had a terrible time trying to keep him clean at all. Finally they told us that the car was ready and we started off. Immediately the motor boiled over and so back we went. They agreed to run the motor overnight and thought it would 'loosen up' and be all right in the morning. And back to the motel we went.

The next morning they agreed to take something off the price and remove the guarantee. We, and of course they, knew that we were heading for California so the guarantee probably didn't mean much anyway. So we started off again going only 30 miles an hour until the motor got 'broken in' a bit.[7] We were not able to go through the high

---

[7]   In those days cars had to be broken in gradually, and this also applied to a new or even rebuilt motor. You started off at 30 miles/hour for about 50 miles. Then moved up to 40 miles/hour for about 100 miles and so forth. Also you couldn't climb steep slopes right away.

peaks of the Rockies but had to go north through Wyoming where the land was flatter and the slopes more gradual. Gradually we were able to speed up a bit and finally got to Salt Lake City, Utah. Here Larry talked a Sears store manager into selling us a new tire that he had saved back for himself. So we replaced the worst of the old ones.

One of the most exciting things to me was driving through the high Sierras. Remember that I had never even seen a mountain in my life let alone anything that high. And coming across Nevada all was flat desert and still winter dormant. It was about the first of April and as we gradually climbed up to the top of the Sierra the roads became bordered by about 10 foot high snow banks on both sides. After the highest pass, as we drove down the far side the snow gradually disappeared, and eventually we ended up in the same day surrounded by green fields with flowers and butterflies everywhere. It was a spectacular trip for me like nothing of which I had ever dreamed. Finally we had made it to California and I can't tell you the tremendous feeling of relief as we got there. We drove on into Berkeley where we spent a few nights in a hotel with a tub and a clean carpeted floor for Pete to crawl on.

Harbor Gate

As a veteran, Larry was allowed to rent a very small, roughly built two bedroom house about a half hour drive north of Berkeley. It was one of a group of small houses that had been designed and built speedily for the shipyard workers during the war, in what was called Harbor Gate, a section of Richmond, CA, down near the San Francisco bay. They were primitive facilities, tiny kitchen, bathtub made of poured cement, kerosene furnace, no refrigerator but only an 'air cooler', using air from under the house fed through slots in the shelves. There was no phone in the house but we could use a public one about a half block away to make calls. But we were glad to have it and there we lived for over three years while Larry went to school and worked. There were other graduate students living in Harbor Gate, going to school and working in Berkeley, so the men were able to form a car pool so that we wives would have cars part of the time to do our shopping and not be completely stranded.

Learning to Drive

But in the beginning it didn't help me much because I still didn't know how to drive. Larry taught me to drive that ancient Studebaker during the first year that we were there. One funny thing that happened when he took me to take the driving test. The only place he found to park was a very tight spot, which required parallel parking. So when the man came out to give me my driving test, being a bit nervous anyway, I could not get the car out of the parking place. So we had to go away, while I practiced some more, and try again later. The next time Larry found a more appropriate parking place and this time I managed to pass. Quite a test of our marriage because I was so upset, but it survived,partly thanks to Larry's patience.

House in Harbor Gate near Richmond, CA
(and the Studebaker)

In the first years at Harbor Gate, the wartime shortages continued for a while. In one letter in August, I told triumphally of finding a bag of flour, the first since May 1st. there were shortages of fats of all kinds, raisins, gelatin, soap, jam, cream and canned fruit. We did have plenty of fresh fruits and vegetables. I even learned from some of the other wives how to can and I proudly put up 20 quarts of local fresh peaches. Larry had even put in a small garden and we spent time pulling weeds and had some fresh corn to eat.

After about a year, Larry's parents retired and decided to move from Sioux City to Santa Ana, just South of Los Angeles. They bought a very nice house there in the middle of what had been an orange grove. Having always lived in the cold of Sioux City, it was a real thrill for them to have several orange trees in their back yard and Grandfather Peter had a great time growing flowers.

Williams Family Happenings

In the two years after we left Chicago in March, 1946, many things happened with my family back in Chicago. Unfortunately, since as graduate students, we were very poor, much to my sorrow we were unable to go back for all the occurrences. On June 26, 1946, my sister Kitty married Bob Kallal, a Chemical Engineer that she had met in graduate school at the University of Illinois. Her wedding was much more elaborate than mine, partly because the family was better off by then and partly because Bob was also a Catholic so Mom regarded it as a more 'proper' wedding. Both of Mom's brothers, Arthur and Jack Atkinson, and her sister Isabelle Soule came for it. This made it the last time that Mom's family was all together before their Mother, Gaga, died.

Atkinsons (bk, l-r) Isabelle, Jack,
(fr l-r) Arthur, Sarah, Dorothy

On August 7, 1947, my sister Dottie married Robert (Bob) Carter. Bob had worked with Enrico Fermi on research reactors at Los Alamos during the war. Dot and Bob had met in graduate school while both were studying physics at the University of Illinois. They had really become attached on a group skiing trip during the previous winter to Aspen, CO. Their wedding however was very quiet (Bob also was not a Catholic) and most of the rest of the family weren't able to be there either. In the year between these two weddings the remainder of the family moved back to Ferguson near St. Louis where we had spent our early childhood. Kitty and Bob Kallal took her on her first airplane ride to get her to St. Louis. Shortly after this, our grandmother, Sarah Atkinson, Gaga, died on July 5, 1947 at the age of 89.

My sister, Kit, and her husband, Bob, after their marriage had moved to Boston where he was to work on his doctorate in Chemical Engineering at MIT (Massachusetts Institute of

Technology). While there, Kit gave birth in May 1948 to a baby girl, Ginny Lou. In the following September Kitty with her 3 month old baby, was planning to come from Boston to Ferguson for a visit. Well, I decided that poor or not, we had enough money I could afford to take the 24 hour train trip to St. Louis to see her and the rest of my family after two years separation. Larry thought that he would not be able to go because of his studies and work so Pete and I were planning to go by ourselves. At the last minute Larry decided that he could afford the time to go so the three of us took off on the 24 hour train trip.

Ferguson Again

The train was so crowded that for the first leg of the trip, we had to sit on our suitcases. After a few stops, it emptied out a bit and we were able to get seats. I had just discovered that I was pregnant again which made the trip particularly wearing. At the end when we arrived, it was great to be back in Ferguson again after all those years. It was amazing how much it had changed since I had left there at the end of 6th grade (1932). The trees were all much, much bigger so the shade made the grass not grow well. The woodland to the west now had two houses built on it and the field where the cow had chased us now had a road just behind our lot and two houses in the field beyond. No more cows. Dot was also there for a visit with her two month old baby, Tricia. I was so excited that Kitty was coming and couldn't wait to see her.

A day or two later, Dad, Mom, and my sister Sally went to the train station to pick up Kitty and her baby. Sally tells me that Kitty looked so different when she got off the train that something was obviously very wrong. Mom and Dod didn't even recognize her at first. Mom said "that's not my Kitty". Apparently while on the train, Kitty had gone into a deep depression but still managed, probably with some help from kindly strangers, to care adequately for the baby.

Kitty's Mental Problems

When Mom and Dad returned from the train station and Kitty got out of the car, something was to me very obviously wrong. Kitty mumbled something strange about Boston and hardly seemed to know me. I was shocked at how strange she looked and acted. She seemed far away and almost unaware of her baby. Dot and I took care of her baby as best we could, changed diapers and gave her bottles. But what was wrong with Kit? We are still not absolutely certain what was actually wrong but it was probably what is now called postpartum depression or psychosis[8]. Later, after we went back to California, her husband Bob came from Boston and he and Mom had a big argument. She blamed him for sending her off in such a state but she had been fine when she left him and he had no idea what would happen. With the help of Bob's sister who was a nurse, a psychiatrist was found who took on her care. She spent September to December in a private mental hospital in a St. Louis suburb where she was treated with electroshock and eventually came out of it. I guess that I was very lucky not to have had any problems like that. I was also very lucky to have such a wonderful and supportive husband and only knew that I didn't want my Mother around after delivery as she always upset me.

Much later Kitty told me that the last thing she remembered was being on the train with her baby until several months later when she came to herself in the hospital wondering where on earth she was. Apparently she had been very isolated in Boston and her husband was working terribly hard so didn"t have much time to help

---

[8] Postpartum psychosis: Apparently this is a fairly common result of the major hormonal changes accompanying childbirth. Nearly ten percent of women experience some depression but a full-fledged psychosis is uncommon— approximately one in a thousand births. Apparently women need more help after childbirth than is usually recognized.

her. While she lost some recent memories as a result of the shock treatments, she was fortunate to retain her long-term memory so was still able to teach Chemistry at the University of Delaware in later years. Furthermore she has not had any recurrences when her later children were born. She says that the Doctor told her at the time when she recovered from the breakdown, that some women 'crack up' every time they have a baby but others have only one episode and never have any more trouble. No one knows why. He also told her that she must be intelligent enough to help in this prevention by taking good care of herself. She certainly did try hard in the future to take care of herself, but I'm sure she was very nervous each time her other four children were born.

My Own Tragedy

Meanwhile, while we were still in Ferguson, Larry decided that since new vehicles were coming on the market now and might be cheaper in the midwest than in California, we could afford and by now needed to replace our old clunker which had limped out to the west coast earlier. Dad went with him and they bought a small Jeep Station Wagon for us. So we set out to drive back to Harbor Gate in California via Santa Ana. We had planned to stop and visit Larry's parents in Santa Ana south of Los Angeles on the way back. My sister Lydia was coming back with us. She had graduated from the University of Illinois with a degree in Economics but hadn't been able to find a satisfactory job in St. Louis. She was going with us to look for a job in San Francisco where she thought that she might have better prospects. However, on the way, we had our own tragedy. As usual I couldn't convince Larry that we needed to stop sooner than he wanted to so we continued until late in the night. That night, I started bleeding a little bit. By the time we arrived in Santa Ana, apparently I was into a full miscarriage. By morning I was bleeding profusely all over Grandmother Asprey's daybed and ended up in the hospital. Larry and sister Lydia drove on up to Harbor Gate and Pete and I stayed behind with my parents-in-law until I recovered. Eventually Pete and I took the train back up to Harbor Gate.

Important Visitors

Back in Harbor Gate, we enjoyed several important visitors over the next year. The first was my only brother, Grant Williams. He was going to school at the University of Missouri on a Navy ROTC program and part of his duty was to serve on a summer cruise. The first year he was to cruise out into the Pacific from San Francisco. So he came and visited us for several days first. As a hostess gift he brought a record called 'Down to the Sea in Ships' with sea chanteys that Burl Ives had collected and sang to his guitar playing. Pete and I enjoyed it so much, that we played it often enough that both of us memorized all the songs and eventually wore out the plastic record.

The next interesting visitor was my oldest cousin, John Soule (son of my Mom's older sister, Isabelle) with his wife Adelia and two children. He was a Colonel in the Army Engineers and was on his way to Seoul, Korea. This was before the Korean War by several years. They ended up seeing a lot of interesting parts of the world including Karachi, Pakistan, and Teheran, Iran, and ending up in France for several years.

A sad thing that happened during those years was one December when we were going down to visit Larry's parents for Christmas. Larry was so eager to get there that again to my great annoyance, I couldn't get him to stop for food or to let us go to the bathroom. It was late and we didn't know the way very well. He took the wrong turn after dark just south of Los Angeles. Trying to get back on the main road, a stop sign was hidden behind a branch, so unknowing, Larry ran it and was sideswiped by an oncoming car and badly wrecked. There were no seat belts, so I can remember throwing my body across Pete trying to protect him. My sister Lydia was in the front seat and was the only one really hurt. Her arm was badly damaged and took several hours of surgery to repair. My strongest memory of the affair was desperately needing a restroom and the tremendous relief when I found one at the hospital. We called Larry's Parents in Santa Ana since our car was no longer drivable and they came and rescued us.

After three and a half years in California, Larry finished his PhD degree in Chemistry and was offered a job in Los Alamos. Also, I was again pregnant and having lost my last pregnancy, I was trying hard to be very careful this time.

Chapter 11

To Los Alamos, 1949-53

A fter Larry finished his PhD in the Summer of 1949 he was offered a job at Los Alamos, NM. However, it turned out that there were problems. Los Alamos was building houses for new workers as fast as possible but they wouldn't be ready until Fall. They would be glad to have Larry go sooner and stay in a hotel room but there would be no place for me and Pete and they wouldn't pay for us to stay in the hotel. So he needed to put off leaving until September and asked for his job back temporarily at UC Berkley to which, fortunately for us, they agreed. However, since our expected baby would be due in early December, we didn't want to wait any longer than September. So all three of us, Pete, Larry and I, came to New Mexico in September. It was a first airplane flight for Pete and for me and so to both of us very exciting. While being flown up in a small four person plane from Albuquerque, I commented on the big brown fields of what I thought was grass in the Sangre de Cristo mountains to the East. The pilot laughed at me and said "no, those are aspen trees without their leaves, not grass". I just wasn't used to seeing trees that far away and have them look like grass.

Fortunately for us, my sister Dottie's husband, Bob Carter, who had worked on the Manhattan Project in Los Alamos during the war had been offered a job there in 1947 while we were in California. As one of the few experienced experts on reactors at the time, Los Alamos had been glad to hire him back. Dot and Bob, with one small baby, had a small two-bedroom house in Los Alamos. They welcomed us but could only offer a space to sleep on the floor in their baby's bedroom until our house was ready. So sleep on the floor, we did for several weeks, and were very grateful for the shelter!

Our House is Finally Ready

The duplex that we were to rent was finally ready in late October (1941-41st St.). We moved in and also slept on the floor there, until our furniture arrived in mid-November! While the house may have been ready, the yard was not. Since it stood on a hill, I can still remember the difficulty, while very pregnant, of climbing up a dirt bank to get to the front door. The houses were not well insulated either. I can remember when we had a cold snap that winter, the plumbing under the houses up and down the street all froze. When it warmed up, water was shooting everywhere. The plumbers were all very busy taking care of the water pouring out from under each house. Fortunately the houses were rented so that wasn't our problem.

In the first week of December, I thought that it was surely time for the baby to come and Larry took me to the hospital. It turned out to be false labor, a not unusual problem. One thing, strange at the time, the nurse thought she got the heartbeat on the left and the Doctor said "Oh no! it's on the right". The Doctor was neither my regular Doctor nor the one who finally delivered me. The hospital was an old Army one that had been built in a big hurry by the military during the war years. They were still very cavalier about how they treated patients. Babies were delivered by anyone who was handy at the moment. It was several years before they built a new hospital with more up-to-date and patient friendly facilities. They sent me home for two more weeks and I felt truly gigantic. I remember not being able to bend over at all to vacuum the floor, so I had to sit down on a chair to vacuum.

Twins, What a surprise!

Finally Dec 16, 1949 arrived and this time I really felt that I must be ready to deliver. Particularly since the 'actual due date was on my birthday, Dec 21, which was now only five days away. So off to the hospital we went at 4:00 PM in the afternoon. They put me to sleep, as they usually did in those days, and when I came to they gave me the startling news, "You have twins!" Through the fuzziness of the anesthetic, I said, "I don't believe it" and the nurse said, "You say that you don't want them?" And I said "Oh No! I'm thrilled about them!" And I was! I was actually delighted.

My regular Doctor had missed them completely but she had not seen me until seven months when it was hard to tell just from the outside. X-rays were rare in those days. It also explained why the Nurse heard the heartbeat on one side and the Doctor on the other! I heard later that for missing twins it cost my Doctor a round of beer for the medical staff! Then when the nurse came out to tell the new father and he stood up, she said "You better sit down, Sir". Wondering what on earth was going on he sat down again. She told him the surprising news, "You have twin girls!".

For twins, they were amazingly good sized and fortunately for me well behaved. No wonder that I had been so huge. Elizabeth Anne (Baby A) was born first at 5 lb. 6 oz. Six minutes later, Barbara Alice (Baby B) was born at 6 lb. 3 oz. Before we knew it was to be twins, we had planned to call a girl, Margaret Susan (after me) but we couldn't think of a name that we thought paired well with Peggy which we wanted to call her. So we settled on Barby and Betty and had our Peggy later. And they were beautiful babies and really as easy to care for as twins could possibly be. The nurses in the hospital couldn't believe that I could nurse both. Having had so much milk for Pete, I was sure that I could, so insisted that they let me try. Probably if it had been my first delivery and I hadn't had so much success nursing earlier I might have given up more easily. I asked them to weigh them before and after each nursing. When they did that, they found that each got six ozs of milk and agreed that I could indeed nurse both. I proceeded to do so for 10 months and they grew well and were completely healthy. I always enjoyed nursing very much but it did take a lot of time for two of them. I guess that you could say that I was a good cow!

Four Born in Los Alamos, 1949-1952

Betty   Barby

Bobby   Peggy

Emergency

About a week or two after we came home from the hospital, I suddenly had abdominal pains that they couldn't immediately identify. They put me back in the hospital for a few days leaving Larry and Pete with two very unhappy babies to try to bottle feed to which they were completely unaccustomed. As for me, I had to try to pump two very uncomfortable breasts. Fortunately the pains went away and I came home after a few days and had no more complications. I'm sure the family was very glad to see me and was I glad to see them and continue nursing! One long lasting effect was on big brother Pete who was only four and a half at the time but remembers it very vividly. As he says now. "I remember being propped up with pillows giving one a bottle. And with awe being 'allowed' to help change wet diapers. It gave me confidence beyond the actual effect." The help involved removing the dirty one and putting the clean one under the baby. Then Larry pinned it. He thought that Pete might stick them with the diaper pins which we used in those days.

Despite being genetically identical and looking much alike when small, they have turned out to be very different. It took several days for us to tell them apart, so we left the hospital bracelets on until we were sure. One basic difference, Betty is left handed and Barb, right handed. Some place I have read that mirror image twins like these are more alike than usual identical twins. The theory is that the egg splits later during gestation after the left-right division has been laid down. Since our girls have turned out to be quite different in their interests and lives, I'm not sure that theory is true.

One small problem, Barby had been crowded enough in the womb that one foot was a bit twisted so she had to wear special orthopedic shoes for awhile. (Grandfather Asprey was very proud to be able to tell them apart by the different colors of their shoes). As a result Barby was slower to walk than Betty who walked at 12 months while Barby didn't walk until 14 months. During those two months it was very strange to have them so much alike and yet one could walk and the other couldn't! The foot straightened out by the end of her second year and Barby has had no trouble with it since.

Six Weeks, Enough Family?

When I went to the Doctor for my six weeks checkup after the twins were born, the nurse said, "A boy and now two girls. Now you really have your family". Well, I didn't feel that way. I just couldn't get enough of babies even after having twins. Believing as I do now, I probably would have agreed and stopped there. However, at the time I didn't realize how crowded the earth was becoming. Having come from one, I thought that big families were necessary. I felt then and still believe that we were the right people to have a big family. We both enjoyed them so much and were able to do a reasonable job and had adequate, if not excessive money, to care for them reasonably well. And as they have turned out I believe that the world is better a place as a result of our big family.

When the twins were eight months old and I was still nursing them, I had one period and then no more. Again that Summer I was pregnant! With our growing family, we were finally able to get a larger house and moved to 2505B 36th Street which had four bedrooms rather than the three in our first house. Also it was all on one floor which made life a little easier for me not having stairs to climb. Also it suited our needs better because the school where Peter would be starting that Fall was just across the street. Otherwise he would have had to take a long walk or to ride a bus. The only bad part about this location was that it was in the middle of a steep hill. In Winter, when it was icy, it was a little hard to get in and out.

Back to St. Louis Again

The following September we flew back to St. Louis to show off the new twin grand babies to my parents. When we took off from Los Alamos, we flew in the small nineteen passenger plane to Albuquerque. Norris Bradbury, director of the lab, with his wife was right behind us. She very graciously offered to help by holding one of the babies. At nine months they were at that nice stage where they will accept anyone and yet are easy to hold and enjoy.

While in St. Louis, my teenage sister, Rose Anne, was such a big help with the two of them that Mom suggested that she come out to Los Alamos for the rest of her Junior high school year to help out. We were flying back but Dot and Bob, who also were visiting, would be driving back with several small children themselves so volunteered to bring Rose with them. And she was a huge help with the twins particularly when the next baby was born. Rose now tells me that everyone back in St. Louis believed that she came out to have a baby. But not so, I had enough for both of us. Little hard on her reputation however, although I never thought about that at the time.

One of the tricks that I learned that winter, while Larry was at work and Rose was in school, the twins would cry to be picked up. Being four or five months pregnant with the next one, I simply was unable to pick them up. I learned to sit on the floor and let them climb on me to their hearts content then they would go away and play and I could get some work done. Either you learn these tricks or you don't survive!

A Mischievous Pair

Of course being two of them they became very good at thinking up mischievous things to do. One time I stepped out the kitchen door to hang a few things on the clothes lines and when I came back they had figured out how to lock the door and of course, all the other doors to the house were also locked. Finally, I managed to talk them into unlocking the door and letting me in. Another time, I had just put a load of dirty diapers into the washing machine. The drain from the washing machine also used the sink drain by hooking it over the front of the sink. They were playing in the sink but they had never paid any attention to the drain hose. So I didn't even think about it when I again stepped out to hang a few clothes. This time however, the washing machine started the drain cycle so they noticed it, They thought it great fun to spray each other and everything else in sight with the dirty diaper water! When Larry came home for lunch shortly thereafter, he found me frantically mopping up dirty water and crying. It had even gotten into the drawer where I kept crackers and bread as well as all over both of them and left several inches on the floor. What a mess! I never thought that hanging laundry could be so dangerous!

Barbie and Betty Sharing a Table

Some of their tricks were just fun. One example, when they were about two, Larry made them a small table and two little chairs. Betty liked meat and potatoes and Barb liked salads and veggies. Each would eat what she liked, then they would trade places and finish off the other plate! Once we caught on, we wouldn't let them do it any more, but they thought it great fun while it lasted.

The Next Arrival

Well finally, May came. This baby was due on May 5, but days went by and no baby. Finally on the 22nd, over two weeks late, I was sure it was finally time. Larry took me to the hospital in the evening and the Doctor checked me out. He said, "No, it will still be several days yet". Well I was so depressed and discouraged at being so late, that when I heard this, I burst into tears. Larry said to the Doctor, "Can't you keep her overnight and see how things are in the morning?". The Doctor grudgingly agreed, admitted me and went away. In the night, I needed to go to the bathroom and got out of bed and started down the hall. A nurse found me and scolded me for being out of bed. I said, "But the Doctor said that I should go home that it would be several more days yet". She said, "Even so you should call for help if you need to go to the bathroom". So after going to the bathroom with her help, I went back to bed and to sleep. About two hours later, I woke up and felt like the baby was coming right now. So I rang for the nurse and she came in very angry and said. 'What do you want now?' and I said, "That baby is coming now!" She took one look at me and fled to get a gurney.

She loaded me on, took me to the delivery room and barely got me on the table when there he was! Was I triumphant the next morning when the Doctor got there! He wasn't even around for the delivery! On May 23, 1951, Robert Russell at 6 lb. 7 ozs had joined our growing family. The Robert was for Larry's brother, Robert Brown and the Russell was for my father, Russell John.

Bobby, What a Calm Child

Fortunately for me, Bobby was even easier to manage than the twins were. He was the most serene baby of all those that I have had. As an adult he was still a calm kind of person. Nothing seemed to bother him much. He went to sleep at the drop of a hat, anytime, anyplace and slept longer than anyone else in the family. At three months, a friend from Chicago, Aggie Morley (daughter of the Margaret that I was named for), came to visit. The guest bed in which she was to sleep was in the room in which he was sleeping. I told her, "Don't pay andy attention if he fusses, I'll come in and get him". At 11:00 AM the following morning, both of them were still sound asleep! My one complaint about Bob was when he got his first tooth at about six months. While nursing he bit down and when I yelped and jumped he grinned. Well, the breast got infected so he ended up on a bottle earlier than most of my babies.

Finally we have our Peggy

While I loved babies, I had finally decided it was time to start limiting my family somewhat. So I had been trying to use the Rhythm Method and was taking my morning temperature to identify the time of ovulation. In September when Larry returned from a trip to a meeting in New York, according to the thermometer we should have waited a few days. But I couldn't say no to him and suddenly I was pregnant again. You could say this was really a 'love' child, usually supposed to be the best!

Eight months later, we finally had our Peggy! Margaret Susan was 6 lb. 6 oz when born on June 25, 1952. This time I had prenatal classes given by a nun from Medical Missionary Sisters of Santa Fe, who ran a clinic for women's health. As part of their approach, Sr. Patrick convinced me that it was better for the baby if mothers didn't have an anesthetic during delivery, not that I could see it did any harm to any of my others. However, Bob had been so fast and easy, since they didn't have time to give me anything, that I was determined to try it this time. The delivery did take a few hours, but really wasn't that painful.

Sleeping with Three Climbing on Me

When I came home from the hospital with Peggy, the most difficult thing was getting enough sleep at night with so many other small ones around. Several times, I remember being so sleepy, when it was time to nurse the baby in the afternoon, that I lay down on the bed. I locked the door so the twins and Bobby couldn't get into mischief and with three of them happily climbing on me I fell sound asleep.

After Peggy was born with no help, except for a girl from Santa Clara Pueblo who cleaned for half a day, I was really busy. I had four still in diapers but loved every minute of having four live dolls to play with. The house was getting crowded and while we were on the list for a bigger house in Los Alamos, they were hard to get. As a left over from World War II and the developing Cold War with Russia, Los Alamos was still all SECRET and the whole town was behind guard gates. If people came to visit and you didn't want to see them the guards would keep them out unless you signed them in. At times it was something of a nuisance because our household helper who came up from Santa Clara Pueblo down in the Espanola Valley would sometimes forget her pass. Then I would have to dress all four babies, put them in the car and drive down to sign her in. It rather negated any help she gave me.

Fortunately, about now Larry and I found that we had very different sleep habits. When I first went to bed I was very cold and had to pile on the covers to get to sleep and then fell deeply asleep so even crying babies didn't wake me. On the other hand, Larry was always hot when he went to bed and had trouble going to sleep and woke easily, so could take the early shift. Later in the night, things reversed, he slept deeply and was cold but now I was hot and slept lightly. So I could throw the extra covers on him and took the late shift.

A Different Kind of Baby

Peggy was completely different from any of the others, particularly from Bob. She was difficult to get to go to sleep and was always awake at the crack of dawn. She was lively and full of fun. When she was a toddler, we got a big black Labrador puppy. He would run up to her to lick her face, knock her down and run over her because he couldn't stop. It didn't bother her a bit. She would get up laughing and head right for him. In personality and other ways she was extremely different from Bob the next oldest. However in other ways she and Bob were like a second set of twins, because she developed so fast that she was always catching up to her brother.

At this time all the houses in town still belonged to the Government and you could not even rent one unless you worked there. When the man in a house not too far from us died, his family had two weeks to move out! If we wanted to paint a room, they chose the color, not we. Larry had planted a vegetable garden behind our house and they proposed to build a fence right down the middle of it during midsummer when it was growing at it's best. After many protests, they grudgingly moved the fence location to spare the garden. We became more and more annoyed with having the government telling us what we could and couldn't do with 'our' house. So we decided to look for a bigger house in Espanola, a half hour drive away, where we could own our own home and do what we liked. In March of 1953, we did just that and lived there for nearly 17 years while Larry commuted to work, usually in a carpool, to Los Alamos.

Chapter 12

Early Espanola Years, 1953-60

Nearly Losing One

The first few years in Espanola were generally good ones but with a few disasters. The worst was when Pete and the twins got dysentery. One morning Pete woke up with an upset stomach which didn't seem too serious particularly since the twins had been through something similar for some days before. Larry went off to work. By 11:00 AM Pete seemed a bit disoriented and began to talk strangely. He now says that he was seeing dinosaurs in the dark vigas of our house. With no car, no phone and four babies, I could do nothing. I thought maybe when the babies took their nap, I could go borrow a neighbors phone and try to get some help. But when I did, the only Doctor that I knew about was not available and I was afraid to stay longer and keep trying. We had been unable to get a phone because there were no lines available and what phones there were in the neighborhood were already on a truly old-fashioned party line.

In the late afternoon, when Larry came home from work at 5:00 PM, he put Pete in the car and took him to a new Doctor who had recently moved into the neighborhood. This Doctor took one look at Pete and said "Take him to the Emergency Room and I"ll meet you there". Pete says now that he remembers it being dark and snowing and that they barely made it up the hill to the hospital. He was admitted to the hospital and spent two days on IV's. He also says that he doesn't remember anything about the following two days. For years, Dr Akes who later became our family doctor, said several times when he saw him, "Never saw a kid come any closer to dying and survive". That will scare a Mom any time. It would have been nice if we could have made changes to prevent things like that in the future. But we couldn't because there were no phones available nor could we afford a second car.

Williams Happenings

Back in Ferguson during the fifties, my sister Lydia graduated from the University of Illinois; Grant, from the University of Missouri; and Sally, from St. Louis University. In the next year or so, Grant was married to Kathleen Concannon from St. Louis and Sally, to Al Lemker from Cincinnati. Grant received his wings from the Navy in October 1954 with our Mom proudly pinning them on him. During this time I was restrained from visiting all these affairs by my crew of small children more than by money. However, I had rather gotten used to the idea that I couldn't go and was rather resigned to the situation.

Grant and His Plane

In 1955-56 my Dad finally retired. His Mother, GraGra, became ill and they spent some time caring for her up in Chicago before she died. Her ancestral home finally left the family when they sold it. Dad and Mom also sold their house in Maplewood and moved to a tiny one in Webster Groves to live out their retirement. By now all their kids had left home and so a one-bedroom house was easier to care for and all they needed. They did have three children, Grant, Rose and Susie close by for help if needed and to house we wanderers when we came to visit.

Lick and the Chicks

One of the early Espanola incidents that I remember vividly, involved our big black Labrador puppy, Licorice Stick, (called Lick for short). We had gotten him from a neighbor, the Brashars, shortly after we moved to Espanola. One early Easter we bought a half dozen baby chicks at the local feed store for the children's entertainment. A day or two later, I was out in the yard in the morning, with several of the four preschool kids running about playing. I suddenly realized that the chicks had escaped from their box and were out in the large empty field next door. There was a three foot wide irrigation ditch and a barbed wire fence between me and them. Furthermore the field was full of large desert sticker weeds as it had not been plowed for the new year yet. What to do? If I tried to go after them, even if I could catch them (which was doubtful), I would have several small kids hanging on me and getting tangled in the weeds and barbed wire. If I waited until Larry or Pete got home from work or school, the chicks would probably be long gone.

As I stood there forlornly wondering what on earth to do, suddenly our big black dog went racing by me. Well, I thought, that will take care of the chicks, one bite from his big jaws will be the end. But no! To my amazement he chased one down, picked it up in his mouth, brought it back and laid it completely unharmed at my feet and back he went for another and another until I had put them all safely back in their box. From where they were, they had obviously been over there for quite a while to get that far, and Lick had paid no attention to them at all until I noticed them. Somehow he got the message from me that this was a problem that needed to be solved. Instinct is not enough to explain why he only reacted when I became aware and started to worry. He had no training at all in catching birds and retrievers usually collect dead ones. So how did he know how to do it? Labs do have a soft mouth so maybe it's not surprising that he could pick them up without harm, But how did he know that it needed to be done and that he was capable of doing the task? It was an astonishing and impressive experience for me who had very little experience with animals of any kind, even dogs. I have concluded that animals, dogs in particular, know more of what's going on around them than we realize or give them credit for.

Early Days in Espanola

Original House

Barb, Betty, Pete
Peggy, Bob (l to r)

Bill Pushes Dad
into New Pool
Bob & Tom Look on

Fourth Grade Picnic

Another very memorable incident occurred when I volunteered to help out with Pete's Fourth Grade class picnic at the end of the school year in May. One other Mother, Carmen Cook, volunteered to drive her family's large flat bed truck to transport the 43 kids of the class, since the parochial school was too poor to afford school buses. (Nothing like that would be allowed in our security conscious society now.) I volunteered to drive the nun, teacher of the class, in my four-door, Ford Sedan along with my four preschoolers. Again no seat belts.

It was a gorgeous, warm Spring day and the children climbed aboard the back of the truck with lunches in hand. Driving up to Santa Clara Canyon, about a mile before we reached the picnic site, the motor on the truck broke down. Well the kids could run that mile with no problem and I drove my car to the site. Carmen hailed a passerby to get a message back to her husband, Roland, who was a mechanic, to come out and fix the truck and rescue us and then she came on to join the picnic. Games were enjoyed by all and lunches eaten by about one PM when suddenly the weather changed abruptly. The temperature dropped about 30 degrees and it began to rain and/or hail. Most of the kids didn't even have sweaters The only shelter of any kind available was our sedan. My four preschoolers piled in and as many small girls as we could cram in. (I counted a total of 21 little heads) The boys, the bigger girls, Carmen, Sister and I all huddled together in the bushes as best we could.

After about an hour of this miserable downpour, Roland and the repaired truck turned up and everyone hastily got aboard and we all went home. That day, I learned an important lesson about mountain weather. Always expect the worst and assume that it will turn cold and dress accordingly.

A Girl Scout Camp

Always being too ready to volunteer to help kept getting me into trouble. One of the young priests at the church thought it might be helpful to the local girls if the parish sponsored a Girl Scout Troop. He asked me and Yolanda Gallegos, an older sister of Pete's buddies Leonel and Carlos, if we would lead such a troop. Yolanda, who was working at her Father's clothing store, would be the leader and I the assistant and committee chairman. Yolanda would meet with them weekly and I would help take them hiking and camping.

The only major thing that I remember vividly about the troop was a camping trip we took them on up at Bandoleer National Monument in Frijoles Canyon behind Los Alamos. Yolanda couldn't be there for some reason, which I have forgotten, so Larry and I took thirteen hispanic girls, Pete, Leo and Carlos, and our four preschoolers for a camp out. None of the girls had ever camped out or even cooked over an open fire before Well we got through the dinner all right and after a little singing around the campfire, settled down to sleep in whatever gear everyone had. Our four little ones were in our tent close by; Pete and his friends were off by themselves but we stayed outside in our sleeping bags close to the girls.

It was a bright moonlit night and I had trouble going to sleep. Suddenly I noticed that there were several skunks wandering about the fireplace and table looking for food. I didn't know what to do. Everyone else seemed to be asleep and the skunks didn't seem to be hurting anything but I was very afraid of their smell. Suddenly one walked right across the foot of our sleeping bags and I sat bolt upright and woke Larry up. He said "Oh they won't bother anything. Go to sleep" And eventually I did and he was right, they didn't bother anything. The next morning, the three boys were very angry with me when they heard about it. Why didn't we wake them up? I guess we didn't tell the girls about it either because I can't remember any response from them which I'm sure there would have been.

When I told the park ranger about the incident, he said "Oh the wood pussies. They're around all the time and don't hurt anything". No but how can one be sure they won't spray this time.

Expanding the House

After a year or two, because it was still a little small for our growing family, we began to expand our new house. It had been built by an eccentric from Los Alamos and not really finished, because his marriage broke up and he had to sell it. Originally we had two small bedrooms and a large unfinished and unheated room which was supposed to be a family room. We combined one of the small bedrooms with the large unfinished room into two medium sized heated bedrooms for kids. We added a very large family room. Later we converted the garage into a second bath, bedroom and space for a washer and dryer.

Family Room Added to Espanola House

Building a Swimming Pool

The decision made to build the pool happened while I was in the Hospital with some sort of flu. I was so sick that I didn't care about anything. Larry told me in the hospital about the great deal that he was considering with our neighbor, Bud Brashar. By buying two swimming pool kits and building them together, one at each house, we would both have a 12' x 24' in-ground pool for $2000 each. Well it might be a good idea but I was too sick to care. I just said "Do anything you like just let me alone". So they went ahead ordered the two kits and flipped a coin to see which would be built first. And Bud Brashar won the toss so they made all the mistakes on theirs but they had a pool first.

To build ours, we had a local man with a back hoe dig a big hole slightly larger than the right size for the pool. Then we had a load of sand delivered and Larry, Bud and the kids shaped the hole to the proper dimensions and spread several inches of sand on the bottom. The treated wood edges and heavy plastic liner from the kit were installed with 2' x 8's around the top. Then we had a concrete pad installed around it with the small diving board from the kit. Finally we filled it with a garden hose and, voila! the kids were ready to swim. We, of course, had to build a fence with automatic locking gates around it. And fortunately we were in a back corner of the community bordered by open fields and orchards, and never had any problems with any living being except for an occasional lizard falling in and drowning. I always worried about kids or animals falling in but we never had any problems.

In between the pool and the kitchen, we added a large porch, screened from the bottom and over the top. Larry had found the screens in the surplus being sold from the Los Alamos Lab. Apparently they were from some project that involved screening equipment from magnetic interactions but worked fine for a porch. Later Larry also found a gas water heater at lab surplus and we had it installed so we could extend the swimming season. The hole, cement, heater, fence and porch of course added to the cost but for a heated in-ground pool with a fenced porch it was all pretty cheap.

In fact the pool was one of the best things we ever did. The kids all learned to be excellent swimmers and are completely at home in the water. I liked it because during the summer, it was the center for the neighborhood so I usually knew where my kids were and what they were doing. To some extent I could watch them from the kitchen window. All of them are like fish in the water. One of the things that I never knew about until Bob told me as an adult, they used to jump off the top of the screened porch into the pool. It was a miracle that they didn't kill themselves on the cement around the pool.

Creations:
Canoe & Pool

School at Holy Cross

In the mid fifties when the twins started school, they also were among mostly hispanics. One boy was half anglo and besides there were the two of them so I guess it wasn't too difficult. At least they have never complained. At first in the early grades, the teacher couldn't tell them apart and they thought it great fun to switch seats and confuse people. At home as well as In school, Barb was usually the leader and would speak up for her sister if needed. such as 'my sister doesn't have a pencil'. Although very much alike, they do have definite differences, mainly in personalities and interests although not much in looks.

When Bob and Peggy started school I guess they had problems being the lone minorities but by then we felt so at home there that we didn't worry much about it. I guess they survived although perhaps I should have worried more. In second grade, Peg's teacher was worrying about her because she talked too much and didn't concentrate on her work. I said that it was too easy for her and she was bored as I had been in school. The nun proposed advancing Peggy to third grade along with another boy who was having similar problems and they did. So Bob and Peggy went all the way through the rest of the grades and high school in the same class. Being of different sex and with very different personalities, as far as I could tell, they mostly ignored each other. They each went their own way and had their own friends. Although I gather from what she says now, she worried about Bob because the teachers gave him a hard time. He was not a good student and didn't always do his homework. In particular, the man who taught seventh grade, gave him a very hard time until he put Bob in the back of the room where there was a shelf containing a set of Encyclopedias. Since, like his Grandfather, he enjoyed reading them, he caused no more trouble and probably even educated himself better because he was no longer so bored.

Some More Surprises

Over four years went by without any additions to the family when surprisingly enough on January 25, 1957 along came Thomas Arthur at 6 lb. 13 ozs. Just why the break in the family is hard to say. One hypothesis we had was that before the twins came and I had trouble getting pregnant, I was told that I had a prolapsed uterus and given exercises which I mostly didn't do. Difficult to believe now that we ever even worried about such a thing. Now just before I got pregnant with Tom, we had poured the large cement floor in our large family room. One of the tasks which was needed to make very smooth concrete was to trowel the cement on hands and knees for a long time with which I helped. It was exactly the position given me for the prolapsed uterus! So maybe that's why the last two turned up but I still enjoyed having them.

Except for the fact that I had bad allergies during the summer that I was pregnant with Tom, I can't remember much about either the pregnancy or delivery. One incident that I do remember vividly, occurred when I was about six months pregnant. Bob who was in first grade came up and said something to me and being busy about something else, I didn't pay much attention. Then I said 'what is it Bob?' He said, 'can I show you the neat trick that I learned at school today?' Innocently enough I said 'Sure, what is it?" He put his head down and butted me as hard as he could with his head in my very pregnant tummy. It might have been a good trick for another first grader but not for a pregnant Mom. I practically lost my breath and yelped. His Dad really landed on him and I tried to say 'he didn't mean any harm but was just not very wise about how he showed me the trick'. All I could hope was that the baby was unharmed and fortunately he apparently was.[9]

---

[9]   Recently Bob accused me of lying to him around that time. Several dogs were doing their best to procreate in our yard and he came in and asked

Tom like all the rest was an easy baby and very quiet and pleasant. Peggy had not started school yet so was a great help with him and enjoyed playing with him. One funny incident about Tom while sitting in his highchair. Someone put a dill pickle on his tray which he had never tried. He tasted it and made a funny face. The family burst into laughter at this and he looked around and realized he was the center of it and kept pretending to taste it and making a face amid gales of laughter. What a clown! The girls had a little doll carriage and loved to dress Tom in doll clothes and put him in the carriage. He seemed to enjoy it as much as they did.

Tom Being the Baby Doll

me what they were doing. Without even looking, I said "Probably fighting". When he went back outside and told the boys what I said, they laughed at him. My response was "I'm sorry but I was just too busy to pay attention. I no more meant to lie to you than you meant to hurt me when you butted my in the stomach". I hope that made him feel better.

Again We Have a Pair

Thirteen months after Tom, again we had another boy to complete a pair. William John (Bill) was born on March 14, 1958. at 7 lb. 1 ozs. The name William came from my maiden name of Williams and for my father who was Russell John (John being his grandmother's maiden name). It was an easy delivery and for the first time Larry was allowed to stand in the door of the delivery room. Things were changing and the Doctor who delivered him was now our local family doctor. He lived near us and by this time knew us well. He also put the baby on the gurney with me while I was taken back to my room. Again something new.

When the two youngest boys were babies, the twins, Barb and Bets were just the right age (six and then seven) to be little Mama's to them. They loved taking care of them and enjoyed playing with them so were a big help to me. I've always said that one child is the hardest and from then on with more it just gets easier as they take care of each other and work off the rough edges. Granted there is more cooking, laundry and cleaning but it's not as overwhelming and they learn to help with all that to some extent. You have to have a big family to realize this. Unfortunately it no longer seems right to have big families for financial reasons as well as the burden on the environment so most people can't or really shouldn't have the experience.

Once again, we had a pair who were almost like twins but here there was a big difference. Bill, like Peggy, was a year younger but grew and developed so fast that he almost caught up to his brother Tom. In addition, there were two boys, Matt and Royce, in the houses next door on either side that were born the same Spring that Tom was. So the foursome played together constantly. I even used to have a 'play kindergarten' for the four in our large family room and they thought it great fun and maybe even learned something. We would play games, sing songs, learn numbers, color and so forth. When I had had enough I would send them out for "'recess".

Bill is a Lost Soul

When the day came that his older brother Tom and the two neighbor boys that he had always played with, went off to school and Bill had to stay at home alone, he was a lost soul. As an adult he told me that at the time, he believed that he was the same age as the other three and couldn't understand why he was being discriminated against. Even now he has trouble believing they were really older. A few weeks after school started, Tom's first grade teacher became very ill. Sister Jeannine, the nun who was principal of the grade school, knew our family well and knew that I had some college education particularly in math and science. She proposed that I should teach the 7th and 8th grade, and give them some math and science, while she would take the 1st grade which she thought would be too much for me. Bill could go into the first grade for the time being with his brother Tom. Everyone thought it was a great solution. So Bill was temporarily in first grade for nearly three months and according to his teacher, Sister Jeannine, he was doing everything as well as the rest and really should be in school but according to the law, they couldn't start him at his age.

When the first grade teacher recovered and returned in December, Bill and I went back home for the rest of the year. Sister Jeannine suggested that when Bill started school the next year he should take a full year of first grade to get some basics; then skip second grade and go on into the third grade. So our two youngest boys ended up going through the grades and high school together just like Bob and Peggy had done. This was not so successful because both being boys they were very competitive and always trying to outdo each other. Tom not surprisingly, being a year older, did just a little better and resented his younger brother, Bill, for doing almost as well. On the other hand, Bill thought he was just as old and should be doing just as well but resented his brother Tom for doing better. I worried about them but I didn't know what if anything I could do about it since no other acceptable schools were available. I hoped at the time that when they got to high school, they would take different classes and the competition would ease.

Medical View of Having Babies Changes

One of the things that really surprised me over the years is the way things changed in hospitals and medical techniques. With my first baby Pete, I was kept in the hospital for 10 days and not allowed out of bed until the 9th day. Seems silly now but that is the way it was. My daughter Peggy says that it doesn't seem silly to a new mother who was sent home the next day after delivery with no help at home. With the twins it was down to eight days in the hospital and we were allowed up by the third day. The stay in the hospital continued to decrease and by the time I had Bill, my seventh child, it was down to two days and I was up the next day. Apparently some of this came from a stubborn patient who had abdominal surgery and refused to stay in bed as long as the doctors said he should. And to the amazement of the medical community he recovered faster and better than most. This apparently made them challenge some of their ideas and it got extended to delivery.

The same sort of change has happened in starting babies on solid food. At first none was allowed until about ten months. With the twins it was eight months. It kept moving earlier and earlier until at one time it was allowed by about three weeks! I've heard since that it has gone back up again to about three months and even to six months because of allergy problems. My conclusion is that they really don't know the correct way to do things. They just sort of guess, follow tradition and hope for the best! What bothers me is that they don't do much, or at least not enough, research or keep records which could be used to verify such things. I guess that's the reason why they call it the 'art' or 'practice' of medicine. I hear now that things are changing and they are trying to research the problems. It is very true that medical research is very complex and difficult and takes a lot of time and money. It's not easy to do research on human beings.

Barranca del Cobre

At the end of the fifties, in the Summer of 1959, Pete was in Boy Scouts and Larry had gotten involved. Under the leadership of Richard Lucero, then the local Boy Scout Executive (and now the Mayor of Espanola), they went on a fabulous trip to Chihuahua and then to the Barranca del Cobre in Mexico similar to our Grand Canyon. At the time the Mexicans were building the railroad through their Southern extension of the Rocky Mountains. They had been told by some French Engineers who had considered building it, that it couldn't be done. But the Mexicans were stubbornly doing it themselves anyway and had gotten almost as far as the takeoff for the Barranca. The Scouts rode the work train out as far as it went and then hiked the rest of the way and down into the Barranca which is almost as deep as our Grand Canyon. They did have a few burros to carry some of the gear but mostly they carried it by backpack. Apparently at the base it was completely tropical so all the trees and vegetation were different from anything the scouts had ever seen before.

Some stories that I have heard about this trip were really funny. On the way down, they met with a group of hosts in Chihuahua and Richard, being fluent in both English and Spanish, was going to translate for those who weren't. As the speaker started off, something was very obviously wrong because Richard was translating from English to Spanish and back again to English. After a few minutes and much laughter he realized what he was doing and got straightened out and settled for going only one way.

Another, maybe not so funny thing, was that, while we don't pay much respect to doctoral degrees in things like Chemistry, the

Mexicans make a big deal of El Doctor with other kinds of degrees. When the scout troop came up out of the canyon, they were were shocked to find that the train had broken down. They had to hitch a ride on the back of a local coke truck. Larry, the assistant leader, respected as El Doctor, could ride in the cab of the truck with the driver while, Richard, the primary leader, had to hang on the back with the kids. When they stopped for lunch they were asked what they wanted for lunch. One possibility was roast goat. Well Larry said "yes but it should really be young". The man brought out a very old and very pregnant goat. Larry said "No, no, she's too old". The man pointed at her belly, very young. I don't know whether they accepted that.

Chapter 13

Sixties in Espanola, 1960-70

In the sixties our family really reached it's peak as far as number of people goes and the diversity of activities. When I say 'family', I also mean the 'Williams' family. Between 1955 and 1960, fifteen new babies including Tom and Bill, had entered the Williams world. Many complicated things happened during these ten years. This chapter will give a picture of who we all were and many of the interactions among us and how the children grew and developed. Now I'm talking about the Larry and Marge Asprey Family. Our oldest five went off to college and Pete, the very oldest, took time off to spend four years in the Navy. We were still living in Espanola with a large garden, many fruit trees and the pool we had built which, along with the horses we rented for two years, kept the kids busy during the summers. The horses were just nags but the children enjoyed them.

Exchange Students

In the early 60's we decided that we wanted to help young people from round the world so signed up to sponsor high school students from other countries. As long as I was home anyway, an extra kid or two around really didn't make much difference. Besides, teen agers can be very helpful. We also thought that it might be good for our children to learn something about other countries. Our first student was Arnoldo Cruz Saenz from Cartago, Costa Rica, who arrived August 1961.

Arnoldo Cruz

Arnoldo at 16 when he arrived, was a very exceptional person to say the least. While he was the third from a family of six, they were reasonably well off and lived on sort of a ranch. One of the things he told me was that several of his uncles played on Costa Rica's polo team. He was very proud of the fact that all his ancestors were from Spain. He wanted to be very sure that I understood just what that meant. His eyes were green and his hair was not very dark. He definitely did not look hispanic. He was excellent at languages. Although he had only spoken English in his high school class before he came to this country, he very soon spoke it fluently. He as a Senior and Pete as a Junior rode a local bus to attend St. Michael's High School in Santa Fe. Many of the kids riding the bus were local hispanics and of course chattered away in the local version of Spanish. Arnoldo spoke only English until they made fun of him one day when he said 'I am Spanish'. They said "No you're not. Because you don't speak Spanish". I guess he finally convinced them. He also told me that the local Spanish was very bad and not at all grammatical. But that was typical of him. He wanted to learn English so spoke only English. I hoped he might practice with me since I was trying to learn Spanish but he refused. He would let me read to him and correct my accent and I did the same for him in English but no conversation in Spanish.

One day he asked me "Where is your Academy?" And I said "I don't know what you mean by Academy". He said "You know, the place where they control the language. Ours is in Madrid and the French one is in Paris. They tell us what is correct and what is not". I had never thought of this before but I could only say, "As far as I know, English doesn't have one. The English teachers would probably like it but I don't think there is one. We're much too independent to be told how to use our language. We just say what we like or go to a dictionary. On further thought and from what I've learned in linguistics, I think they only try to control the language without much success. Languages keep changing all the time whether the teachers and academies like it or not.

Arnoldo was a very determined person. One time that first summer, we rented a couple of horses for the kids to ride. We also rented a burro, thinking because he was small, the smaller children could ride him. Big mistake! First try he just threw them off. Well Arnoldo said "he just needs to be trained" so he set out to ride him and was promptly thrown off. He got up thrashed the animal well and got back on. This went on for half a day and finally Arnoldo could indeed ride him but no one else could. We gave the animal back to the owner because he wasn't worth it since no one but Arnoldo could ride him and he really didn't want to. As far as I can tell, he felt that he was an excellent rider and he was not going to be conquered by a mere burro.

When school was in session, the minute that he arrived home from school, Arnoldo instantly sat down with his books and began doing his homework. With this example, Pete got some of the best grades for that year that he ever did in high school. On the other hand, when school was out for the Summer, Arnoldo only wanted to party. Apparently this was the custom in his country. I remember him teaching us a sort of a round dance that was popular in his country to the popular song "Summer Place". After being here for just a year, Arnoldo graduated with his class earning the Honors Medal, the Math Medal, the American History Medal and even the English Medal over all native English speakers! Later we heard that Arnoldo had come back to the US to go to college at the University of Ohio where he earned a PhD in Chemistry. Eventually we heard that he became a Vice President for ALCOA (Aluminum Company of America) as a result of some impressive invention that he had made over the years. He has married an American and has a home in Pittsburgh. For a while I had lost his address but recently we have gotten in touch again. He and his family are currently living in Europe and he is supervising Alcoa plants all over the continent.

One time when Peggy and her husband Dick were in Costa Rica they visited the Cruz family who welcomed them with open arms. One of Arnoldo's brothers picked them up at the airport and apologized for being a bit late. It seems he was a Doctor and had been doing heart surgery! Peggy tells me that we should visit them for an exciting time as they have a very impressive place plus a home on the beach. Maybe someday I will, who knows.

Rony Guerra

Our second student was Jaime Guerra from Bolivia and was called Rony. He was not the student Arnoldo was but he was a happy-go-lucky sort of person and was fun to have around. Another difference between the two besides scholastic abilities was in their approach to life. When I asked Arnoldo to do something, he would stand there and make me say it over and over in different ways until he understood exactly and then go do what I wanted. On the other hand when I asked Rony to do something, he would say 'Yes! Yes!' and dash off without the slightest idea of what I really wanted. I would have to go after him and bring him back and try again to explain what I wanted. And Rony didn't win any medals when he and Pete graduated from high school that year. But graduate they did. After he went back to Bolivia, Rony went over to Brazil to college and ended up with a degree in Physics and worked on Solar Energy in his own country. So he really was quite bright just not as determined or focused. Many years later, our son, Bill and his wife Susan were down in Bolivia, and they looked up the Guerra family. They too were welcomed with open arms and a great feast was spread for them.

Pete, the Oldest

Of course the household mainly consisted of all seven of our own children for at least part of the decade. Pete, our oldest, had started school while we still lived in Los Alamos and was in second grade when we moved to Espanola. What I had not realized when we entered him in Holy Cross School in Santa Cruz, was that he would be the only non-hispanic in his class. It is one way to learn about racial prejudice! Fortunately for him, he was bigger than most of the boys so could at least defend himself to some extent. I guess he had some problems and not many friends, until two new boys arrived from Colorado. Leonel (or Leo) Gallegos, in Pete's class, and his brother Carlos, a year younger, while still hispanic, were also outsiders and they and Pete became fast friends. I am convinced these friends helped him adjust to the change in schools.

Although Pete went through St. Michael's High School in Santa Fe without too much trouble, and graduated with Rony in 1962, he couldn't seem to get going in college. He went to New Mexico Tech for one year and was on the edge of flunking. He thought it would be easier at UNM (University of New Mexico) in Albuquerque so transferred there. And of course it really wasn't any easier.

During this period, as a summer job to pay for his college expanses, he recently reminisced about an experience he had working for a telephone company. The job was to install trays for cables in a large empty room. There was a pile of metal sheets and material for frames. The sheets were to be cut to the proper length, the frames screwed to the wall and the metal sheets fastened into the frames. The usual way to do it involved laboriously cutting metal sheets with a saw. Well Pete had a better idea of how to cut the sheets. He scribed a heavy line on one metal sheet and then broke it over another. It broke cleanly, exactly where he wanted it to, and avoided all the slow and painful sawing which would be needed otherwise. It worked so well that when the boss came back to see how he was doing, Pete had the job almost completely done. The boss' jaw dropped in shock since he had expected it to take several weeks. Pete laughed and said it was worth the price just to see the look on the man's face. After a few minutes of keeping him in suspense, he finally told him how he had done the job so well and fast. Since he was just a temporary summer employee, he was let take it easy for the rest of the few weeks but the only recognition that he received, aside from his salary, was from his immediate boss.

Later, the boss asked him to write up the procedure that he had used which he did and never thought anything more about it. He kept in touch with his former boss and a few months later, he showed Pete a new issue of a training manual printed by the company which described the procedure in almost exactly Pete's words! I asked "Didn't they even give you an award for your idea?" He said "No. The boss said that if he, the boss, had invented it, they would have had to give him an award or at least a raise but they couldn't acknowledge that a summer temporary had come up with such a good idea that their own trained engineers couldn't". And he said again, "But the look on that man's face was worth the price any day. And I was just a student and was well paid for my time". He had no complaints but was just glad not to have had to do such hard, obnoxious work.

Pete in the Navy

Now it was the mid 60's and while he had a draft deferment as long as he stayed in school, if he flunked out, he could be in the Army heading for the war going on in Vietnam. He says now that his early troubles in college were that he just needed adventure. He finally decided in 1966 to sign up with the Navy which should give him some of that adventure.

Here are a few of the experiences that he has told me about his time in the Navy but most of them will have to come from him. I know that he spent several years on the destroyer, the USS Lofberg, in the Pacific on Vietnam tours. They spent some time sailing around the coast of Vietnam during the war there and as he put it, 'bombing outhouses'. He did tell about getting very sick one time and being airlifted to an aircraft carrier by helicopter. He was so sick and weak that he almost slipped out of the harness holding him and fell into the ocean. He was grabbed by the shirt by a corpsman and kept from falling, quite probably saving his life Another time he told about being the one steering the destroyer in a wild storm (Probably a typhoon, equivalent in the Western Pacific, to our Atlantic hurricanes). He wasn't at all sure that he could do the job but hung on and they made it. But he did say he felt terrified at having the responsibility of the entire ship resting in his hands. I believe his experiences in the Navy changed and matured him more than he thought.

Barb & Bets

"They look different to me" is Bobs answer when people ask him how he could tell our twins apart. This is not too surprising since he has known them from his birth. He also tells about watching in a mirror while one combed her hair and thinking it was Barb but when she turned around it was Betty! Since Barb is right handed and Betty is left handed, we think that they are what is called 'mirror image twins'.

When Barb and Bets graduated from 8th Grade at the local Holy Cross parochial school in May 1962, there was a problem of where to send them next. The public high school in Espanola started with the Sophomore year and the local public junior high did not have a good reputation, so this made a problem. Pete (and our exchange students) had gone to St. Michael's, a Christian Brothers four-year high school in Santa Fe for boys, a thirty minute ride by bus. The equivalent for the girls would be a nun's school in Santa Fe which was not anywhere near as good a school as St. Michael's. It also was more expensive and meant them having to catch rides to get home in emergencies. Not only would the cost be doubled for the two of them, but, while we didn't like it much for the boys, it was just not acceptable to us to have girls thumbing rides. So Larry suggested having them commute with him on the forty minute ride up to Los Alamos. The schools were willing to accept them as children of an employee. I think that he liked having their company too. They had to wait for him after school for a few hours in the library, which wasn't ideal but seemed tolerable.

School in Los Alamos

While in school up there, they became friends with a girl named Cherie who had been given up unofficially for adoption by her mother to a rather strange woman who treated her badly. Cherie was so unhappy at the way she was treated that she kept running away and Catholic Charities had finally taken custody of her. The twins came to me and asked if we couldn't take her in for a while since she had no place else to go. Well we no longer had exchange students, so we decided this would be a good way to help young people who had problems so we agreed. Catholic Charities interviewed us to be sure that it would work out for her and not cause troubles in our family. So we found a bed for her and had another adoptee for several months.

Our Tragic Loss

When Cherie came into our house in October, I was about seven months pregnant with a baby due in December. In November, the baby decided to come but it was not a normal delivery but what is known as a 'hydramnios'. The baby was not normal and couldn't live beyond a few minutes. Instead of the usual pint of amniotic fluid, there were seven quarts. Something had gone very wrong with the development process. Unfortunately it is not unusual for babies born to mothers in their forties to have problems like this. As far as I was concerned, while I was sad that any baby couldn't make it, with seven wonderful children already at home, I really felt that we had a big enough family. So while I was sad I only cried briefly and then turned to the future. I was put into a room with a young girl who had given up her baby for adoption so I guess we cried together.

When I came home all of the children were unhappy about the lost baby. However, Cherie was the most upset of all so I think of her in connection with this loss. Recently Peggy told me that Larry cried over the lost baby when he brought the mini casket home for burial. The children had never seen him cry and it shows how much he cared about all his children when he would cry over the lost eighth. They were amazed that daddies cry too and this made a deep impression on them. He chose to name her after his mother, Gladys Mary, and buried her in the local cemetery.

Later the following February, Catholic Charities worked things out with Cherie's regular birth mother and she went back to her own family. She was an interesting addition to our family for a while. She now lives in Albuquerque and the twins, Barb and Bets, have seen her a time or two.

After a year in Junior High, in Los Alamos, the twins moved to Espanola High School where they got a reasonable education. When the twins graduated from Espanola high School, they both won scholarships to UNM and NMSU. They decided to go to NMSU and spent the first year living in the dorms. Some of their friends were also going there so I guess this was part of their desire to go there. Barbara got a job in the Computer Center to help pay her way and Betty spent a semester working at the Los Alamos Lab on a co-op program.

Bob—Success at last

Bob reminds me very much of one grandfather, Russell Williams. They both liked to fix things and my Dad was something of an inventor although he never did anything with his ideas. I remember hearing about him making an electric curling iron long before they were sold in stores. Bob always said from the time he was small that when he grew up he wanted to be an inventor and he did achieve that. Strangely enough though, he is also like Larry's dad, his grandfather Asprey, in that he remembers and likes to tell jokes. It's really strange how those genes get mixed up. To me, it's one of the delights in raising children to see how these combinations play out. Just don't expect them to be copies of you. They are completely themselves and not extensions of their parents.

I worried about Bob when he was in High School. His grades were so bad that I thought he would flunk out. A neighbor boy bought an old junk car to fix up and Bob started to work on it with him and suddenly everything changed! He seemed more willing to do homework and his grades improved. At school, he seemed to have no friends since he didn't bring any home. nor did he go to the houses of any beyond the immediate neighbors. Yet when he was a junior, a group of the boys from school came and asked me if they could have a surprise birthday party for him in our house. They would bring all the food and clean up afterwards. I wouldn't have to do a thing! They were as good as their word and I really didn't have to do anything about it. They gave him the gift of a large (about 10 inches tall) seated monkey bank! And they all seemed to have a good time.

A Very Special Peggy

As I said before, although Peggy was only 13 months younger than her brother Bob her personality was extremely different. After being advanced a year in second grade, this meant that Peggy would be in class with Bob for the rest of the grades and high school. As far as I could see though, this didn't seem to bother either of them very much. Just why Bob and Peggy were not sent to Los Alamos for 9th grade as the twins were is something that I can't now remember. The same problems of distance and expense of going to Santa Fe and attending St. Michael's and Loretto High Schools were of course still valid. My best guess is that the twins hadn't liked the experience of Los Alamos Junior High very much and Espanola High hadn't turned out to be as bad as we expected. However Peggy tells me now that the Junior High was terrible and she really regretted not being able to use the scholarship to Loretto that she had won.

Another little tale about Peggy that I remember. She did not like meat much. When Larry made her eat some she would chew for a while and when no one noticed she would slip a chunk of it into a space above a table leg. She got away with it for a while until the dog discovered it and tried to get it out so we found out what she had been up to.

Another incident that I remember with Peggy was one time when I told her to do something that she didn't want to do. She became very angry and threatened to run away. I said "If that's what you want to do you'll have to do it or do what I say" So she flounced off and was gone for a little while but shortly after, turned back up and did what she was supposed to do. Many years later, I asked her what happened when she ran away that day. She laughed and said "Oh I got down to the end of the subdivision that we lived in and decided that an ice cream cone would taste good so I came back". She's the only one that I can remember running away, aside from Bill, and that didn't last very long either.

Tom and Bill, Our Third Pair

Tom and Bill however, as a pair were not at all like the twins who were so alike or Bob and Peg who each had their own friends and mostly ignored each other. These two were so different in personality, (rather parallel to Bob and Peg) yet both being boys, they fought much of the time despite having many of the same friends.

In April of 1962, Tom and Bill both had measles. Tom didn't have too much trouble with it but Bill was quite sick and even had some hallucinations when he had a quite high fever. But as far as I could tell they both survived and recovered completely. Like most small boys, they had a few accidents. On time when he was about four, Tom was eating peanuts a day or two before Christmas. He managed to inhale one by mistake instead of swallowing it. We had to take him to the hospital because the doctor said it might cause him to get pneumonia. Larry tells about going to see him in the hospital and saw Tom running away from a nurse. As soon as he spotted his Dad, he ran like a rabbit and climbed him 'like a tree'. Eventually Tom apparently vomited up the peanut because they couldn't find it in his lungs anymore although the doctor had earlier spent a lot of time chasing it around. Since Tom was in the hospital, we of course had to hold up Christmas for a few days, which everyone agreed to do, until he came home. When they did get to the gifts it made them seem even better.

The worst disaster occurred late one summer afternoon. Dad was away at a technical meeting and the kids and I were out in the yard when I noticed that our roses were covered with aphids. Usually, Larry took care of things like that so I really didn't know what to do but looked for some insect spray and found a bottle of malathion. I read the instructions, measured out a tablespoon full and set the spoon down while I sprayed thinking Bill at three was old enough to know not to touch it. Bill decided that it looked good to eat, picked up the spoon and put it in his mouth. Of course it tasted bad and he yelped and dropped it. I realized immediately that it was bad stuff and that I should have been more careful. I tried washing his mouth out and tried to find a doctor to see if I needed to do anything more. Well it was late Saturday afternoon and I couldn't reach anyone so what could I do but hope he hadn't been harmed. Unfortunately from his experiences over the years, I'm afraid more damage was done than I realized but at the time he seemed unharmed.

The Fighting Pair

Being in the same class in the grades, Tom felt put down because his younger brother did almost as well as he did. On the other hand, Bill felt put down because his brother, although a year older, did somewhat better than he did. I worried a great deal about their interaction and fighting, but didn't know what to do about it because there were no other satisfactory schools available. I thought maybe when they got to high school, they would take different classes and get separated naturally. But not so! Despite the very different personalities, their brains and interests were still very much the same. In high school they each took all the advanced math and science that they could find and they still ended up in class together. Tom is rather quiet and reserved and Bill is cheerful and outgoing. Tom hardly ever had girl friends in high school although the girls were interested enough to call but he didn't respond. On the other hand, Bill usually had a girl friend or two around.

A Major Family Tragedy

The worst family tragedy of all occurred in April 1964. My only brother, Grant Williams, as a member of the Naval Air Reserve lost his life when his jet plane crashed. After graduation from the University of Missouri in Aeronautical Engineering in the mid fifties, he was obligated, in return for his college education, to spend four years in the Navy. So he flew jets off a Navy Carrier for awhile. Along the way though, he had gotten married and had several children. When his term of service was over, he had so fallen in love with flying that he couldn't bear to give it up completely. He did not want to leave four half orphans as was very common with his fellow pilots. But he agreed to stay in the National Air Reserve as a weekend pilot which seemed fairly safe, so he could get some flying in. At the same time, he took a job with McDonnell Douglas in St. Louis as an engineer, communicating with test pilots flying new jets.

After several years, he and his wife Kathleen had four preschool children including a brand new baby. He took off on a weekend flight to Jacksonville, FL. which was to be his last flight. He took off into a cloudy sky on the return flight, turned around, came back through the clouds and crashed. His wing man followed him up, turned around but saw in time that he was going to crash and managed to avoid it. If the cause of the accident has been determined, we have never heard what it was. The next day his poor wife heard the dreaded knock on the door and was told that her husband was dead. While heartbreaking for all of us, it was a particularly terrible blow to my parents because he was their beloved only son. At the funeral the casket was closed because the body was destroyed in the crash. All sisters came from all over the country. Mom's faith seemed to support her because she took it well despite the overwhelming pain that we knew she must be feeling.

And of course the biggest victims of the tragedy were his four small children and his wife Kathleen. She now had to raise them by herself which she has done very well. She had been a school teacher and gradually went back to school to get an advanced degree so could return to teaching. She had only one sister who lived in Cincinnati, OH. Every Christmas after spending Christmas evening and morning with Dad and Mom and her parents, she took a train to Cincinnati for the rest of holidays. The local family all tried to help but there was not much that we could do being so far away. Being nearby Dad and Mom, Rosie and Susie were able to help some. Grandpa and the uncles living close could help fill in as male role models and helpers. Many years later, Kathleen married a good friend Jim Mannion whose wife had died of cancer. Each had four partly grown children so the wedding was quite spectacular with four paired couples of children as their attendants.

Summer of 1966

1966 was one of our more hectic summers. It began with my graduation in May from the College of Santa Fe with honors in Mathematics and Chemistry. Chapter 15 has more details about this.

Politics in Rio Arriba

When we had first moved to New Mexico, we registered as Independents. In time we found out that this left us out and our vote became meaningless. The Republicans essentially had no candidates and only members of major parties could vote in the primaries. This meant that he who won the Democratic Primary won the election. So we reregistered as Democrats. We tried to do a little to help clean up politics in the area and being a Judge in a local Bond Election was one of Larry's contributions to this endeavor.

During that bond election, the sheriff who was the big party boss in Rio Arriba County came in wearing his gun and insisted that he had to 'help people vote. His actual unspoken goal of course, was to be sure that people voted 'correctly' so they could get patronage. There was even one case where the Principal of a local Junior High School insisted that he couldn't read or write so needed help with voting (so he could keep his job). Larry stood up to this and wouldn't let the Sherif in with them. If anyone went to help anyone vote, Larry went.

Changing Politics

Matt Chacon was our Lawyer when we bought the Espanola house so we became friends. He also had children in the same school including the one who was advanced with Peggy into the third grade. Matt too was trying to improve local politics and even managed, when he got elected to the state legislature, to pass a law that they had to publish the precinct meetings where candidates were selected. Believe it or not, when we first moved down there it was impossible to find out when precinct meetings were held. After the law was passed, the politicos were very unhappy and tried to fight it. One time we went to the place announced (the back of a bar) and things were all dark. On the door in the back and in the dark, there was a notice that the meeting had been transferred to another place. By the time we got there, the politicos were coming out saying "Oh the meeting is all over. Sorry you weren't there." In another precinct, it was held in someone's house and only those who got there early and had seats were allowed to vote. Any people who were a few minutes late didn't have seats so couldn't vote

This type of shenanigans went on for some years but eventually they accepted the fact that people had a right to be involved. However, I remember one time when we went to such a meeting. We took a flash camera and took pictures of the proceedings which made them very nervous. Not that it really mattered because we didn't see anything really wrong. They were very used to doing things their way and they just didn't like voters watching.

Family Activities in Rest of 1966

In July, we had a family back pack-hike in the Pecos Wilderness which was fun for the whole family except for Pete who was off in the Navy so missed out. I don't really understand why it should be such fun to climb hills carrying a heavy pack, eat limited amounts of dried food cooked over a campfire, some times in the rain, and sleep in a tent on the hard ground but we all thought it was. I only wish that I could still do it! All of the children like it too and have continued as adults.

Backpacking:
(T, l to r) Larry, Barb
(B, l to r) Bill, Betty

Up Top on Sangre de Cristo Mtns.
Some wild Life Friends

Looking at Vassar

Finally that September, Larry took his three daughters, Barbara, Betty and Peggy, with him on a business trip to New York. They did some sight seeing including the Stock Market. Apparently it's the custom when young women appear in the visitors gallery to stop business for a few minutes and all turn and look at them. The three girls were embarrassed at the attention but it amused Larry no end. After his meeting was over, he took the girls up to Vassar College in Poughkeepsie, NY, to visit his sister Tim. She was a graduate of Vassar and after getting her PhD in Mathematics from the University of Iowa, was now a Professor of Mathematics and Computer Science. As I have mentioned earlier, Vassar was an Asprey family tradition, his Mother, Gladys Brown, and Grandmother, Winifred Learned, both being graduates in the days when few women went to college at all. I guess that the family hoped that at least one of our girls might be interested in continuing the tradition but it didn't work out that way. None of our girls, the only granddaughters, were interested enough or had good enough education and grades to manage it.

Summer of 1969

This too was a hectic Summer. In May to celebrate our 25th Wedding Anniversary, Larry and I decided to take a trip to Mazatlan, Mexico. Since Peggy was 17 and Bob 18, we thought that they were old enough to manage the household in our absence and they agreed to do it. The twins were already off at school at New Mexico State University in Las Cruces, and Pete off in the Navy. It was a delightful trip and we enjoyed it very much. On our return, Peggy had a feast spread out for us with the dining room curtains closed and big letters in silver spelling out "Happy Anniversary". What I did not suspect at the time was that the curtains were closed to hide a broken window which had happened too recently to have been fixed. I'm not sure what the cause was but probably a fight between our third pair of kids, Tom and Bill, who were now in 6th grade and still fighting.

Getting Ready to Move On

About now we had decided to sell the Espanola house that we had enjoyed for so long because it no longer would suit our needs. Bob and Peggy were almost ready to take off for college and this would leave us with only Tom and Bill at home. Because I was now working in Los Alamos, I was not too happy with the idea of being so far from them in Junior High, without an older brother or sister to help out in emergencies.

The house had been on the market for some time without any luck. Houses being hard to get and expensive in Los Alamos, we had been fortunate to buy a very small two bedroom, one bath house there. It was on a fairly large lot and we planned to enlarge it for the four of us. We had an architect in Pojoaque, drawing plans for this remodel. In late July, Larry had a six week business trip to Japan and Australia planned and had invited his sister Tim to go with him and take their two elderly Aunts from California (Alice and Emily Asprey). I of course was unable to go because I could not afford the time from work and caring for the house and kids. In June Larry had taken Bob down to NMSU to get him oriented and signed up for school in the Fall. Peggy's appointment to do the same was in early August, so I was to take her later.

A Hectic Weekend

That year the Fourth of July was on a Friday so we would have a long three day weekend and I was looking forward to getting the house and yard in as good shape as possible. With Larry gone, besides working full time, I would need to maintain the house that we were trying to sell and in midsummer, things grew very fast particularly the weeds! On the side, I needed to keep in touch with the architect so we could get going on the remodel. I would also need to get Tom and Bill registered for school up in Los Alamos. They could ride up with us until the house in Los Alamos was ready.

All this was on my mind when Larry picked me up after work on that Thursday evening. We of course, rode together driving the thirty miles to work daily between Espanola and Los Alamos. He told me that he wanted to stop at the local LA Inn for a drink with some of his friends which he liked to do occasionally. There in front of everyone, with no prior discussion, he announced that he had the weekend all planned: Friday evening we were having neighbors over for fireworks; Saturday he and his best friend, Bob Ryan, were going fishing; finally Sunday he was going hiking with a bunch of graduate students and friends up in the mountains in the morning, while everyone was invited for a pot luck Sunday evening at our house in the Valley. To say the least, I was a bit upset by all this. I had planned to cut grass, pull weeds, clean house and such and generally get ready for having him gone for six weeks. But I had had a drink so was a bit too fuzzy to say much but I was unhappy. Maybe it was about this time that I quit drinking at all. We called off the pot luck but everything else went about as he had planned.

Chapter 14

My First European Vacation, 1965

In June 1965, Larry was to give a professional talk in Moscow, Russia, and decided that if we could arrange it he would like to take me with him for a vacation in Europe before he went on to Russia. But what to do with the kids? At this time Pete was in college and had obtained a co-op job in Chemistry in the Los Alamos lab. So there were only six other children to worry about. I talked to three of my sisters, Kit, Dot and Sal, who were married and lived on the Atlantic coast with their families. They agreed to share our kids around among them for two weeks if we drove them to the coast. With the youngest six, we took off in our Greenbriar[10] Van to drive first to Bethesda, MD, where my sister Dot and her family lived.

---

[10]   The Greenbriar was a van made by Chevrolet in the 60's with an air-cooled motor in the rear. And yes, it was green. In addition to a bench seat in the front it had two facing benches in the back along with a cargo area in the far back. No seat belts as yet of course. We used it for many years to take our own seven plus temporarily adopted children on camping and backpacking trips.

Driving to East Coast

The first part of the journey was successful and straightforward with Larry driving most of the way. Dot drove us to the Dulles airport in Washington DC. where we took off at 5:00 PM for England leaving our kids aged 15,15,14,13,7,and 6 in the Carter house with her own nine kids aged two to sixteen. Dot was obviously a spectacular person to take on a mob like this. The other two sisters, Kitty and Sally who lived in Delaware and New Jersey respectively were to come and pick up some of the kids to stay with them. Dot kept some of the boys, Kit took most of the girls, and Sally, since she had only two boys, took another group of the Asprey and Carter boys. All of the children thought it was a great ongoing summer slumber party. At least that's what my kids say now. I owe my sisters a lot for this and have tried and even been able at other times to pay them back in other ways with their children.

London

After landing in London at about 7:00 AM and spending two days there, mostly sleeping to make up for the night flight from Washington, we flew to Rome for three days. As guide to Europe we were using the book "Europe on $5.00 a Day" by Arthur Frommer. Rather out of date now but it was great then. He particularly stressed the Bed-and Breakfast (B & B) idea along with cheap little out of the way restaurants. Not only is it cheaper, I actually think it made the trip more rewarding because you really get to meet local people. To start off we stayed in a B & B in Rome which he recommended. It was on the third floor of a building combining small businesses, restaurants and apartments overlooking a square in the center of the city. After riding up in the elevator, the door opened on the main entry to the facility which was a small restaurant with about six tables along with the 'hotel' managers desk. Off the restaurant a short hallway leads to the left and our room was just off this hallway. So when you came out of the bedroom, you were almost in the restaurant which didn't bother us too much. Farther down the hallway were other rooms and a communal bathroom which we shared. The sleeping accommodations consisted of two single beds. This was the beginning of our long running battle over beds in Europe. Well this didn't suit us so we complained and the smiling maid, who spoke no English, brought a piece of foam to bridge the center and tied the center legs together and made it up as a double bed. Very different from a typical motel or hotel in the USA but this would work for us.

Adventures in Rome

On the floor below our room, was a beauty parlor and since it had been nearly a week since I had washed my hair and it also needed a cut, I decided to give it a try. Since I spoke no Italian and they didn't speak any English it was an amusing experiment in hand signals. But at the end my hair looked OK if different and it was at least clean when they finished and the ladies seemed much entertained by the experience.

Driving in Italy

Another amusing experience happened when we went out for dinner that night. It seems that the Italians don't normally eat until after 9:00 PM so when we arrived at 7:00 PM for dinner, the restaurant was open but completely empty. They welcomed us enthusiastically. Again not knowing any italian we used the point and guess technique. Most of it was fairly normal restaurant food but at the end I decided that I wanted something exotic and different so I pointed. To Larry's vast amusement, the waiter brought me a plate bearing a sharp knife and a whole orange! I had ordered an 'aranche' and that's what I got. Not quite an exotic dessert but amusement for Larry.

After three days of Roman sightseeing, we rented a car and took off to drive to Paris. We first drove North to Florence where we spent some time in the many famous art museums. Next we drove west to Pisa. On the way there, we stopped at a filling station out in the country for gas. We both dug out all the lira we had to pay for it, but it was not enough. We offered them some travelers checks but they would have nothing to do with them. We had been told that dollars were accepted most places in Europe but not here! What to do? Then Larry had an inspiration. He was carrying one of those four color pens that were popular in the 60's so he offered that to the man and his face lit up with a huge smile. He was thoroughly pleased with our payment for gas and we got on our way to Pisa and the leaning tower.

Lunch in Pisa

We arrived in Pisa about 1:00 PM that day and were really hungry but most of the restaurants seemed to be closed. One looked like there were people inside. A man came to the door and said it was closed until our accents told him that we were Americans! Then he threw the door wide open and said "Welcome". It seems the large family was having 'dinner' and they would be delighted to have us join them. He spoke the most amazing English with a strong Brooklyn accent. It seems during the Second World War when the Americans were moving up the coast in Italy, he had worked with some great soldiers from Brooklyn and they had taught him English and been very good to him. So we benefitted from the kindness of our soldiers to Italians. While editing this, our daughter Peggy told me that she and daughter Barb had the same experience years later in Naples. It's amazing how often kindness to strangers pays off.

After a good lunch, we drove towards Genoa through the edges of the alps where they come down to the edge of the Mediterranean Ocean. The road was two lane, curved, hilly and narrow with much traffic. So the driving was terrible. Along the way we found a place to spend the night. Since the traffic along this two lane road had been so bad, we decided to get up early the next morning (5:00 AM) and stop along the way for breakfast.

Getting Lost

Well the traffic this morning was even worse than the night before and the roads were not any better, so by 7:00 AM we had not found any place to stop or even to pull over. As we came into Genoa, the roads widened but the traffic was even worse with many great big trucks and still no place to pull off and stop. Driving straight along with what we thought was the regular traffic, suddenly we were on a side road and the traffic had thinned way down. The only thing that I could figure was that we had missed a turn when we had trucks on both sides of the car. We proceeded not knowing what else to do and all of a sudden the road came to a complete end! We turned around and headed back the way we had come, we thought, when we came to a guard gate! We hadn't seen it going the other way but here it was in our way. The man wanted to see our passports and papers. He didn't speak any English but I thought that I could understand from his Italian, which is very close to Spanish, that he was asking what ship we had come from. We showed him everything we had and he was not satisfied. Finally he came around to the other side of the car, opened the door and motioned me to move over and he got in. He indicated by hand signals that we were to drive and he would show us where. He took us to a four story building and up to an office on the top floor.

The man behind the desk also spoke no English but he did speak some French. We gave him the passports and papers. In his broken French and my school girl French we went over things and finally it turned out that we had indeed gotten down on the Genoa docks by mistake, just how we'll never know, and the guard had indeed been asking what ship we came from. The problem with the papers was that when we rented the car, we were supposed to have been given special coupons for cheap gas, designed especially for tourists. Apparently, since we didn't know anything about them, we were not given any. Since we didn't have them, apparently the guard could only think that we were fakes but certainly more than he could handle. The man in the office couldn't explain how we got there either but he told us how to get back on the main road and straightened out our papers as much as he could. By this time it was 10:00 AM, five hours since we had left the hotel and both of us desperately needed a bathroom. When we asked for one, he said they had none we could use in the building. We could go next door to a bar which had one. Thankfully we got on our way again. By the time we found a place to eat in Genoa, it was lunch time so we had to skip breakfast completely but were glad at least to be able to stop and to eat. What a relief!

Back on the Road

The maps that we had been able to obtain for this trip were almost as bad as the roads and the signs along the way. We were trying to drive from Genoa to Nice and which road to take wasn't too clear. The signs along the way were never for 'Nice' but for the next little town which had no interest for us. There were dozens of these little villages and the names on the map were tiny and on top of each other. By the time you matched the sign on the road to the one on the map you were past it and trying to find the next one. Despite all these problems, we managed to make it to Nice which turned out to be very nice!

Made it to Nice

When late in he day we arrived in Nice, we went first to the B & B picked out of the guide book and checked in. Here they had a double bed for us but it was up on the third floor. Then we went to find something to eat. We hadn't had much to eat during that wild day. We found a small restaurant and had a pleasant dinner. But when it was time to pay, we had not had time to get any French francs, so tried to pay with our remaining lira. But the restaurateur would have none of it despite the fact that we were still fairly close to the border. We offered him dollars and travelers checks both of which he refused. This was before the days of the convenient credit card. So I tried to explain in my limited French, that we had just come into the country and had not had a chance to get any francs but if he would take our dollars, first thing in the morning we would come in and exchange them for francs. Reluctantly he took them and we left. When we returned in the morning after visiting the bank, he had the dollars still sitting on top of his cash register and eagerly got rid of them. Not everyone is open to the world and it's exchanges. It is their country. We don't take francs, pesos or euros over here, not even close to the border.

Language Difficulties

By now we had been on the way for well over a week, so when I spotted the French version of a laundromat, I collected our dirty clothes. The signs on the machine weren't too clear so I tried to ask the manager about how some worked in my limited French. Well she was of the school that believed that if you talked louder and faster, people would understand better. A young girl waiting for her laundry said in English, "Can I help". And I said, "Oh yes if you only could". She asked my questions and got some answers for me. Then, while we waited for the clothes to wash, we talked. It seems that she was a student in English at the University of Nice, working on her Masters Degree and had just flunked her orals! When she found out we were Americans, she said that she would love to spend a day talking to us and practicing. And I said "But of course, we would love to help out that way". She said "Would you like to see something of Nice?" She would be glad to show us around. I said, "We're eager to go to the beach while we're here". She said "Wonderful, I know a lovely little quiet beach where I can take you. I will bring lunch and will drive you there. I can also show you where Brigitte Bardot lives" (She was a popular movie star of the day and, unlike us, most Americans would be eager to see where she lived). We agreed on a time for the next morning.

Nice People in Nice

About ten the next morning she showed up at our B & B in a bright red convertible with her boyfriend, plus a big friendly gray french poodle, and a nice lunch with a couple of bottles of wine. Well it was a great start to the day. Off we went for the beach. It was the time in the mid-sixties when the French were first allowing women to appear on the beach topless which was of course never allowed in the US. When we arrived at the beach, our hostess took off her coverup showing that she was topless like most of the women on the beach! Well Larry was a bit overwhelmed and didn't know where to look, (but held up bravely). it was a fun day and we enjoyed it thoroughly. We kept in touch with our young friends for a while but by now we have lost touch and I can't even remember her name although I still have a picture. She did write that next time she tried, she passed her English orals successfully so maybe we helped her a little.

Nice young Friends in Nice

After the lovely day in Nice, we continued driving up toward Paris with the roads still not able to handle the traffic, in particular the many big trucks. For a while we tried to drive between 1:00 and 3:00 PM when some people ate lunch and took a siesta. It helped a little but was still bad as other people had figured that out too. So we decided, because we really weren't in a big hurry, to go cross country, take some side roads and explore the country side. This was definitely better if slower and we had some friendly experiences at some of the B & B s we found in the guide book. One time we stopped at 7:00 AM at a tiny little gas station with just one gas pump. The lady came out in her bathrobe to pump the gas and then invited us in for breakfast. We hadn't even realized that it was a restaurant but it was, if small. So we had a very simple but good and very friendly family style breakfast.

By now, I had found out several memorable things about struggling in foreign languages First of all you can divide most people you meet who don't speak your language into two classes. One, the minute they hear a foreign accent, they are terrified and immediately flee for help from someone more experienced. Second, are people who find you an interesting challenge and are willing to work with you and make suggestions of words when you get stuck. They almost seem amused by your problems but are not threatened by them. Even better, I have learned not to ask 'Do you speak English?" No they don't. Period. But if you ask 'Do you understand a little English', they will agree that they do 'a little'. This gives you leave to throw in an occasional English word if you're stuck and they don't feel that they have to say anything in English unless they choose to. It's a crucial difference.

Collecting the Kids

Eventually we made it to Paris and after a day or two Larry put me on the plane for Dulles Airport in Washington DC while he prepared to go on to Moscow to the seminar where he was to give his talk. In Washington, Dot picked me up and I collected the Greenbriar and some of my kids from her. After a short visit in Bethesda, MD, we drove to Wilmington, DE, to my sister Kit's house for a visit and to collect some more kids. Then it was on up to New Jersey, Sal's house and the rest of the kids. I can never thank my three sisters enough for giving me that once in a lifetime opportunity. We had a few days visit at Sal's and we spent one of those days at the 1965 New York World's Fair. It was my first visit to New York and the kids loved it.

Driving Back to New Mexico with Six Kids

From New Jersey we set out cross country heading first for St. Louis where my parents still lived. Since none of the kids were old enough to drive, I had to do all the driving and those were very long days without a break. I remember when my neck would ache, Barb would massage it and that would help. They were good kids but still kids and they got restless and tired too. We made it safely to St. Louis with only one stop along the way somewhere in Ohio. In St. Louis we stayed with two of my sisters, Rose and Susie, for a day or two while we visited with my parents. Then we took off on the final leg of the journey to Espanola.

And everything went surprisingly successfully, until we reached the middle of Santa Fe, NM. Then the trusty steed, the Greenbriar, threw a rod and refused to move a step farther. Guess It felt that it had done it's duty as far as it needed to. We pushed it into a nearby gas station. It was then about four in the afternoon, so I called Pete where he was working at the Los Alamos lab. He had our old station wagon with him at work so I told him of our predicament and he came on down to Santa Fe and picked us up and took us home to Espanola where we still lived and was I glad to be there! I couldn't help but think since it was mid-July, how disastrous it would have been if the van had decided to quit out in the middle of the hot long miles that we had just driven through Oklahoma and Texas. But fate was with us and that disaster didn't happen.

Chapter 15

Back to School and Working, 1964-1981

S ome of my early jobs as described above, were the usual baby-sitting, clerking, etc. that many students do. Both my work at the Marshall Fields store in the Chicago Loop and on the Manhattan Project at the University of Chicago were meaningful and satisfying at the time. However, neither were what would really be called a 'career'. Being a 'Chem Tech' and member of the so-called 'Shotgun' group on the Manhattan Project that measured neutron absorption in materials from Nuclear Reactors, were moving in the right direction but were still only a beginning. Probably the Project jobs were the most dangerous. The rumor was that we would all be sterile or our children deformed. Even if they admit to being a little weird, our children have all been healthy and have done well. The rumors appear to have been much exaggerated.

Raising Children

As was said earlier, it was generally accepted, in those days that once a woman had children, she was not supposed to work. And it was true that I enjoyed my children so much that I wanted to be with them as much as I could while they were little. So for nearly twenty years, I was Mama and a housewife. I did fill out income tax forms in a CPA's office for a few months before I became pregnant with my twins. I had a chance to do this because my sister Lydia was staying with us out in the Bay Area. She had returned to California with us to look for work. After an auto accident where she was injured, she was not able to work, so stayed with Pete, my oldest son, while I worked briefly instead.

After California we moved to Los Alamos, where four children, including a set of twins, were born in less than three years. Then to Espanola where two more were born. I continued to read magazines like 'Scientific American' to feed my passion for science and worked my way through the textbooks that I had, such as Calculus and Chemistry, working most of the problems. But after a while, this was not enough. My Husband understood somewhat. I remember him surprising me with a new-baby-gift, when Tom was born, a four volume "World of Mathematics" that I had seen advertised and craved. I dearly loved it and read it from cover to cover.

What to do Next?

Gradually I became more dissatisfied and restless. I guess it was what is now called a mid-life crisis although, at the time, I didn't recognize it as such. It came to a head one day when Larry took off for a week of hunting, leaving me at home with the seven kids. After weeping and seriously considering suicide for a while, even figuring out ways, such as poison, in which I might do it, I finally decided that as unhappy as I might be, I I could not do that to my beloved children. I had quite a conversation with myself.

I asked myself, "Well what is your problem? What do you want? Do you want to go hunting or fishing?"

Answer: "No, I just want to have some vacation from the kids and some fun like he does".

"Well, why don't you? Do you expect him to arrange it for you?"

"Yes, I guess I do, but that doesn't make sense because he doesn't know what I want".

"That's the key, you have to decide what you want and then arrange it yourself! He's a good husband and I'm sure will cooperate in whatever you work out".

I thought about taking a weekend with some women friends and staying in an Albuquerque motel, shopping and taking in a movie. But no, I realized that I did not want to do that. Shopping bores me and so do most movies. What I really wanted to do was to go back to school, finish my degree and eventually go back to work. As a young girl, I had never been interested in teaching. Now, however, having worked enough with my own children and tutoring some of their friends, as well as working with Boy and Girl Scouts, I thought that I might enjoy teaching. I decided that being a Secondary Math teacher was something that I could do well and that was always badly needed. The daily and monthly schedules, would fit well with the remaining part of raising my children, who were still pretty small, so they would not be neglected too much.

But how to finish up my degree? I wrote to both of the colleges that I had attended earlier, Rosary and the University of Chicago, to see if they had anything useful for me to extend into a degree, but they didn't. All they offered were Great Books, Philosophy and things like that. I tried UNM (University of New Mexico, Albuquerque) and they did have some correspondence courses for secondary teachers who needed to maintain their certificates. So I successfully took one of those by correspondence. However, it was a two hour drive to Albuquerque and, while some people do it, to me it did not seem practical to make the four hour round trip five or even three days a week. So this was certainly not a long term solution.

First Teaching Job

My first chance to try actual teaching came about almost by chance, one evening in 1962, when Larry and Richard Lucero, then the local Boy Scout executive, were having a meeting about the Boy Scouts in our house. Richard asked me if I would be interested in a job teaching in the evenings. One of his Den Mothers had been doing it but was tired of it and was planning to quit. 'But', I asked, 'Don't I need a degree?" and he said "No, she didn't have one, she had just worked in an office. That's all they require" and I had certainly done that as well as having attended Business College. So he told me where to apply to the principal who was running the project at the local high school. When I applied, the principal took one look at my resume. He was astonished because the President of Rosary College, River Forest, which I had attended earlier near Chicago, was a dear friend of his! What a small world it really is! So he hired me on the spot.

The job was part of a 'Manpower Development Program' designed to help develop skills for girls who had graduated from high school. They had some business training but had not enough skills to be able to find jobs. The local high school facilities were being used after regular school hours. One teacher taught typing from 3:00 to 5:00 PM; another taught shorthand from 5:00 to 7:00 PM and the third was to teach Office Practice from 7:00 to 9:00 PM. This last was to be my job. It included filing, spelling, grammar, simple math, taking notes and things like that, which all seemed well within my capabilities.

Amazingly, after I did it for a semester I was apparently quite successful because some years later, I ran into several of my former students from that class. They thanked me profusely, because, they said, it had been just what they needed and they were now working quite successfully. And the really surprising thing was that I had actually enjoyed it. Furthermore, since I always had dinner ready before I left, my family seemed to survive it without much problem. The people in charge of the program were pleased with what I had done but had decided to transfer the program up to the technical school at Ojo Caliente. They wanted me to go up there and continue teaching, but it would be a two hour round trip drive, sometimes through winter snow. So I didn't believe it would work out with so many of my children still at home and I declined to continue. However that one semester was a great way to test out my taste for and potential for teaching

College of Santa Fe

My next efforts toward a degree came at the College of Santa Fe. At the time it was an all male school run by the Christian Brothers called St. Michael's College. They had opened their evening classes to the general public so I found a useful Sophomore English course there and drove the 30 miles twice a week for a Spring semester with a teacher friend from Holy Cross School. Then the following Summer, they saw the need for teachers to maintain their certification and opened Summer school classes to women where I found a full schedule of classes. When Fall came and I wanted to take Math and Chemistry courses, they decided that as an older woman, I wouldn't corrupt the boys too much. Besides they didn't have very many students in those fields and an addition there was welcome. As it turned out there were only two of us in one Math course and three in a Chemistry course! About then they changed the name of the school to College of Santa Fe and gave up on the limitation on women. I ended up being one of their first three women graduates in 1966. I believe the other women were also like me, somewhat older, and had done almost all of their classes at night.

My graduation was with honors, no less, in Mathematics and Chemistry and with a Secondary Teaching Certificate. Not only was my accomplishment picked up by the national news, but my picture, with six of my children, appeared on the front pages of both the Albuquerque Journal and Santa Fe New Mexican on Mother's Day two days before graduation on Tuesday. I received congratulatory letters from far and wide, including, one from the Governor of New Mexico. In addition to my great happiness at my success at graduation, I was particularly pleased and surprised that my father who had never seemed to pay much attention to me, came by himself for the ceremony. I guess he was more aware and interested in his children than I gave him credit for or ever realized. I guess he cared more than he had been able to show. He was such a quiet and retiring sort of person that he wasn't able to express his feelings very well. He told me many things, during that visit, about his life but unfortunately I didn't write them down right away so that many have been forgotten. How I wish that I had a recorder at the time! Many of the things in the earlier Chapters about him came from this period. When he went around Espanola with me on shopping errands many people knew me and had seen the papers and heard the news so they congratulated me. And of course when I Introduced him as my Father, he shared the spotlight with me and just beamed.

Approval of Graduation by Children

Father and Husband

Teaching Junior High

While I had taught for most of a year at the local parochial school which my children attended, my first real full time professional job after graduation was teaching junior high math. I had applied to teach Mathematics and Chemistry in the Espanola Senior High School, but since a position there was not available, I was offered as an alternative the 7th and 8th grades at the John F Kennedy Junior High near San Juan Pueblo (1966-67). I They promised that if a position opened up in the High School, I would be transferred there.

While I liked the actual teaching, I couldn't get along well with the management. The Principal of the Junior High started out at a preliminary teachers meeting, by saying, "We're sure glad to have you because we really need a girls PE (Physical Education) Teacher". Startled, I said "But I I thought I was to teach math. I don't know anything at all about PE." He said, "Oh well yes, but really as a woman, you should be able to teach PE and a little Math on the side but that isn't very important." Disappointed, I said, "I'll try but I really don't know anything about PE and I hate organized sports of all kinds. Furthermore, I don't think I'm qualified". Then he said, "In addition, we would like to have you sponsor the Cheer Leader Squad". Since I especially disliked organized sports and this was voluntary, I declined this completely which was not well received. I said "If you want a math, games or science club, any of those I'll be glad to try out". But no, they had no interest in any of those.

So I was assigned two math classes and four of girls PE. It was obvious that I was going to be the proverbial square peg in a round hole. After several weeks, they found that I was quite right. I wasn't qualified to teach PE. So they had to rearrange the schedules and they didn't like that at all. Now they gave me five math classes and one so-called study hall with all girls, where I could have the girls run around the playground, do some exercises, and maybe do a little studying on the side.

Tom and Bill in the Grades

At this time, my two youngest boys were in 5th grade and I worried a little about having them come home alone from school before I could get there. The very first day of school that Fall they went off to their Holy Cross Parochial grade school and I to my Junior High. Before I left, I told them that I had a dental appointment in Santa Fe right after school so they would be home by themselves until the older children (Bob and Peggy) came home from High School. Well the first unexpected thing that happened, Tom and Bill were let out of school after only two hours and came home to be alone for the rest of the day. Of course I didn't expect this or even know about it at the time. Then the Dentist's office called the house to let me know that my appointment had been canceled because the dentist was away, so I shouldn't come to Santa Fe after school. Well those two 5th graders had the sense to recognize that they needed to get that message to me at school to keep me from a useless trip to Santa Fe. They did not have the phone number but managed to find it and call the Junior High office and get the message to me. Was I ever impressed and decided that they were quite capable of managing on their own when necessary.

Fighting the Administration

At the school, my next battle was over the candy store. They had an excellent hot lunch program and according to my understanding of the law, they were not allowed to sell candy in competition with it. But that was exactly what they were doing. Kids could buy candy, ice cream, coke etc. or hot lunch but not both. This seemed wrong to me and I wasn't afraid to say so. They protested, "but that's how we get our money for sports equipment so we have to do it that way". The most demeaning thing that happened at the school, was that the principal listened in to my classroom over the loud speaker system.

He would chastise me over the intercom in front of my class if they were noisier than he thought they should be.

Another problem of teaching in this school was that the only other Math Teacher, Mr. Vigil, had originally taken no Math classes beyond High School Algebra so by default with a college degree in Math, I was the head of the two person department. Of course it didn't mean much about control over what went on in the school. The texts we used had been selected and ordered by Mr. Vigil the previous year and were very unsatisfactory because they were completely beyond the capabilities of the students. Sadly the students there were all at least two years below their supposed grade level. They couldn't even read the text, let alone do any of the problems in it. This meant that, if they were to learn anything, I I had to prepare work sheets for them practically every day, which meant a lot of work for me. I tried to get some work books for them and even made a special trip to Santa Fe to the Text Book Depository to pick them up. These helped some because the problems and text were designed for 3rd and 4th grade and thus appropriate for their capabilities at the level at which they were. But even though the work was appropriate, unfortunately the workbooks were clearly marked for the 3rd and 4th grades. The students as 7th and 8th graders felt demeaned to use such books even though they could work the problems.

At the end of the year I really didn't want to continue and the school district didn't want me back. This was despite the fact that as shown by the standardized math tests given at the end of the year, my students had advanced on average a year and a half while the other math teacher's students had only advanced an average of nine months. They really didn't care about the students learning. To them I was just a nuisance and they were glad to be rid of me.

At about this time a position teaching Math in the Senior High School did open up, but I I was not offered the job as had been promised. On the contrary, a cousin of the Superintendent was brought in from Ojo Caliente for the job, not me. However, even if they had offered it to me, the chances are that I wouldn't have taken it because I was so disgusted with the attitude of the administration and their lack of interest in the kids learning.

Introduction to Computers

One thing that did come up during that year of teaching that turned out to be very useful. In June, 1967, I a week long introductory seminar on Computers was offered for Math teachers in the state by New Mexico Tech in Socorro I signed up along with about 300 other Math teachers from around the state. In the morning lectures were given on the underlying theory of computer operations. Then in the afternoons we were assigned a program to work on their local computer. The problem: Solve the equation (x = sin ax) for x by iteration, with input of a value for "a" and print out the results. A simple enough problem but I was fascinated and couldn't wait to get the program running. I think that possibly I was the only member of the group that actually got the problem running and I was hooked on computers. I I found the whole idea of how computers work completely fascinating then and still do.

Fortunately for me, that summer, I also had a call for an interview from the Los Alamos Lab (where I had applied earlier). This was 1967 and computers were starting to come on line. There were no degrees in Computer Science in those days but my Math and related Chemistry skills were applicable to the potential job. Of course, that seminar at Socorro may have helped me get the job as a Staff Member. At any rate, I was hired and my salary doubled overnight!

A Second Life

In a way it was a second life for me. I came to realize that I could have both children and a scientific career, not in parallel but sequentially. In a way I went back to being the person that I was before I was married. It was very different from being only a wife and Mom. I realized that I was much more comfortable in a work or class environment than I was at home or in other social situations. Except for when I was seeking a mate and thought that was a way to find one, I always hated parties. I couldn't understand why others liked them. During the nearly 20 years that I spent raising children, I had also done a lot of volunteer work in the Church, School, and Community and hated every minute of it. I felt it was required so I did it but it was nothing that I ever enjoyed. Once I went back to work, I simply didn't have time so felt fully justified in dropping out of all those activities. What a relief! It may have been hard on my children but. from what I've heard, I don't think they suffered too much.

Early Computers at Los Alamos

At the Lab my principle job, in the beginning, was in the Theoretical Division (T-1), and I was to work on large codes (or programs) that calculated the expected behavior of neutrons in nuclear reactors and nuclear weapons. Since neutrons are what cause elements to fission, their behavior is key to both reactors and weapons. All of the codes were written in what was then a brand new programming language, FORTRAN, short for 'FORmula TRANslation' which I first had to learn. Until that point in time, the large codes, written in FORTRAN, had been kept completely in big drawers of punch cards. They were now in the process of being moved on to large magnetic tapes. The computer still read a control deck of cards and then took information from tapes as requested by the cards. After the problem had run, the computer printed out a listing which then had to be read and errors in programming found. The program was then corrected by punch cards in the control deck. The card deck was then resubmitted to be run again. This cycle continued until the results were correct as shown by test problems.

When I first started, the "Stretch" computer which filled an entire large room and didn't do much more than a typical modern PC, was just being discontinued. With Forrest Brinkley's (my first mentor and teacher) help I actually ran a job or two on it before it completely disappeared. Another earlier computer that was still being used a little in the beginning, was the MANIAC (much like the ENIAC) but which ran a system written at Los Alamos called MADCAP, somewhat like FORTRAN but only used locally. (Actually, I personally thought that it was a better language). One of my interesting early jobs was to do a translation of a program from MADCAP to FORTRAN for Roger Lazarus.

The computers that were the real work horses at the time when I first started, and actually running practical problems, were two IBM 7094's that, along with Stretch, had been developed jointly with IBM. After further development, IBM, then went on to use them for business computing. My first group, T-1, which had been involved with this early development, was led by Bengt Carlson. I Over the years he spent a lot of time going back and forth to Poughkeepsie, NY working with IBM. The computers had been primarily designed to calculate neutronic and hydrodynamic behavior in nuclear reactors and weapons. These are both extremely complex problems and are essential to development of weapons and reactors. To give an idea of how complex neutronic calculations are, I have seen pictures of a huge roomful of people doing them in England, when they were developing their nuclear weapons shortly after WW-II. The "computers" (people were called that then), performed calculations on mechanical calculators. Each passed their result to the next person who then performed their share of the calculation. This was the way they did the required neutron calculations at that time. It's clear what an improvement the big computers were over doing them that way.

Shortly before I was hired, the Lab had just received two new CDC (Control Data Corporation) 6600s. I Then shortly after I started, two more CDC 6600's arrived. I A few years later these were followed by two CDC 7600's, still larger and faster. Finally, the CRAY computers began to arrive. The Los Alamos Lab bought the first CRAY for their own work, helping Seymour Cray have enough money to build another. He had been senior designer of the CDC machines but wanted to start his own company and do things in a way that he thought better. These were the best computers that we had for a long time and were the last that I I worked on. All were 'fed' small control decks and then read the program and/or data from tapes or other storage devices as needed. About the time that I stopped doing computing, the Lab moved on to having terminals at each desk and people could load in their own material, so card decks eventually disappeared. Even later I actually had a Personal Computer (PC) of my own on my own desk but that was in the middle eighties.

Moving Back to Los Alamos

In September 1969, we had been able to find a house in Los Alamos which we could afford and so moved back up to Los Alamos. With Pete in the Navy and Barb, Bets, Bob and Peg now all in College, and thus only Tom and Bill still at home, we didn't need as large a house as that in Espanola. In addition, Bill and Tom were just starting Junior High so I felt better about having them closer in case of emergencies. With both of us working, it was also a great relief not to spend so many hours on commuting. Actually the house was close enough to the Computer Center where I worked, that I could even walk to work in half an hour. To be sure it was across a canyon and so meant a several hundred foot climb down and back up again or a half mile around to go across a bridge. During those years, the walk helped me keep in shape!

Computer Division Formed

A year or two after I started, computers were expanding so fast that the group T-1 which ended up furnishing computing for most of the whole Lab, had grown to nearly 100 people. This was much too large for a group which usually was supposed to consist of around 20 to 30 persons. So the decision was made to form a new Division-Computer or C Division. The then group leader of T-1, Bengt Carlson, was old enough that he did not feel up to taking on such a challenge but wanted to go back to doing research on neutronics, his specialty. He would maintain a small group, T-1, for people who would work on neutronics. Since I had become fascinated by this topic I decided to follow him rather than transfer to the new C-Division being formed.

T-1 Didn't Work for Me

Shortly after this change, a new man, Kaye Lathrop, joined T-1 and the administration of the group was turned over to him. What a disaster! Bengt had been an effective and considerate leader. Perhaps the kind of person he was, was partly behind the big success of the Laboratory in computing. But Lathrop was something else. Most of the time I worked directly for Forrest Brinkley so was unaware of the change. However when Forrest was away for a few days one time, I had to work directly for Lathrop for a few days. He was completely inconsiderate. At 8:05 AM he would page me and complain bitterly because I had not instantly, on arriving at work, dashed upstairs to hand him the particular listing he wanted to work on. I guess that he was too lazy to go down and get his own listings from the computer room as everyone else did, but he expected me to run up and down stairs for him. What made it particularly bad is that I had recently been diagnosed with an ovarian tumor and was about to have surgery I just wasn't in shape to do what he expected.[11]

Shortly thereafter during my annual review, in December, he informed me that since I wasn't doing well enough to suit him, he was not going to give me a yearly raise. That did it! I immediately went down to the new C-Division and applied for a job there which I Immediately got. I It seems that Lathrop had also refused to do neutronics work for the weapons design groups because it would be classified and therefore couldn't be published! His career was all he was interested in. So they needed someone to work on the corresponding neutronic codes for the weapon design groups. I was to transfer after I had my projected surgery which happened in January. The transfer occurred at the beginning of March. In C-Division, now headed by a great guy, Roger Lazarus, I was treated very well by my group leader, Bob Frank, and the assistant group leader, Frank McGirt. What a huge difference good leaders can make!

Now followed one of the best periods of my nearly twenty years of work. in addition to the interesting programming that I enjoyed doing, at noon while we ate lunch we played duplicate bridge. There were two tables and each table dealt and played four hands of bridge with duplicate boards. Then the boards were exchanged and we each played the ones the other table had already played. Afterwards, we could, and many people did, compare results of the two groups which is always fun. Three other ladies were part of this bridge group. One was another programmer in my group, Jenny Boring, and two were secretaries in the Division Office, Dee Stewart and

---

[11]   And it wasn't just me. A woman friend who later worked in his division had been invited to give a keynote address a t a national meeting but because she was a woman, Lathrop refused to send her. Only men would be sent by him. She could go but had to take vacation and pay her own way. There were also rumors that he took other peoples work and published it as his own. People used to say of him, that they were tired of the footprints he left on their backs.

Marjorie McCormick. One time the four of us decided to take an afternoon off and go to Santa Fe for lunch and arranged with the restaurant to let us spend the whole afternoon playing bridge there. It was really fun and we promised ourselves that we would do it again but somehow we never did. And soon thereafter, Jenny left and transferred to Sandia in Albuquerque where my son Pete met her later.

Nuclear Engineering

At first, in the Computer Division, I worked primarily on Nuclear Weapons Programs for the Weapons Design Groups. Although the mathematics and physics were applicable to both weapons and reactors, they used different engineering. There was a lot to learn and as time went on I became more and more interested in the subject of Nuclear Engineering. In a year or two, I began to take night classes in Computers, Physics, Math, Engineering and anything else that I could find.

Chapter 16

Losing Parents/ Watching Kids Grow Up, 1970-80

As described in the last Chapter, my professional life went on at LANL as did my life at home. In late 1969, as described above, we had moved back up to Los Alamos where we lived for this whole decade. The period from 1970 to 1980, while highly satisfying, exciting, and almost overwhelming in some ways, was very sad in others. In particular it was very hectic with a tremendous amount going on. In fact going back over my records and notes, I'm amazed at how many complex things overlapped. As the decade started, in the Fall of 1969, Bob went off to start college at NMSU (New Mexico State University) in Las Cruces where the twins already were and Peggy started at UNM (University of New Mexico) in Albuquerque where Pete already was after coming back from the Navy. So that meant that we had five kids in College all at once. The last two boys, Tom and Bill were just starting Junior High in Los Alamos and later went on to Los Alamos High School. During the decade all seven of our children earned at least one college degree, BS or BA, and several, as well as I, also received an

MS or MBA.[12] They are summarized in a footnote. Unfortunately I couldn't attend all graduations, much as I would like to have but I was pleased and proud of the achievements of all of them.

We had begun backpacking in the 60's and continued this into the 70's. We also took many interesting trips which were interspersed with the backpacking trips. Both Larry and I learned to fly, received our pilots licenses for small planes, and even ended up owning our own Cessna 210, 3705Y (yankee). The saddest part of the decade was that in the early seventies the end of life came for all four of our parents then in their eighties.

Help for Larry's Parents, Gladys and Peter

To begin with, taking the last first, in July 1971, Larry got a call for help from his Mother, Gladys, in Santa Ana, just south of Los Angeles. His Father, Peter, had fallen while working outside and had been unable to get up. He called for help but his wife, Gladys, couldn't hear him so he lay there for a long time. Finally a neighbor heard him, got him up and helped him into the house. Now he was

---

[12]   Degrees from 1970 to 1980

May '71	Barb	BS, Math, Computers	NMSU (New Mexico State University
July '71	Betty	BS, Biochemistry	NMSU
Sept. '72	Betty	MS, Animal Genetics	UC (University of California), Davis
Sept. '73	Pete	BS, Operations Research	UNM (University of New Mexico)
Feb. '74	Peggy	B, Math, Computer Science	UC Davis
June '75	Tom, Bill	High School Graduation	Los Alamos High School
June '75	Pete	MS, Operations Research	UC, Berkeley, CA
May '76	Barb	MBA, Computers	NMSU
Dec. '78	Bob, Tom	BS, Electrical Engineering	NMSU
Dec. '78	Mom	MS, Nuclear Engineering	UNM, Albuquerque, NM
May '79	Bill	BS, Geophysics	NMSU

in bed and couldn't even turn over by himself and, his wife being in pretty poor shape herself, was physically unable to turn him or care for him in other ways. So Larry went out to help and survey the situation. While they could and did hire temporary help, it was obvious that they had reached the stage where they could no longer manage on their own. Betty and Peggy, then out at UC, Davis, CA, volunteered to go down and help for a few weeks which they did. However a major change was obviously needed.

Moving the Senior Aspreys to Los Alamos

As it happened, the house next door to us in Los Alamos had just gone on the market when the owner had died. It was a three bedroom, two bath house, small but adequate and all on one floor. After consulting with Larry's sister Tim about it, we decided that the best solution was to buy that house next door and move Larry's parents from Santa Ana into this house in Los Alamos. While this meant leaving behind their friends and the life that they had chosen, we were the closest relatives they had and they did need help. The senior Aspreys certainly didn't seem to want to move back to New York where Tim was. And none of us, children or grandchildren, could afford to abandon our lives and move out to California to care for them. Tim went out for the summer to help them sell their house and some of their furniture. With her help they then packed up and shipped the things they wanted to keep to Los Alamos. So for the next four years, they lived next door to us and, with the help of our two youngest sons, Tom and Bill, then in high school during those years, we did the best we could for them. With the extra house to look after, it kept us pretty busy, particularly since both our jobs were strenuous and demanding. At the time it never occurred to us to worry about the effect of the altitude (over 7000 ft) on them although perhaps, from our experiences since, we should have.

One of the first things we did was to install a buzzer between the two houses with buttons by each of their beds for emergencies. I remember one time about one in the morning, Mother (Gladys) woke up and called "Peter" several times. When he didn't answer (not surprising since he was quite deaf and had his hearing aids out) she got up to check on him. She got as far as the door to his room and fell and couldn't get up. She lay there in the cold and made enough noise that she finally woke him up and had him ring the buzzer for help. Of course we came and rescued her and chastised her for trying to get up by herself. But this sort of thing happened many times. As time went on, and Gladys was in a wheelchair most of the time, we installed a bridge-walkway between the two houses and were bringing them across regularly for dinner. I remember one time taking Mother to the hospital and after they took X-rays of her hurting knee, the doctor asked me when she broke it. Well I didn't know and he looked at me like I was an idiot for not knowing. But how could I know? At that time they had only been with us for a few months and I knew little of their life before out in California.

One unfortunate thing that happened, at the time it had not been easy for them to sell their house in California. So they held a second mortgage for the man who bought it, a man named Eady. He was a bachelor Lawyer and turned out to be something of a deadbeat. He sized up the situation and decided that he could afford just to stop paying on the Second Mortgage. The monthly amount of about $32 was small and didn't mean much to us. However it meant a lot to Peter Asprey. He had been very poor in his childhood and small amounts were very important to him. Each month he would get very upset because the check didn't come from Mr. Eady. The money wasn't very important but his being upset was. Both their son, Robert Asprey, and grandson, Peter Asprey, at different times, went out to California to try to get him to pay but to no avail. He faced them both and flatly refused to pay anymore. Of course that means he can't sell with a clear title and I've often wondered what happened about it after they died. So many things in life remain unresolved despite our best efforts.

In some ways the years in Los Alamos were good years for them as they had a chance to really get acquainted with their only grandchildren, (which they mostly couldn't have so far away in California), both the two who still lived at home and the other five who still visited frequently from Albuquerque and Las Cruces. I think it was also important for the grandchildren to make contact with their grandparents. Unfortunately, by the time they moved there, they were incapacitated enough that they couldn't easily make new friends in their age group. Dad particularly missed this because he was such an outgoing person who liked people and he really seemed to miss having friends of his own for conversations. In some ways it might have been better if they had come sooner but it was a little late to decide that.

Getting Acquainted with my In-laws

I too had a chance to get acquainted with them and they were whimsical people in their own way. I remember Gladys telling about when she was a little girl, she came running in one day and said to her Mom "There are a million cats in the yard" and her Mom said skeptically "How many?" She said, "Well maybe a hundred" Her Mom said again "How many?" She said "Well our cat and another". That became a family retort for anyone who exaggerated. One of Peter's favorite stories which he told many times was about a little girl who went on a picnic with some friends. After going to the bathroom behind a tree, she came running up to her mother and said with great excitement. "Mom come see. Jimmy has the neatest little gadget to take on a picnic". Again this became a family saying.

Getting Acquainted with Larry's Siblings

Another bonus from having them there was that Larry's sister Tim was able to arrange a year's sabbatical in 1972-1973, working in the Computer Division at the Los Alamos Lab. She was able to use that third bedroom and gave us a break from looking after them but also the children and I got to know her better. Also during that period, Larry's brother Bob came from Spain for several long visits. Since I had hardly known him at all before, this was the first chance I had to get acquainted with my unusual brother-in-law. He was a US Marine in WW II and had been in the first wave in the attack on Iwo Jima Island and after the war was stationed in Japan for quite a while. Since being discharged from the Marines, he has remained a bachelor, lived most of his life in Europe and made a living writing books on military history. Among others, he has written on the German Generals in WW I, Frederick the Great, War in the Shadows (Guerrilla Warfare) and his latest, two volumes on the life of Napoleon. When he visited, he, Larned and our youngest boys, Tom and Bill, took several canoe trips down the Rio Grande which seemed to have been enjoyed by all even if they did upend the canoe occasionally.

Pete—College, Marriage, Working

The only one of the grandchildren who had been able to really get acquainted with his Asprey grandparents before they moved to Los Alamos, was Pete while he was out in California in the Navy. While stationed in San Diego during the late 60's, he would go up to visit them in Santa Ana near Los Angeles when he was on leave and had some good visits with them then. They used to speak with affection about him sitting on the floor playing the guitar during those visits. When Pete came back from the Navy in 1970, he went back to school at UNM (University of New Mexico) in

Albuquerque where he had had so much trouble earlier. Now it was a completely different story, he did very well without too much trouble. He also taught for several years as an adjunct professor at UNM Graduate School. He also taught later at a Junior College in California.

At this point his sister Peggy also was in school at UNM and she introduced him to Cindy Cornil who was in the same dorm as she was. Cindy and Peg met when Peg was complaining to a friend, Renee, that her feet were too big because she wore a shoe size 10. Renee said, "Come here and I'll introduce you to someone who really has big feet". They went down the hall and she introduced Peg to Cindy who wore shoe size 12 and says laughingly, "When I swim I don't have to wear flippers because I have my own built in". Cindy was a champion swimmer and a lifeguard, so she wasn't only kidding! As a result of this relationship, Pete and Cindy met and decided that this was it and they were married a few months later (Jan 1971) in the chapel at UNM. Cindy was the third child in another family of seven from Roswell. So while the wedding was almost all family, it was still pretty big. As a teenager, Cindy had endometriosis so the doctors weren't at all sure that she could have children at all. So Pete and Cindy were delighted when their first healthy child, David was born Nov. 1972, in Albuquerque.

Pete to California

When Pete finished up his BS in Operations Research at UNM in September 1973, they went out to California. There, Pete went to graduate school at UC (University of California), Berkeley, and received his MS in Operations Research in June,1975, after two difficult years of study. While out there, to their great delight, their second child Jenna (Jennifer in Jan 1974) was safely born. But that was to be it. They have had no more. But since they have two wonderful kids they really can't complain. For a while Pete worked in California with a small business. He then got a job back in Albuquerque working for Sandia Laboratories as a Data Base Designer, and has been with Sandia very successfully ever since until his retirement in January 2005.

Betty & Barb, Not so Identical

The next in line, our twins, Barb and Bets, got Bachelors and Masters Degrees in this decade. The fields they chose are symptomatic of the differences in their interests. Betty chose the field of Animal Genetics, while Barb has worked on computers. Betty has worked in a Chemistry Lab like her Dad and Barb concentrated on computers more like what I did. To be sure it was business computing while mine was science and engineering.

By 1970, it had been decided that since the University of California was running Los Alamos Laboratory, the children of employees were eligible to attend the California schools like resident students. So Betty went out to graduate school at UC Davis. As Betty says, she was ahead of her time by getting a degree in Animal Genetics, because she could not find a job in her field then, although now it is growing like crazy. When Betty graduated, Sept. 1972, she first found a job in Indianapolis working for a medical equipment company, American Monitor. There she met and married her husband, David Strietelmeier (May 1975). For two of the years that they worked for that company they were managing a plant in Belfast, Northern Ireland. Since those years overlapped the year (1981-82) that we spent in Germany, we were able to spend Christmas with them in Northern Ireland, and they came down and visited us in Germany as well as sharing a cruise trip through the Greek Islands with us.

Barb's first degree was a BS in Mathematics and Computers. She then went on to earn an MBA, work in the Computer Center and even teach classes at NMSU. In January 71, she was married to a fellow student, Jeff Ray. This marriage however, did not last because as we suspected, they were both pretty young and had rather different ideas about what marriage meant. They were divorced in 1974. In Jan 1977, Barb married Art Whatley who was a professor in the Business School at NMSU with whom she had been working. Before she met him, he had been married and divorced with two boys. Barb and Art lived together for nearly a year and then got married. Almost immediately Barb got a job up in Albuquerque at Sandia Labs where she worked with her brother Pete on data analysis. This marriage also seemed to be having trouble lasting but fortunately there were no new children involved. In fact I understand that was one of the problems. Art was somewhat older and already had two boys and really didn't want any more. On the other hand Barb was younger and had no children but still wanted to have some. This made for a problem between them and eventually they too got divorced. [13]

Bob, the Inventor

From the time he was in grade school, Bob always said that he wanted to be an inventor. When he went to college in 1969, he started in Mechanical Engineering and worked part time in the University Computer Center to make enough money to help pay his expenses. During this period, he did something that convinced me that we had something very special in our Bobby. We bought a used refrigerator and the ice maker didn't work. I called a service man and he came and looked at it but couldn't figure what was wrong with it. So he detached it and took it away. A few weeks later he

---

[13] ironically, after this, Art got married to another woman and actually had a little girl. He and Barb have remained friends and still keep in touch. She even says they were better friends after the divorce than when they were married.

brought it back, very shamefacedly. It seems that he had it all apart on his desk with the parts laid out in order and his three year old got into them and mixed them all up so he couldn't possibly repair it. So he brought the mess back, all apart with the pieces in the ice holder pan, and of course didn't charge me. I put it on the shelf and we continued to use ice cube trays. When Bob came home from school, I said to him more in jest than seriously. "Here's a puzzle for you Bob: and handed him the 'mess' and told him the story. He took it away and some time later brought it back, plugged it in and turned it on and it worked perfectly. Was I amazed! He had never even seen it together and yet was able to figure it out and get it working. This takes a very special type of mind.

An unusual phase in his college career took place in December about half way through his Junior year. He got angry with some professors about something. He never would tell me what it was but I guess it was because of his refusal to turn in homework that he knew how to do perfectly well but was unwilling to go to the trouble of writing up. He continued to believe and argued many times with me that he shouldn't have to do homework if he knew how to do it very well and can still pass all the tests. My argument is that he may think he knows how to do the work but the Professor does not and the Professor has to give him a grade based on something. My words fell on deaf ears.

At any rate, he went down, resigned from all his ME classes, went to the EE (Electrical Engineering) Dept. and asked if they would take him. They said yes but that he had to go back to the beginning and take the EE sequence starting with Freshman classes. So he registered for a beginning EE class and went and asked the Computer Center for a full time job, instead of the part time he was then working, to help him pay for the extended time he would need to finish up. Since he was apparently very good at computers, they cheerfully agreed and he spent several years catching up—and having fun on the side! Apparently, not being in a hurry, and as an employee he could take one class per semester for free, he decided that this was a good deal and continued to take one class at a time.

Gradually Getting a Degree While Having Fun

Among other things, he learned to parachute from a plane; learned to fly and helped to develop the computer system, SOLAR (Student On Line Academic Records), for student records at NMSU. He had rented a house on El Paseo Street just across from the University. When it was being sold a few years later, he told us about it. We thought it might be a good investment so bought it with what little money we got from Larry's parents when they died and rented it to him and his two younger brothers for the same rent.

In July 1978, while Bob was still slowly working on his degree, he met and married a fellow student, Joanne Joyce (aka Jojo) Raabe. She has a degree in medical radiology. They met while Jojo and her sister had a small store on the Mesilla Plaza. Bob and his house mate Charley came into the store one day. Jojo said later that they were such a scruffy looking pair that she wasn't sure she even wanted to have them in there. Even wondered if she would have to call the police. He asked her for a date and she told him she couldn't go because she had a small son and couldn't afford a baby sitter. He said 'so what, bring the kid along'. This rather changed her viewpoint on him and after a while they decided that this was it. Surprisingly enough when Jojo brought him to meet her sister Ginny and her husband Jed. The guys each said "you!" It seems they had been neighbors and friends for a long time before either met his wife and so remained good friends as brothers-in-law. After all these adventures, Bob finally ended up graduating more by accident than anything else, at the same time as his six-year younger brother Tom, both as Electrical Engineers (Dec 1978).

Peg, Something Really Special

While Betty was getting her MS degree at UC (University of California) Davis at Davis, Peggy who at the time was at UNM in Albuquerque, decided it would be more challenging out in California and that she might get a better education. So she went out to stay with her big sister Betty and get her degree in Math and Computers. After graduation in 1974, she found a job in Silicon Valley where she has been ever since. She did programming at all sorts of companies even a startup, David Systems, which unfortunately was badly managed and failed as so many of the startups do (I have heard that the ratio of success is about 1 in 7).

At one point she was getting ready to go to Boston with a male friend, when someone else discovered her. As she puts it "Who was this nerd with socks that don't match, who keeps hanging around me?". Apparently they had been in the same circle and known many of the same people for several years but hadn't happened to meet each other. This one night when they did meet, Richard (Dick) Lyon decided that this was for him and insisted on seeing her home. And it wasn't long before they decided to get married, which they did in Los Alamos, July 1981. Dick grew up in El Paso, TX, only about an hours drive from Las Cruces, so is from the same general area. His parents are retired there and we see them from time to time. His father was an electrical engineer with El Paso Electric Co. Dick had graduated from Cal Tech (California Technology) and worked for many years for Apple Computer Co doing research as well as consulting weekly with Carver Meade also at Cal Tech.

Losing My Parents

When in 1969 we had moved from Espanola to Los Alamos, all our parents were still alive but in their 80's. In July 1971, we, took five of our children and drove to a resort in the Ozarks in Southern

Missouri, to help celebrate my parents' 50th wedding anniversary. The actual anniversary had been in January 1971 but they had arranged the actual celebration for the summer when the children were out of school so more of their children and grandchildren could come. Six of my siblings and their families also came. There was a swimming pool, tennis courts, a stream for fishing and rafting running through the resort and places for camping as well as cabins for the older people. Many games of chess and bridge were played. On the last night a Mass and ceremony was held, followed by a traditional feast.

Celebrating 50 Years of the Williams Marriage

But this was to be the last celebration for them. In May of 1972, less than a year later, the first to go was my father who, back in St. Louis died apparently of a stroke or a fall down the basement steps or both. No one seemed to be certain just what the actual cause was, but at his age it's bound to happen sooner or later.

Two years later in February 1974, Larry and I had planned to take my mother with us to an American Chemical Society (ACS) Fluorine Chemistry meeting in a beach resort south of Tampa Bay, Florida. Among the Chemists, there were large groups of Bridge and Chess players. In between meetings, everyone liked to play various games. We were sure Mom would enjoy it since she loved to play both games on the beach. The week before we were to leave, my sister Susie Hartenbach, called from St. Louis to say that Mom was in the hospital with a stroke.

Mom had been playing a last difficult game of chess when she began to feel poorly and ended in the hospital. By the time I got there to visit Mom she was in a nursing home for rehabilitation as a result of the stroke and very unhappy. I can still vividly remember her crying when I walked in and begging to be taken home. At the time this didn't seem possible because she was confined to a wheelchair and unable to do much for herself. She was certainly not up to a trip to Florida so Larry and I had to go on by ourselves. After the meeting as planned, we flew over to the island of Eleuthera. It is a beautiful place in the Bahamas, for a weeks vacation to celebrate 30 years of our marriage. The whole time I was worrying about Mom but didn't know that I could do anything for her.

Later, my sister Susie took Mom into her home for a while but it was pretty rough because Mom couldn't do anything for herself and didn't accept her disabilities very well. She would do what Larry's mother had done. She would try to get out of bed by herself, fall and not be able to get up. One of the advantages of a big family is that there are many to help carry the burden. So my sisters in St. Louis were on hand to help Mom out, as difficult as it was. Also my Sister Kitty, whose husband was from a farm in Southern Illinois, always came home to St. Louis during the summer for a visit. During the final Summer, she took over for a while to give Susie some relief. So when Mom finally died quietly in the hospital, Kitty was the one who was there at the end (Aug. 1974).

Losing the Senior Aspreys

For a while, when in July 1971, we had brought the senior Aspreys to Los Alamos, we had an extra house to care for, along with our own house, two jobs and two teen agers. We hired as much help as we could but there was still much extra for us to do. Tim's sabbatical year at Los Alamos Lab working in the computer division, helped for a while and let us take some vacations with the kids.

One unfortunate thing was that Tim had promised her Mother that she would not let them go to a nursing home. Like many people, they had visited friends in one and hated the thought of it. This was all very well, but Tim was not willing to give up her position teaching Mathematics and Computers at Vassar College back in New York to come to Los Alamos to take care of them. Or for that matter, to take them back there with her but she still expected us to keep on caring for them. This rather made for bad feelings between us for a while. She blamed us when we finally gave up and felt that we had to put them in a nursing home when we could no longer manage them and their house. This disagreement has however been smoothed out over the years and we ended up having a reasonably good relationship with Larry's only sister but we don't see much of her since she's so far away.

A final big change occurred in August of 1975 when our two remaining boys, Tom and Bill, went off to College at NMSU in Las Cruces. Over the years, when the older children went off to college, we had hardly noticed the change because there were still so many left behind. But this time it was very different because at the end of that September, we decided that we just couldn't manage the parents and their house any longer. We convinced them to move to Grenada de Santa Fe, a relatively pleasant nursing home in Santa Fe. We were a bit sneaky about it because we told each of them that it was needed for the other. On that basis each of them agreed. Mother was in bad enough shape that we had her taken in an ambulance and I rode along. Larry drove dad down in the car and met us there.

Shortly thereafter, Tom & Bill asked "Is Zonta (the family dachshund) your dog or our dog?". They were living with Bob in the rental house down in Las Cruces and would love to have him. And of course we said, "Take him, he's yours". So all of a sudden, what had been a noisy, busy house was almost overwhelmingly quiet. We continued to visit the nursing home several times a week but it wasn't long before we began to notice that Larry's parents really didn't know who we were. Mother began to complain about this strange man who was always following her around. We tried to explain that he was her husband but she didn't seem to understand. I remember Mother holding my hand while Larry stood at the foot of the bed and she asked who he was. I told her that it was her son Larned and a few minutes later she asked him where I was.

In October of 1975, Larry and I took a weekend backpack trip up over the Santa Barbara Divide in the Sangre De Cristo Mountains, for a break from our sadness over visiting them in the nursing home.[14] It did help to get off in the wilderness by ourselves. Within

---

[14]   The last time we had visited the nursing home, we had given Dad a gift with a big red bow. A lady passing by was very excited by the bow and Dad graciously presented it to her as a gift. That picture was in my mind as iI wrote the following on the back pack trip.

The Divide
All through the golden afternoon we walked,
While the aspens whirled their wealth along the trail.
The pack straps bite and the path is steep,
But oh how sweet, tonight's starlit sleep.

Strange how little warn the azure sky and lingering warmth
Of the ice and cold so soon to come.
Or the towering pines, of the barren tree line
Up the trail

a few months they were both dead, Peter in December 1975 and Gladys in March 1976. So from all being alive in 1970, by 1976 all four of our parents had died. However, fortunately the next generation goes on and we tried to look ahead.

Tom in College

Again the difference between Tom and Bill (and also from Bob) showed up when they went to college. Tom knew what he wanted to do from the beginning. He started off in Electrical Engineering, kept with it and went straight through in four years. Both Bob and Bill started in one direction, changed their minds, fooled around and got there eventually but it took them awhile. An observant comment was made to us about Bob and Tom by one of their professors, Eldon Steelman, in the engineering department at NMSU. Many years later he remembered them both very well and said "Tom was an excellent student. Always there with his work done. Now Bob was different . . ." Then he hesitated. "He was an interesting student. You never quite knew about him." We laughed at this and Larry said "You mean he only did his homework if he thought it important enough". He laughed too and said, "I guess that's it". Although Tom and Bob were six years apart in age they graduated together in May 1979.

So, in the autumn of my life,
My strength refuses to accept,
The winter rigors just ahead,
When life thins down to a slender thread
Of a good nights sleep or the taste of bread;
When all life's treasure is a shiny bow
Or a memory flash from long ago.

Only the mind aware takes note,
And trembles at the wintry prospect
Of death's approaching chill,
Without the promise of returning spring.

Bill Traveling the World

In high school and at first in college, Bill was always restless. One of my most vivid memories was in early August 1974 when I had a Gingivectomy on my gums. When I went back to work after the surgery, I was still unable to eat solid food. I was still feeling pretty shaky when I had a phone call from Bill. It seems he and Tom had had a fight and he was in Santa Fe and was running away from home and was thinking of going to Los Angeles. I swallowed hard, thought fast (he was now only 16) and said. "I know summer is hard and you two have trouble getting along but it seems to me that running away doesn't really solve the problem. If you need to get away for a while, why don't you take the family Jeep, the dog Zonta and supplies for a day or two and go backpacking over in the Sangre de Cristo Wilderness for a few days." He thought about it and decided that maybe that would be a good idea. So we got past that crises but it was only temporary.

In college, he started out in Mechanical Engineering but it was all classes and no fun lab work. I suggested he try changing to Physics which had labs. So he did that and liked Physics better. Then he signed up for an Engineering Co-op Program which alternated a semester of co-op work with a semester of school. This meant of course that it would take longer to finish than if he had just taken courses. His first co-op job was with a Sewage Plant down in Arlington, TX, between Fort Worth and Dallas. Well he stuck this out but didn't like it much. Of course, part of the idea of the co-op program, is to find out what kind of work you do and don't like.

A year later, he was given a job on an oil survey ship in the North Sea out of the Shetland Islands off the coast of Northern Scotland. While this was rather scary and I know he was glad to be back home, he did get interested in oil geology because he ended up getting his degree in geophysics. When he came back, I was appalled to hear that he had started out on the trip with only $7.00

in his pocket, a plane ticket and a charge card. I had assumed that the people who arranged the co-ops would check on things like this. But no, they assumed that the students would take care of it and Bill had expected the banks to be open on a day before he left and they weren't. Fortunately he went with a friend who had $80 and was willing to share. But they still came close to trouble when the planes in northern Scotland were grounded by weather for days. Fortunately for them, the clouds cleared for one day to let them get to the Island where the ship was before they starved completely.

One of the things that we had insisted on when they were in college, they were not allowed to own a motorcycle as long as we were supporting them. But when Bill came back to the US from Scotland, with a large amount of money from the job, he felt so independent that he bought a motorcycle on the East coast and rode it back cross country. We were appalled but still didn't feel we could stop him even though technically we were still supporting him, because he had been through so much and was essentially on his own.

Learning to Fly

The 1970's were full of all sorts of changes in our life. One of the more fun things for us in 1978 and 1979, Larry and I learned to fly and obtained our Private Pilot's licenses. Our first instructor was Rob Mosely, a young man still in his late teens who learned to fly from his father, before he learned to drive a car. He was amazingly good and patient with us oldsters. An experience that I will never forget was my first solo landing while the instructor waited by the runway. We used to fly at 6:00 AM in the morning before work because it was the best flying time and the winds were light. The morning after I made my first solo landing I felt like I could fly without an airplane! I walked into work with a colleague that morning and couldn't resist telling him all about it. I was so exhilarated that I was walking on air.

Our new Plane
Cessna 210-3705Y

Marge—After
Receiving License

Walking on Air After Getting Pilot's License

One incident that I particularly remember was, one of the special requirements for a license, a solo cross country flight. One is required to make a triangular trip with at least one leg of 100 miles. I started from the Santa Fe Airport and was heading for the airport at Carrizozo, NM. When I started, the weather was quite calm and not much wild weather was expected. However, by the time I reached Carrizozo, NM, a strong wind had come up unexpectedly from the South. The runway ran East and West so it meant a cross wind landing at which I was not too experienced. The first time I tried to land, I didn't put in enough adjustment for the cross wind so was being blown off the runway, so had to go around and try again. When I turned back toward the runway to try again, I couldn't find it at all! The airport was so small that the runway looked a lot like a small road so it wasn't too surprising that I couldn't recognize it. Finally I did find it and landed successfully. When I taxied up to the building, there were two men sitting on the hood of a pickup truck. They had seen me flitting about and came out to the airport to see what was going on. I said I was all right but wanted a cup of coffee (and a bathroom). They said there was none out there but there was a loaner car that I could use to drive into town and get the coffee. I got my coffee and restroom and went on my way to Fort Sumner, the second leg of the trip. I still remember vividly that desperate lost feeling of not being able to find a runway to land on! I eventually logged around 200 hours flight time before I decided that my eye sight wasn't good enough to continue.

Getting My Next Degree

I finally completed my MS in Nuclear Engineering in December 1978 (which was awarded in May 1979) and my pilot's license in February 1979. My Sister Sally came to visit the same week that I was to take my flight test and waited at the Santa Fe Airport while I was put through my paces by Dick Brown the FAA inspector. Then in April 1979 we bought a Cessna 210, with retractable landing gear (3705Y). Most of my flight time was actually logged in this Cessna which we bought from a man named Ed Schelonka who also checked us out in it. He had been in the US Air Force, then worked for a while at the Los Alamos Lab and now was going back to school to acquire an MD degree. We recently found out that he has done just that and is now down in Belize running a clinic with his wife who is a missionary. We became so comfortable flying the 210 that we made many trips in it including a year of commuting from Los Alamos to classes toward my residency for my PhD at UNM in Albuquerque.

Cessna 3705 Yankee. What fun we had Flying it!

A Flight to Meet New In-laws

In his last semester at NMSU, Bill had gotten engaged to a girl, Lynn Kujawa, from Long Island, NY, and after they graduated from college in May 1979 (Bill, BS in Physics). They were planning to be married in the middle of August. We decided to fly them back to Long Island so we could meet her parents. We got as far as Cape Girardeau, MO, where, on landing, the nose wheel broke and the propeller was damaged. No one was hurt but we are all really shook up and I guess Bill and Lynn were terrified. Since Lynn and Bill were a bit nervous about flying anyway, I guess they were glad to change to ground transportation. The plane could not continue without major repairs, so we rented a car and drove the rest of the way. We took turns driving through the night to the far end of Long Island, where we met her family. However, this marriage was not to be because a week or two before the planned date in August, they decided to cancel. I don't know any details as to why, because the decision was made back in New York between the couple and her parents, when we weren't there. When the plane was repaired, we went back to Cape Girardeau to pick it up in June.

Xmas Grab Boxes

One of the last Christmases in this decade I tried something new for fun! When cleaning out a buffet in our dining room, I realized that I had a lot of family heirloom dishes that I never used that I thought the children might like to have. With seven children, I didn't have enough of anything to give one to everyone. What is the solution? The idea that I came up with was to get seven large cardboard boxes, all about the same size. Then I randomly put things in them until they were all pretty full, as equivalent as I could make them. Then I sealed them up, wrapped them in Christmas paper and put numbers from one to seven on them. Then on Christmas after all other gifts had been exchanged, I had everyone draw a number from a bag starting with the youngest. They then were to match their number to one on a box. There were a few mismatches like Bill getting a set of knitting needles! However a little switching took place and everyone agreed that it was fun. Since I may have to move soon into a smaller place, I might do the same thing but we may have a problem getting all children together at one time for the distribution. In fact it can probably never happen again.

Flying to Mexico

One of the final things that we did in the decade, was in the Spring of 1979. We found a motel on the tip of the Baja California with a private landing strip. We decided to fly down there to celebrate our 35th Wedding Anniversary and see what it was like flying in Mexico. It was the first time that we had flown over water, almost out of sight of land, across the Gulf of California. It was also the first time that I had landed on a dirt landing strip. It was a very nice, quiet place and Larry had great fun fishing off the coast. When we flew back we brought back an ice chest full of dorado (a fish not a dolphin).

Chapter 17

Some Fun Trips
between 1975 and 1981

Among other unusual hobbies, son Bob, during his college years, had a most unusual pet, a burro, better known as Juan-Too-Many or JTM for short. Bob had a small gray GMC (General Motors Co) van, which he called the 'Elephant', and used to ride around town with JTM in the back looking over his shoulder. We (Larry and I with Tom and Bill) actually went backpacking in the Gila Wilderness with them one Spring. We thought that maybe JTM would carry some of the gear. But no, he carried the ice chest with the beer! First things first! JTM was such a people friendly animal that one time we tried to leave him in a shady, grassy spot where we thought he would be more comfortable while we had lunch. Because it was away from us, he made such a fuss that we had to move him over nearer to us but this was on some rocks and in the sun. Also when Larry was trying to catch some fish, JTM decided that he had to find out what was going on. Suddenly Larry found him looking over his shoulder breathing down his neck and watching the fish rod. You never knew what he would do next. He was a strange pet. We've always wondered what happened to JTM. Bob said something vague about leaving him with some rancher in the area and then losing touch with him.

Bob and JTM in the Gila Wilderness

Down the Grand Canyon

One of the most memorable trips that Larry and I ever took was a float trip with the Canyoneers, in June 1975, on one of the big so-called 'banana boats' down the Colorado River in the Grand Canyon. The Canyoneers was run by a granddaughter of John Wesley Powell, who was the first man to run it back in the 1800's. We went from Lee's Ferry, just below the Glen Canyon Dam to Lake Powell (Mead) above Boulder Dam. The 'banana boats' were rafts made of four approximately 30 foot long air filled rubberized tubes lashed together. There are wooden seats on the two center tubes for the passengers. Gear and supplies are loaded in the back just in front of the motor and the location for the guide who steers. There were eleven of us from all over the United States in addition to the two leaders. The primary leader was so enamored of the canyon, and had been down it dozens of times and knew it so well, that he didn't want to do anything else.

We were to bring along a tent and sleeping bags, along with minimal personal gear. Everything had to be stowed in waterproof bags because everything got very wet when we went through the rapids. And, of course, we were required to wear life jackets at all times on the river. Food, drink and any other supplies were furnished by the tour company which was managed by a granddaughter of John Wesley Powell, the first man to go down the river in the 1800's.

When we started off, the river was very calm and reasonably warm. But it wasn't long before we went around a bend and there was a small rapid waiting for us and from then on there were many more. If you sat in the front seats, you had a railing to hold onto but you also got the wettest. At first we were floating through pine forests but after several hours, we came to a sandy bank where we were to spend the first night. A portable toilet was set up, a fire was lit by the leaders and we set up our tents. After a 'backpacking' type meal most evenings, and some talking around the fire, we settled in to sleep for the night. Each evening was a little different with one night very special because we had steaks and the assistant leader appeared in a white shirt and tie over a bathing suit! That didn't happen often though, because although they had a couple of big coolers, there was still a lot of food needed for such a big a group and most of it was condensed and/or dried.

On some mornings it was obvious that the level of the river had hugely changed vertically. We were told that it changed often depending on how much water was allowed to flow over the dam above us to generate electricity for Los Angeles. They told us that having the water controlled like that has changed the canyon drastically. The water is much warmer at times than it used to be and the canyon doesn't get cleaned out by spring floods as it used to. As a result they were required to carryout all waste of every kind or lose their license to take tours down.

The Banana Boat

General View
Down Canyon

Heading Into Rapids

Our Viking Leader

End Of Trip

I remember one incident very vividly when going through one of the smaller rapids. I had been sitting on one of the side tubes with my feet over the edge, when the raft jumped suddenly and I got dumped over the side. I had my life jacket on over my bathing suit and had hold of a rope. I hung on for dear life so really wasn't frightened The leader saw me go (fortunately his co-leader was steering the boat) and he was there like a shot to grab my arm and pull me back up. Sometimes on smoother rapids, they even let people float thru the rapids in their life jackets but I really hadn't wanted to do it by accident.

As we continued on down the Colorado River the walls got more rocky and higher and the channel got narrower. The leaders pointed out that these were some of the oldest rocks observable on the planet because of the depth of the channel that the river had cut. The bigger rapids had mostly come from runoff which washed rocks down from the side channels. Sometimes we stopped to camp by these side channels and hiked up them a ways. As we went deeper it also got hotter. As it got hotter, we wore bathing suits all the time, with a shirt underneath or over our life jackets to keep from getting too badly sunburned. It got so hot at times that it felt good to dip the shirt in the river, put it on, soaking wet, and let it drip.

Finally we got to the biggest rapids of all, Lava Falls. The week before this, a big raft had turned over trying to run it with all passengers aboard. Now, after pulling over to one side, our guide was studying the rapid very intensely. Meanwhile, another boat was not willing to take a chance with their passengers. They had pulled off to the opposite side above the rapids and a helicopter was coming to carry the passengers across the rapid. After they were all transported, their guide took the boat through the rapid and picked them up on the other side After our guide was satisfied on how to maneuver through safely, we all loaded onto the raft and away we went holding on for dear life of course. Fortunately we made it through without problems! Since it was the next to last day of the trip, it was a great climax. At the end, we came out onto Lake Powell and had a great time 'sailing' on the lake. Eventually we came to the beach landing site, packed up the boat and said goodbye to all our newfound friends.

Backpacking with Lucy Carruthers, a Coworker at the Lab, in July

In that same very active Summer a coworker, Lucy Carruthers, and I were leaving work on Thursday, the night before the 4th of July weekend, we commiserated with each other over the fact that both of our husbands were away for the weekend. Our children really weren't interested in anything that we wanted to do but had their own plans. We were both free to do anything we liked. We came up with the possibility of taking our dogs and going backpacking together in the Santa Fe Forest over in the Sangre de Cristo Mountains for two nights. It was amazing how different it was packing with another woman instead of just the family. She came up with very different food than we did. I particularly remember a plastic box with celery and carrot sticks. They only were good for the first night but it was great that night.

We had such a good time on that first trip that the next Summer we did it again. This time we went to San Pedro Parks over to the West of Los Alamos. While this also was fun, we had a little problem when we decided to take a path which was not too well marked on the map but we thought looked interesting. Apparently it hadn't been maintained for some time. After we got a way into it, the path became almost completely blocked by huge downed trees. The dogs could run around the ends of them but we had to climb over or walk long distances around. We were to have been picked up by Lucy's husband around noon, but we were several hours late getting there. Fortunately for us he hadn't given up and was still waiting.

High School Graduates to Colorado in August

Later in August that same Summer, partly as a graduation treat for Tom and Bill who had graduated that Spring from Los Alamos High School, I decided to take them, along with a friend and fellow graduate, Walt Silbert, on a camping trip up to Southern Colorado in our Jeep Wagoneer for a long weekend. I particularly remember driving across the top of a high plateau just before the town of Ouray. After driving across the top, we came down the far side toward Telluride on a very narrow one-way (down!) road with many switch backs. Some were so tight that we had to back up a bit to get our big Jeep around the curves with the steep drop-off right beside us. After passing through Telluride, we came to a side road where we found a camping spot beside a small lake. After setting up camp, the boys found some trash wood they used to make a raft and had a great time 'sailing' on the lake. It was cool enough that I didn't feel up to taking a chance on getting wet but they didn't seem to worry about that.

Other trips in That period

There were many trips but too many to do more than summarize a few.

76   Mar Larry and I took Tom, Bill and Zonta (our Dachshund) on a backpacking trip in the Gila Wilderness.

76   June Larry was Assistant Leader on a Sierra Club Hot Springs. led by a friend, Bob Wilkerson, high above Yellowstone Park, Wyoming. Ellen Wilkerson and I were some of the 'followers'. One of the nicest things about this trip was that it ended up after a week in the wilderness without a shower, with a delightful hot springs swimming pool.

77   Jan Larry and I took Peggy on a camping trip to the Virgin Islands. We flew to St. Thomas and camped on the island of St. Johns

Peg and Marge explore old Fort
on St, Johns Virgin Islands

77 Aug. Ellen Wilkerson led us on a canoe trip down the upper Missouri River in Montana. Among those on the trip, besides Bob Wilkerson, Larry and me and along with our daughter Barb, were her husband Art, and stepson, Percy. One wild thing that happened on the way back, driving in a wind storm, the lashing on a canoe came loose and suddenly we saw the canoe sailing along beside us on

the road! Luckily we were able to retrieve it before much damage was done.

Seatrek Hawaii, Jan 1980

One of the more overwhelming trips was one to Hawaii. It was presented as an international one to be supervised by the University of Hawaii and was to give us a real look and overview of the remote but beautiful islands in the very middle of the Pacific Ocean. It began on a beach on the Big Island, Hawaii. We assembled the first evening on the beach and began meeting our fellow travelers. As we met each one, it seems that this one was from Australia. The next also was from Australia and the next and the next. Eventually it turned out that it was school vacation down under and so most of the group were teachers on vacation and all Aussies. One other man was an American from Colorado, boyfriend of one of the three leaders, and we were from New Mexico and the leaders were students from the University of Hawaii but everyone else was from Australia. So my vision of meeting people from all over the world was not to be. They were great people and we enjoyed the Aussies but it was really only marginally International. That first night we slept in our tents on the beach.

The next few days we were driven in small vans over most of the Big Island and then we sailed in a small sail boat, to Lanai, the pineapple Island, which had previously not been open to the public. We toured the pineapple fields and met some of the workers in their village. After this we went on to the island of Maui where we were to camp in a Girl Scout camp. Well it seemed there had recently been a typhoon, the Pacific equivalent of an Atlantic hurricane, which had just passed Maui a few days earlier. Many large trees were down and the electricity was down everywhere along with them. We arrived late in the day at the camp not realizing that there was no electricity or lights and found no one there. Fortunately, we had our flashlights and found our way around as best we could. After setting up camp in the dark and starting camp fires where we could, we fixed food and settled down for the night. In the morning people turned up and the next few days were a bit more comfortable.

Kamehameha King of Hawaii

Hiking in Crator of Volcano Haleakala

Glider on Hilo,
Ridge Behind

The most interesting trip on Maui was to the volcano Haleakeala which was dormant at the time. We first had a talk from one of the Park rangers about the Volcano and what the current situation was.

They monitor it very closely and believed that they knew how it was going to behave for a while. They were completely convinced that it was safe so took us on a hike down into the crater which was very quiescent. There were occasional steam vents in some places, but it looked mostly a little like a moonscape with absolutely nothing living in the area. Climbing back out was very steep and I wasn't at all sure that I was going to make it but I did. As we approached the upper edges of the crater, there were actually a few rugged bushes growing along the edge. They were the first living things we saw in Haleakeala.

Finally, we were flown in small planes to Hilo where the trip ended and we all parted company, again from our new friends. To extend the vacation a bit, we had rented a room and a car in Hilo to do some sightseeing on our own. The first thing we found that seemed to be fun was a small airport on the North end of the Island which offered glider flights. We found that we could go together in one plane although we were pretty crowded in the back because the pilot sat in the front seat. The airport was situated along the beach and there was a high ridge on the opposite side of the runway. We were towed up high over the ridge and then released. My impressions were of amazing quiet with only the sound of wind rushing by. We flew along the top of the ridge first. Then the pilot turned out over the ocean where we flew for a while over the waves. At last he turned into the final leg for landing on the runway. The flight was not very long, it probably lasted about half an hour, but it was enough to be one of the more memorable adventures in Hawaii.

The next interesting thing we found, was a small museum which showed many details of the history of Hawaii. The Polynesians had come here many hundreds of years before from SE Asia. How they found these islands in the middle of the vastness of the pacific seemed really unbelievable. They must have been incredible navigators. At the time that we were there, they really hadn't figured out how they did it, but they were working on it. Much more is now known but it is still an impressive feat. From genetics and confirmed by linguistics, it has been proved that they originally all came from southeast Asia and moved gradually from island to island over the centuries before the Europeans arrived on the scene.

Three-Disaster Trip

In the summer of 1980, we organized a backpack trip up above Vallecitos Lake in Colorado which turned out to be a complete disaster and was the last backpack trip for Larry and me. In addition to our family, we were joined by my sister Lydia and her husband Harold 'Pete' Chadwick along with Pete's sister and her boyfriend from back East. While Pete and Lydia were seasoned hikers and packers, the sister and friend were not. Our son Pete had been offered the use of a cabin near Durango, (which is not far from Vallecitos Lake) by a friend (at Sandia in Albuquerque)

Before we set off on the backpack, on the first day in Colorado, after camping for one night, we went on a short raft trip down the San Juan River, over in the four corners area. That was fun and fairly mild but that night our son Pete's wife, Cindy, turned up with an upset stomach. She was fairly sick so Pete decided that it was best to take her to the Durango Emergency Room. They concluded that it was only food poisoning and not too serious. She felt poorly enough however, that they decided to make use of the offered cabin and not hike with us.

The next day all the rest of us started up the trail carrying our packs, when the next disaster struck. Larry slipped on the edge of an overlook and fell, fortunately not too far, but landed on his side on a fallen tree and, it turned out, broke several ribs. After the boys picked him up and found that while he was hurting badly, he was still intact. Our son Tom took off down the trail to see if there was a way to have him carried out. He felt pretty poorly and we did not know what was actually wrong. Meanwhile the other two boys, Bob and Bill, tried to support him back down the trail. He could walk but with great difficulty and we really didn't know yet how seriously he was hurt. After they got about half way down, Tom came back up to say that there was no way other way get him out, except a helicopter and that was doubtful because of the big trees and would cost us around $300. If he had been completely unable to walk, I guess the only other alternative was a makeshift stretcher of some sort but fortunately he could stumble along if with difficulty. Eventually they got him to a vehicle and took him to the cabin where Pete and his family were. So for the second night, Pete took someone to the Durango Emergency Room, this time his Father. Bill and Bob came back to help me out because now I became the default leader of the remainder of the group.

Pete remembers when taking Larry to the ER, where they took an XRay of his lungs and saw what they thought was a spot on it. Tom came in to tell me about it and bring me out. Pete later found out that It was only a shadow so hiked in nine miles to tell me that I didn't need to come out and then back out to take care of his family. He still remembers starting at 3:00 PM to hike 18 miles in and out. getting back about 10:00 PM.

The next morning when we were ready to take off up the trail, we realized that our two young teen aged boys, Clint (Bob's stepson) and Percy (Barb's stepson) had gone fishing without telling anyone and were nowhere to be found. Well, we didn't want to spend the whole day waiting around for them so Tom agreed to wait for them and get them packed up and ready to join us when they showed up, while the rest of us went on ahead. (And I guess he gave them what-for when they did show up!) Well after a few miles, we found a delightful camping spot by a stream and set up a fairly permanent camp. I was still worrying about Larry but figured I couldn't do anything about him and I was needed to keep the trip going anyway. About now, Bob and Bill decided, I guess, that we were moving too slowly for their taste and they were going to go on up over the continental divide (Chicago basin) to where the trail joined the Durango-Silverton Train. While I didn't think too much of the idea, Bob was old enough, that I believed he could manage to take care of Bill and himself. Things hadn't been much fun for them so far, so off they went over my protests without jackets or sleeping bags.

The group that had started with eleven was now down to five. But there was fishing for those who liked it and it was a beautiful day in a beautiful spot. Eventually Tom and his miscreants turned back up for another night. And eventually a day or two later, Bob and Bill turned up safe and sound. They had gotten to the railroad too late to get a train that night so had to spend the night without a tent or sleeping bags and it gets cold at night up there. But they survived and caught the train the next morning. After a day or two more we decided that we had had enough and went on back down to the trailhead. When we arrived at the cabin where Larry was, we found out that he was OK but just had a couple of broken ribs which would heal in time, and meanwhile there was nothing that could be done for them.

However, the night before, there had been a third disaster. Pete's nine year old son, David, had been awoken in the night by a bat biting him on the neck! Well they caught the bat but thought it wise to take David and bat, guess where, to the Durango Emergency Room! Third night for Pete, his son this time. I think the ER was beginning to wonder about him! While that bat was not rabid, but they could not be certain that it was the one which did the biting. Eventually David had to have the rabies shots anyway after they got back to Albuquerque. Interestingly enough, normally only vampire bats bite and the local department of health did not believe there were vampire bats in that area. They checked the bat that had been brought in and sure enough, it was indeed a vampire bat, so they learned something.

When we got back to Los Alamos, and Werner Maschek, our visiting German friend, who had been staying in our house, heard about what had happened he was even more concerned about David and the rabies possibilities than we had been. I can still remember him walking up and down and worrying. When Pete and his family got back to Albuquerque, they also decided that to be safe he should have the rabies shots. If he actually got rabies they would never have forgiven themselves, so it was understandable. It was a memorable trip but it would have been nice to end on a high note instead of a disaster like this

Chapter 18

Karlsruhe, Germany, 1981-82

B efore we went off to Germany in September of 1981, we thought it would be nice to learn a little conversational German. In February of that year, Sybille Wilhelm, the wife of one of my colleagues, (Siegfried Wilhelm, working with me from Germany), offered a conversation class in German for people like us who were going to Germany. Both Larry and I took it and it really helped, me more than Larry. There were about eight to ten in the class. I got good enough that when we made it to Germany, I was what someone called 'street fluent'. I could answer the phone and ask questions on the street and, usually, understand the answers, while Larry mostly couldn't but depended on me. There's no question that some people, like me, have more facility for languages than others, like Larry.

Sleeping Arrangements

When we arrived in Germany, we were met at the airport by Siegfried Wilhelm and taken to one of a set of apartments used for visitors to Karlsruhe University. The first big problem and one that lasted in one version or another all through our year in Germany was sleeping arrangements. In the visitors apartment, the beds consisted of two narrow cots each with a thin mattress covered with a fitted sheet, and two folded quilts, one the size of the cot the other about half that size. Since for all the nearly forty years of our married life we had slept together in a double bed this was very unsatisfactory. We assumed that the small quilts were to be folded up to substitute for the pillows to which we were also accustomed. We tried to push the beds together but with the separate quilts and pads we simply couldn't curl up together the way we were used to doing. Well we tolerated it as best we could for the few weeks that we were there and determined to find an apartment with a double bed.

Our friend Siegried helped us buy a used 4-Door Volvo. He explained to us that the German' s were very fussy about selling used cars. The law required that they had to be inspected and deficiencies corrected before they could be sold. So we need not worry about buying a used car. Using this car made it possible for us to look over apartments for rent. And after a while, we found one in a good location in Blankenloch, a small farming village, about half way between Karlsruhe and the Institute, Kernforschungszentrum Karlsruhe (called KfK), where we were to be working. And we were assured that the apartment had a double bed.

So we rented it and moved in where we found a nice double bed but looking more closely, we found there was a board down the center and two separate quilts! I complained in my poor German to the landlady who did not speak much English. She said OK! OK! She would fix it but I couldn't see how. Well a few weeks later she brought a foam divider to be put over the board which helped but we still couldn't get close as we were used to doing and the separate quilts still pulled apart all the time. When we visited with our friends the Willhelms, I complained to Sybille, who had taught the conversational German class back in Los Alamos, about the problem and she said 'You could sew the two quilts together by hand,' which I considered doing. Ultimately she took pity on us and volunteered to sew them together for us on her sewing machine, which she did. Since it must have been a difficult, unpleasant job, and while not a complete solution, it certainly made things more tolerable and we were very grateful for her help.

When we crossed the Rhine for trips to France, we had no trouble finding double beds in the hotels. Maybe that's why the Germans consider the French immoral. However, we encountered this problem wherever we traveled in Germany, Switzerland, Holland or Belgium. Also whenever we visited the homes of our friends, we noted that they mostly had separate beds so this seemed to be the tradition in Germany. We never did understand it or get used to it. I even wondered how they generated the next generation! Maybe we're immoral too, although I'd be hard to convince.

Banking Arrangements

Another important adjustment that we had to make was to the banking customs in Germany. When we signed up for our pay at work, we were asked for the number of our bank account. At that point, we hadn't even found a bank, much less opened an account. Well it turned out that we couldn't be paid until we gave them an account number into which our paychecks would be deposited. An interesting man from the personnel department had been assigned to us to help us get adjusted to life in the country. He had been a pilot in the German Air Force during the 2nd World War and was a relaxed, outgoing sort of person. His favorite phrase was 'keine angst' meaning, I assume, 'don't worry'. He showed us where a local bank was and helped us get signed up so we could get paid by deposit. The main bank was in downtown Karlsruhe with a small branch on the site of KfK. Then if we needed cash we could go to the bank to withdraw some. Also the same applied to paying bills.

We gave the bank the account number of our Landlady for the apartment and then they were to deposit the rent from our account into her account. Well a few weeks went by and the Landlady came by with a complaint that I could not understand no matter how I tried. A few days later she brought her son by who spoke better English than I did German. It seems that the bank had gotten the wrong number for her account and she was not getting any rent. Well we finally got it straightened out, got the correct account number, and she got paid. Poor thing!

The Blankenloch Apartment

Aside from the not-so-satisfactory sleeping arrangements, the apartment was interesting from other points of view. The Landlady and her Husband were from East Germany and had crossed the border between East & West with nothing but the clothes on their backs. He described himself as an architect although, as I understand it, he was more like what we would call a draftsman. He was competent enough that he had found work and they had gradually accumulated enough money to buy an old farm house in Blankenloch where our apartment was. This was a small village with homes of the farmers who worked the surrounding fields. When we walked around the town, all the houses had large enclosures with barns, tractors and other farm equipment. Many had chickens and we could hear the roosters crowing in the morning. While our apartment did not have a barn, it did have a building which had been remodeled into a large meeting room which could be used for parties. The courtyard was surrounded by a wall with a locked gate on a side street and a doorbell outside it. The first floor, which fronted on one of the main streets, had been fixed up as a boutique with mainly women's clothes but also notions and such. There were not many stores in the small town so it seemed to be doing quite well. The store also had an entry into the courtyard.

Blankenloch Apartment
—Die Blau Haus

View across the Street
from our Apartment

Courtyard from Balcony
Where I was locked out

They had fixed the upstairs for a rental apartment with a separate entrance out the back into the courtyard. This is what we had rented. It wasn't cheap but not too wildly expensive either and we thought it would serve our needs once we solved the problems of the rent and the bed. The arrangement of the apartment was rather unusual. The stairs from the courtyard, with the entry door about half way up, came up into the living room. At the top, a door to the right went into a study and then on around into a large kitchen with table and chairs in the center. There was a small three burner cook stove, small refrigerator with tiny freezer compartment, a small sink and rather ineffective washing machine, but which did work. There were a few dishes and minimal cooking equipment. There was a very small balcony off the kitchen overlooking the courtyard, where I could hang laundry. From the kitchen, one went down a little hall, through the bathroom and on into the bedroom at the back of the apartment. Rather strange to go through the bathroom to get to the bedroom but it worked all right for a married couple like us.

Locked Out

One of my most overwhelming experiences with the apartment happened one time when Larry was off in France for a meeting of some sort. I was working rather half asleep on a cold, rainy weekend morning on my PhD dissertation which at that time I still hoped to complete, when the doorbell rang. Being half asleep, and not thinking too clearly, I went down stairs to answer the door in the outside wall and the door half way up the stairs closed behind me. It turned out to be someone looking for another address, not ours. So then I turned around and realized the predicament that I was in. I did not have my key with me so I was locked out. It was raining and cold and I had no coat on and was wearing bedroom slippers. What to do? Larry wouldn't be back for a day or two. The Landlady had a key she kept in the boutique but it wouldn't be open for several hours and I would be thoroughly soaked and frozen by then. With slippers on, I didn't want to walk any distance to find a phone. Besides while I knew the Landlady's name, I didn't have her phone number. Across the street (the house shown in the photo), I had noticed an elderly couple who had smiled at us and seemed friendly, so I thought maybe they would have a phone that they might let me use if I could make clear to them what my problem was. So I gathered up my courage and went across and knocked on their door. They of course spoke no English and not even regular German but only what they described as 'Karlsruher Deutch', which I gather is the local dialect. I tried to explain my problem in German and that I would like to borrow their phonebook and phone. I'm not sure what they thought but they were a kindly couple and understood enough to let me in and showed me the phonebook and phone. Without too much trouble, I found the Landlady's phone number, called her and explained, in German, my problem and since she lived only a block or two away, she came, got the extra key and rescued me. Was I glad to be back in my apartment again! From then on I was very careful about going out that door without my key.

Dealing with Bureaucracy

While my German was improving, I still managed to get in trouble from time to time. One of the more amusing experiences happened along in November when we were driving to work. A police car came up behind us with his lights flashing and pulled us over. Larry was driving so of course the officer tried to talk to him and his German was poor enough that he couldn't understand, so I got out and came around the back of the car. The officer pointed to a tail light that was not on. Larry hit it and it immediately came on so it was just loose. However that still didn't satisfy the officer and I could not understand what he said the problem was. So he wrote an address in Karlsruhe on a piece of paper and said that we must go there the next morning for certain. This was Thursday morning and we were to go there Friday morning, he implied, or else.

The next morning, we took off from work and went into Karlsruhe to the address on the paper. It turned out to be just about a block from our bank so Larry took the auto papers and went into the office. Meanwhile, I walked over to the bank to pick up a little cash and then walked back to the address. Well it seems that the problem was that when we bought the Volvo, we were living in Karlsruhe but when we moved the few miles to Blankenloch, we were in a different district and needed to get new license plates which we had not known so hadn't done. Not too surprising that my German was poor enough that I hadn't been able to understand the policeman's explanation of a fairly complex problem.

When I walked from the bank into the office, someone was helping Larry with the German on the application form. Then Larry said, 'Give me our passports (which I carried in my purse), and follow that man' pointing at a German man, who was standing by the door, and who immediately went out the door. So I too went out the door just in time to see the man disappearing down the end of a long hall turning right I rushed after him as fast as I could. As I turned the corner, I saw someone that I thought was the man standing at a payment window. He said to me in German, 'Give them some Deutschemarks' and immediately took off on down that hall. They told me how much and I gave them some money. By now the stranger had gone out the door at the end of the hall. So, completely bewildered, I followed along.

When I went out the door, it was on to a quiet side street but there was no one in sight anywhere. Where had he gone? There was a little park across the street but only one very small building with a sign that said 'Bicycle Shop'. Could that be where I needed to go? Since there wasn't any other choice, I walked over and into the shop. I really hadn't had a good look at the man that I was following but a man at the counter looked vaguely like him and he was smiling at me in an encouraging way. So I walked up and he handed me a piece of paper and said something about waiting there and then left. As I had time to look around, I noticed that in addition to bicycle parts, there were license plates on the wall. So that was what it was all about. They were making us new license plates. And sure enough in a few minutes, they gave me some new license plates.

What I hadn't realized, and found out later, the reason for all the rushing around, was that it was now 11:55 AM and that at 12:00 Noon on Friday, the license bureau closed up tight until Monday morning. That would mean that we would have had no license plates so would have been unable to drive our car for the whole weekend or risk going to jail. I don't know how we would even have gotten home to our apartment. But thanks to the kindness of strangers, and after Larry put on the new plates, we were ready to get back on the road.

Riding the Train

One other neat thing about the apartment, is that there was a train stop a block or two away. We rode it a few times to go into Karlsruhe, but not very often since it didn't stop at the KfK installation where we worked. For going to work we used the Volvo. But one night we had a rather terrifying experience with the train. We had been away on a trip and thought, since we would be gone for about a week, it would be easier to take the handy train back than leaving the car in the station parking lot in Karlsruhe for such a long time. We had looked up the schedule and a train left at about 11:00 PM so we boarded it confidently but when it came to Blankenloch, it didn't stop but kept going off into the night! Now what? So I went up to the conductor who of course spoke no English, and told him we needed to go Blankenloch so what could we do now? He looked at his schedules and told me to get off at the next stop and wait half an hour, when a train would go the other way which would stop at Blankenloch. So at the next stop, we got off and sat on our suitcases in the dark and cold for half an hour. (The stops were pretty primitive around there and there was no waiting room) We weren't at all sure that the conductor had understood me or even if he knew what he was talking about. However, fortunately for us, he did understand me and was quite right. After a while, a train did come along going the other way, and did indeed stop at Blankenloch. Again were we glad to be home in our little apartment!

The Institute

Working as visiting scientists in Germany, was particularly nice because, besides all the nice friends we made, we were able to spend weekends and vacations sightseeing in Europe. Larry worked for the European Union for Trans Uranium Research (better known as TU). A block or two away, I worked at an Institute for Fast Reactor Research run by the German Government. There was a large cafeteria at the entrance to the site where we could and did meet for lunch. The Germans like to have their big meal or dinner at noon so the cafeteria was popular with both the workers and their wives who then could serve a light supper at night. Much less work for the women that way.

We made many good new friends in addition to the ones we had made when they worked in Los Alamos. An example of these new friends was my office partner, who was from East Germany and told me tales of going back to visit his parents and other family relatives that he still had over there and how they were treated. For example when he crossed the border to visit, he was required to bring a certain amount of West German Marks with him to spend in East Germany but was not allowed to bring any back when he returned. All must have been spent or left behind with relatives. This was long before the fall of the Berlin Wall.

Another good friend was Joe Peterson from Oak Ridge and the University of Tennessee where he taught. He worked with Larry at TU (Trans-Uranium Lab run by the European Community). His wife Hannelora became a good friend of mine and we had great fun playing tennis together at a local indoor court. She was a lovely person and I was very sad to hear later that she died of cancer shortly after she returned home to the United States.

Friday Afternoon Beer Busts

One thing that I found quite strange about working in Germany was that, while there was hot water available for coffee, there was no place in the whole institute to get a drink of plain cold water. In fact, plain cold water, with or without ice wasn't even available in restaurants. One had to buy bottled water which was carbonated which I dislike. On the other hand, they thought it a great idea to have a keg of beer on the premises on Friday afternoon to end the work week. I can't imagine anything like that going on at the Los Alamos Laboratory! Alcohol of all kinds was forbidden on site. Strange how different customs can be.

At one particular Friday afternoon beer party, I met a tall, elderly, good-looking German that I had never seen around before. He was quite distinguished looking and came over and sat down at the picnic table where I was sitting. We talked for a while and he asked about me and why I as an American was there. I told him a little about what I was doing. I tried to find out something about him without much success. A few days later, we had a meeting in our conference room in the Fast Reactor Institute and there on the wall was a row of pictures and here was my new friend in the midst of them. I asked my good friend, Werner Maschek, who he was and he told me his name, which I have since forgotten, and something about him. It seems that during WW II, he was in charge of the German reactor program in a cave in the Black Forest. They had tried to build a reactor but were not as successful as Fermi was at the University of Chicago. There was one idea about criticality that they did not grasp, the idea of heterogeneity. Apparently they tried to build a homogeneous reactor and couldn't make it work.

After the war ended, he apparently was partly responsible for getting the Fast Reactor Institute started. Unfortunately, he wasn't around much by now so I never saw him again. Later, I read with interest that a group of German scientists (of which he was probably one), who had been captured and taken to England at the end of the Second World War, were still being held prisoner when our atom bombs were dropped on Hiroshima and Nagasaki. Of course the British had bugs planted and were listening hoping to get more information on the German nuclear program during the war. The Germans were heard to say that they were completely convinced that the stories about Japan were public relations only. Since they had been unable to make nuclear weapons, they were convinced that it couldn't be done. How little they knew and how little we knew of what had gone on in Germany during World War II!

Christmas in Northern Ireland

Since our daughter Betty and her husband David were involved with starting a plant for their company American Monitor in Northern Ireland during this year. As part of their service they had a very nice large house assigned to them, we decided that it would be pleasant to spend the Christmas Holidays with them. We drove to the Ferry to cross the English Channel. Then we drove across England to where a Ferry crossed to Dublin, Ireland. From Dublin, we drove up to Belfast. Their house was indeed nice and it was a great celebration. While 'the troubles' there were ongoing, we fortunately saw very little of them. On the way back to Dublin, there was a man lying by the road with a machine gun pointed at us but let us pass with no problem. A little frightening but pretty minor problem.

I remember one funny little incident in Dublin. At dinner in a restaurant, Larry ordered a bottle of wine. The waitress brought the bottle and uncorked it. Larry took one taste and said "This wine is corked". The waitress looked and sure enough it was full of bits of cork. She took it away and didn't come back for a while. Finally she came back and said apologetically, "We opened all the bottles in the case and they were all corked, so you'll have to order something else", which Larry proceeded to do. It was the only "corked' wine we have ever found anywhere although we had heard of it.

Conference in Italy

Along in the Spring, a group of us were to go to a meeting in Northern Italy on what was being done with Fast Reactors in Europe. A colleague, Seigfried Wilhelm was going to drive down to the meeting and his wife, Sibiella, and their two daughters were going to take the train down to meet him for a family vacation at the end of the meeting. So he invited me to drive down with him and then I could take the train back up to Karlsruhe at the end of the meeting. It made a very instructive trip for me since, besides being a pleasant traveling companion, he was very knowledgeable about much of Europe. He told me many interesting details about the areas through which we drove including the Alps of Switzerland and Northern Italy.

The meeting was informative although it really stretched my German despite most of it theoretically being in English. Some of the accents were rather heavy and the French absolutely refused to use English. They thought that the meeting should really be in French. There were people from all over Europe as well as England. One evening at a communal dinner, I was seated away from my usual German friends and was surrounded by men that I didn't know. I tried to talk to the men on either side of me or across the table, but they mostly ignored me and didn't respond to my comments. It was as if they couldn't understand or see me or I couldn't be of any interest. I felt really isolated. After a while, Walter Maschek who had flown with me at Los Alamos leaned over and said to me across several people, "Hey Marge, it's too bad you couldn't have brought your plane with you when you came over to Germany".

Well it was as if I had been invisible and someone had turned on a light over my head and now they could see me or at least I was of interest. The men on both sides of me turned towards me and the man across the table started to ask me about 'my' plane. Why hadn't I brought it; what kind was it and so forth. From then on they all talked to me. It was a strange feeling and a striking display of the male chauvinism that is so widespread even in Europe. And why hadn't we brought the plane over? It would have been complicated and very expensive. Extra tanks would have to be added to the plane and we would have to hire someone with a special license to fly it over. We would even have to have special licenses to fly in Germany ourselves and the usually cloudy weather over there was not too conducive to flying. So we had decided it made better sense to leave it behind in storage

Germans Give Party for Japanese

Along in the Spring, several Japanese who were working on projects for Fast Reactors, similar to the ones that we were working on, came to visit in Karlsruhe. As I remember, one had been at Los Alamos the year before. At any rate, the Germans planned an elaborate party for them and invited Larry and me. It was to be held at a restaurant in Ettlingen, south of Karlsruhe itself, in an area where we had never been. We were also asked because we had a fairly large car, if we would pick up the three Japanese at their hotel and take them to the dinner, which we of course agreed to do. We were given instructions which were not too clear but we managed to find both the hotel and then the restaurant with Larry driving. Well it was quite a festive evening with much food and wine. I remember one of the Japanese who sat next to me spent a long time trying to teach me the Japanese numbering system. Interesting but I just couldn't seem to get it and can remember nothing about it. Maybe too much food and sociability.

Greek Cruise

Greek Feast as Part Payment

Marge on Burro
Ride on Santorini

Complete Gridlock in
Athens, Greece

When the evening was over and we went out to the car, it was pouring rain. Since I didn't drink and Larry had had quite a few, I was the designated driver and wasn't at all too sure where we were or how to get to the hotel or our apartment. Well we wandered around a bit getting somewhat lost in the dark, but we did eventually manage to get the Japanese safely home to their hotel and finally found our way back to our apartment. What a relief both for the Japanese and for me! Larry seemed completely unworried.

A Couple of Spring Trips

We took a couple of spectacular Spring trips. The first was to visit the wife of Jean Claude Spirlet. one of Larry's colleagues, up in Holland, who was working on a PhD in Oceanographic studies. Jean Claude would go up to visit her on the weekends We rode up on the train and it was a pleasant visit. But the big surprise was that it was that the weekend that we were there, was when Holland held a spring parade with the floats decorated by all the flowers from their huge fields of bulbs. Whether they knew about it and just wanted to surprise us wasn't too clear. Or whether it was just an ordinary thing to them. The parade was as impressive as the Rose Parade in Pasadena, CA, on the first of January and we were able to park right alongside the road. I even remember a billboard made entirely of flowers advertising coca cola. out in the middle of a big field of flowers.

The other impressive trip was down the Rhine on a riverboat. It was a front row seat to view the many ancient castles and fields of grapevines along the Rhine river. We ended up in Mannheim planning to take the train the rest of the way. We had our luggage with us and had assumed that there would be taxis to take us the mile or two to the railway station. Well surprisingly enough there were no taxis. So along with a bunch of other passengers, we started to walk. Along the way, we found out why there were no taxis. We passed a bar jammed to the doors with excited people. It turned out that the soccer finals between Germany and Argentina were being played at that point and all Germans had taken the day off. This was even true at the train station where we found the ticket window closed up tight. So, when to our surprise, a train came along, we got aboard but with no tickets. This was scary because all the signs said that it was against the law to board without tickets but we didn't know what else to do. Either the engineer was listening on a radio or it was on automatic. We thought that under the circumstances maybe we could buy tickets from the conductor when he showed up. But to our surprise, no conductor ever showed up and when the train stopped at Karlsruhe, we got off after a free ride thanks to a soccer match.

Greek Island Cruise

One of the real highlights of the year in Europe was a trip to Greece followed by a cruise through the Greek Islands with a number of our children. Betty and her family flew from Ireland to meet us in Greece. Our children Barb and Bill also met us in Greece. Peggy's husband Dick was giving a talk in Paris at a computer association meeting. They then came on to Karlsruhe by train for a brief visit. We were to drive the four of us in our Volvo to take the plane from Frankfurt to Greece for the cruise. When we got in the car it wouldn't start! So we called for a taxi and asked the driver to take us the hour long drive to the airport. By now, of course, we were somewhat late and there was a question of whether we could catch the flight at all. The driver rose to the occasion and drove like mad to get us there in time and we tipped him well. Ironically when we got back, the silly car started up with no problem. I'll never know what the problem was.

We spent a couple of days in a hotel in the heart of Athens with the acropolis sitting on top of the hill in plain sight. We then took off for the port from which the cruise was to depart. On the way, our bus ran into a complete gridlock at an intersection. I have never seen anything like it before or since. Everyone honked horns, got out of their cars and had a great laugh at the situation. Finally after a lot of backing and filling they managed to get traffic untangled and moving again. I was glad that we weren't driving in such a mess.

On the cruise, we visited Santorini which has the strange round harbor which is apparently, the crater of a volcano which blew about 5000 years ago, and rode burro's up to the town on the high rim. We visited southeast Turkey where the ruins of Ephesus, which 2000 years ago had been a seaport, but now had been moved inland a few miles by earthquakes or earth fill. It was surprising how well preserved those ruins are despite being subject to earthquakes over the years. The taxi driver we hired to take us to the ruins, when we got there insisted on parking on a very special hill in case he had trouble restarting the taxi when it was time to go back. If so, it would be easier to push it downhill and get it started. Fortunately he had no trouble starting up this time.

A great adventure, particularly sharing it with so many of our children: Barb, Bets, Peg and Bill. After we landed at the end of the cruise, Bill decided to stay on in Greece for a while because he had found an interesting girl student from California on the cruise. He was to come back to Karlsruhe later by train, which he eventually did. However when he got there, he had lost our phone number but could remember the name of our village, Blankenloch. He had just enough money left to pay for a train trip, so took the train to Blankenloch but sat in the rain on the steps to the Boutique below us. Our landlady when she opened up at noon, recognized him as looking like us, and offered to let him into our apartment which he gratefully accepted. There he found my phone number and called me at work. And of course I was very glad to see my youngest safely back again. Larry was off giving a talk somewhere at that point.

German Host Dinner
for Japanese and US

Saying Farewell to Muellers
in Strasbourg

Eva & Walter Maschek
Friends at LANL & KfK

Crossing Atlantic on Way Home

Paying some of Our Debts

In July, as our year was getting close to the end, we had a number of parties to repay the people who had treated us so well and helped us out so many times. On July 3 we had a 4th of July party for Larry's friends at TU, and in honor of the British members, Larry made a fake 'Boston tea party' using an opened tea bag and a mini harbor.

I'm not sure they appreciated it but l guess that they were used to Larry and his entertaining nonsense.

On the 16th of July when we had planned a party for some of my colleagues, we got a call that our son Tom was coming into Frankfurt on his way around the world to Penang, Malaysia, on business for Hewlett-Packard. Well that was exciting and in the morning we went at the expected flight time only to be told that the plane was seven hours late! So we drove the hour back home and hours later Larry went back again to pick him up while I started the party. During the following weekend of his visit we took him up to Interlaken, Switzerland, for a ride up the cogwheel train to the top of mountain for the fantastic views of the Alps.

Some other amusing things that happened that summer were a trip we took to Norway; a sailing trip that Larry took with a group from TU on the Mediterranean from the South of France to Corsica; and a talk Larry gave at Julius Liebig University. When they were making arrangements for this last talk, the people doing the planning insisted on Larry reserving a hotel room. He couldn't understand why because it was only about an hour drive away. However when he got there he found out why. The food and wine at dinner went on until midnight and no way could he have driven home in that state. They knew what was coming and planned accordingly. I don't know much about the sailing trip but I gather that Larry had a good time. The Norway trip was a very interesting adventure. We flew to Oslo and took the train over to Bergen. The scenery along the way was very spectacular, including a huge waterfall just beside the tracks. When we got off the train in Bergen, we were approached by a pleasant looking but somewhat older lady who asked if we were looking for a place to stay. It seems she was the widow of a Sea Captain who had died and left her with nothing but her large house. So to make money to live on, she rented rooms. She hailed a taxi and got in with us to show the driver the way. It turned out to be a nice clean place right down on the harbor and a good central location for sightseeing.

Return from Germany

As the year drew to it's close in August, we sold our Volvo and disposed of the bicycles that we had acquired. We also sold the German Schreibmachine (typewriter) that we had purchased, which had special German characters so would not be much use back home. Then we packed up all the gear which we had to take home and had it shipped off.

Finally we took off on the train to catch the Polish ship, the Stefan Battory from Rotterdam, which was to take us across the Atlantic to Montreal, in eight days. It's hard to believe that when the planes can make it in ten hours, it still takes eight days for a ship to make it across the Atlantic Ocean. This is still fast compared to several hundred years ago when it took months. It was an interesting adventure in it's own way and something that we had always been curious about. It was a peaceful journey with no storms but no sunshine either. It was cloudy and rather gloomy almost the whole time. We did lots of reading and found some bridge players to pass some of the time. One time I even played bridge with a Polish woman who spoke German but no English so had to have translations of all the bids since my German was still a bit primitive. Friendly but rather strange. Some time later, one of my bridge partners who was a Canadian came to Los Alamos with her husband for a visit. We have now unfortunately lost touch. The trip was sometimes fun if mostly rather boring and we were very glad when we came to port in Montreal where we caught a plane the rest of the way home.

Chapter 19

Final working Years/ China Trip, 1982-86

A fter our return from Germany, when I returned to work in the group doing Fast Reactor Accident Analysis, the group leader who had supported my work on my PhD dissertation in the past, had moved up in the hierarchy. The man who had taken over the group was not willing to support my degree work at all. Now I had a decision to make and decided to try to find another group which would support me. I was fortunate enough to find such a group over in the Weapons Design Division where I had worked before. I also found a new advisor, Clarence Lee, who was an old friend from my days working on big programs for nuclear weapons design. Since those early days, he had taught Nuclear Engineering at the University of Texas at College Station, TX. Now he was considering coming back to the Lab and this new group very much wanted to hire him and me to work on a special project that we had worked on together before. However this did not work out at all.

One More Try at the Degree and Giving Up

While I transferred successfully, the group leader there who had wanted to hire us also moved upstairs to higher administration. The new leader who took over from him, not only didn't want Clarence Lee, he did not even want me, so again I had to go job hunting. For a few weeks in this period, before I left, I had an interesting office partner, Wen Ho Lee! He seemed like a very nice person and I could not see that he had done anything illegal, which is what I told the FBI when they queried me about him. It was a short period but I soon moved on to a new and very different Division. It was at this point that I decided that so much changing made it time to call it quits on my search for a PhD. A third change of advisor and dissertation topic was just too much and I wasn't getting any younger. It was a painful decision since I had put so much effort into it. It put a final end to such a long cherished dream.

After this next change and an extended higher clearance level, I ended up in a highly secret group working on Nuclear Proliferation. We worked in a 'vault', which consisted of a group of rooms with no windows and a specially secured entrance but it was still inside the Administration Building which had guards at it's entrance. The special higher level clearance took several months to obtain and up to that time we worked outside the vault. Just why we needed this, I never quite understood. Having worked for years with a Top Secret clearance, I couldn't see why that was not enough but for them it wasn't.

Now I was no longer programming computers as I had been before and I did miss that a lot. We were sent material by the CIA (Central Intelligence Agency), DOE (Department of Energy), NSA (National Security Agency) and other 'initial groups' that I don't even remember, if I ever knew what they were. These three however were the principal ones. We were to read and analyze the material as to whether we thought Nuclear Proliferation of atomic weapons (one of the main types of WMD) was occurring. Then we would write reports on what we had read. The area to which I was assigned was, in general, the developing world. In particular I remember reading at length about India, Pakistan, Iran, Israel, South Africa and Iraq! While I knew about nuclear weapons and making them, I didn't know much about these countries but I learned a lot! However, I'm not at all sure that there was anything in the material they sent us that would give enough information to reach any realistic conclusions. Much of it was from local newspapers from these countries which then had been stamped "TOP SECRET". I suppose that it would reveal something if they knew what we were interested in and what we were reading. Seemed rather silly to me and I couldn't see that there was enough information to tell anything for sure.

The one part of the job that I did enjoy was escorting groups from the CIA, State Department and other Washington organizations on a week long introduction to nuclear weapons. These were people who were going over to other countries so we hoped to give them some idea of what to look for during their tour overseas. They were interesting to meet and I enjoyed being the hostess. I gave lectures about the theory of nuclear bomb making. We toured the facilities where Los Alamos had built the early ones so they could get a feel for what was actually involved in building primitive atomic bombs.

Winter of 83-84

In the Autumn of 1983, since our house was still quite small, we decided to have the Kitchen remodeled and the front wall moved out about three feet to make a larger kitchen. The work began in September and was completed in November. The result was a house much pleasanter to live in and made cooking, much easier. When they were built during the war, the Western Area houses seemed quite nice but now as time went on they began to seem small and needed some upgrading.

That November, a colleague of Larry's, Lew Jones, asked me if I would be interested in going to the local Duplicate Bridge Club with him. His wife wasn't interested and neither was Larry, so we decided to give it a try which we did for about five months. And while it was fun for a while, the members were all rather heavy smokers, which I found quite unpleasant. They were also very fussy about details in a way which made it so restrictive that I decided spoiled much of the fun for me. The final blow occurred one evening when Lew misplayed by accident and he didn't even notice it. I didn't notice it either and it did not affect the outcome but our opponents did notice and called the director. That was the last straw for me and I decided to call it quits.

ANS Meeting in New Orleans

In June of 1984, I had a paper ready to present at the next ANS (American Nuclear Society) meeting which was to be held in New Orleans. Never having been to that city it was particularly appealing to me. An also attractive feature of the period was that there was a World's Fair being held there that Summer. For the very first time the People's Republic of China was first beginning to open it's doors to the rest of the world. They had sent a representation so it made for a fascinating visit to the Fair which turned out to be right next door to my hotel.

My Brother-in-law, Bob Carter (my sister Dottie's husband), also turned up at the meeting and we had a great time sightseeing together. I even remember going to the French Quarter with him which I wouldn't have dared to do by myself. Part of the World's Fair show were some spectacular fireworks sent from China, one of their specialties, and they were shot over the Mississippi River which I was able to watch from my hotel room window. They were the most impressive that I've ever seen, before or since.

ANS Trip to China

The following June, 1985, the nuclear society, ANS, arranged a tour of China with the Chinese Nuclear Society under the People-to-People Program that President Eisenhower had started back in the fifties. Of course it meant paying your own expenses but Larry and I decided that it might be a fascinating trip which it indeed turned out to be. We were asked to prepare presentations that we could make during the trip. I used much of the same material that I had used at the New Orleans meeting. As usual, they had to be pre approved for security reasons. You could say we knew too much and they didn't really trust us to know what was secret and what was not.

Simon—
Our Great
Guide

 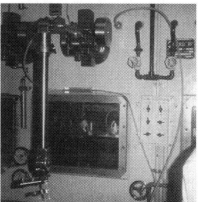

Small Trucks for Building Reactor   Hot Cells for Isotope Production

We first landed in Beijing where we visited schools and labs. There we gave our papers for the first time and then participated in discussions with members of the Chinese Nuclear Society in smaller groups. Our special tour guide, Simon, a young man in his early twenties, was a good example of the changes taking place in China. His parents were architects who had learned to speak Russian but spoke no English. Our young guide had been to graduate school in Seattle, Washington, and spoke excellent English but no Russian. He loved Western classical music. On some of the long bus rides he and I passed the time seeing who could sing and recognize the most Beethoven, Chopin and others.

As part of the Beijing visit, we did some of the usual tourist things. We were taken to a section of the Great Wall and walked along it with many ordinary Chinese including some of the members of their military. We also were able to visit the Hidden City where the Emperors palace was hidden behind many walls. We got to see the rooms for the Empresses and Concubines. The Emperor can have his palace. I wouldn't want to live so confined but it was interesting to see.

In general, I expected their laboratories to be relatively primitive compared to those that we were accustomed to at Los Alamos but that was not the case. The bathrooms might be, and were, fairly primitive, but when it came to technical equipment they were amazingly sophisticated. One thing that worried me is that, like the Russians, they seemed not to have paid anywhere near as much attention to safety as we did. However they seemed very interested in what we were trying to do along that line. This importance ot this since the accident at Chernobyl has become very clear, because the Russians were not as safety conscious as they should have been.

The Los Alamos Equivalent

Our next visit was to Chengdu, their site equivalent to Los Alamos. It was out in the central part of western China and we were flown there by Chinese Airlines. It was a bit scary but they landed safely enough if a bit roughly. We did not, of course, get to see where they built nuclear weapons but we did get to visit a site where they prepared radioisotopes which was quite impressive. We also visited a fusion reactor that they were trying to get to work.

At each institute that we visited, they put on a special feast for us. They have very different customs. Maybe a dozen of us would sit around large round tables, covered with a white cloth. There were no napkins so one just used the table cloth to wipe your hands! The only utensils were chopsticks, of course, and the serving dishes were on a movable 'lazy susan' in the center. You were given a small plate, about the size of what we would use for bread and butter, and you just reached out with your chopsticks and helped yourself to the food in the center. Or if your host thought you were too bashful to help yourself fast enough, he would put things on your plate for you with his own chopsticks! When these small plates got full, particularly with duck or fish bones, you just pushed them off to the side on the table cloth! The food was very good but not at all like what we regard as 'Chinese'. It consisted mainly of duck, seafood, greens and rice.

One big surprise occurred the first night we were in the hotel in ChengDu. The list of room numbers were posted by name in the lobby. We found ours on the first floor and went right to prepare for bed. Before we even got to sleep, there was a knock on the door. Larry answered it and to his amazement, it was a man who he had worked with in Boy Scouts in Espanola. The man was there on completely independent business and had recognized our name on the posted list. An unusual name helps but it is a small world, after all. They had a great if brief reunion.

First Nuclear Power Reactor

One special tour was of the first Nuclear Energy Plant that they were just starting to build. It was far out in the country and they were using what looked to me like tiny trucks and wheel barrows to build the reactor. No large trucks or cranes as you would see in our country. One amusing incident occurred when we first arrived on the site. We drove up onto an open bluff above the valley where the reactor was being built. It had been a long drive out in the country and we drove in the equivalent of a US yellow school bus over bumpy roads for several hours. By then my bladder was calling loudly for relief. As we got out of the bus, one of the men said to our guide "is there a restroom around anywhere". Overhearing this, I ran up and said "How about me too". He answered the man "Well I guess you can go over behind the bus" But then he turned to me and said "But I don't know about you". So I walked over to where the group was looking over the edge at the nascent reactor, and did my best to hold it.

A few minutes later a small open jeep with a Chinese driver drove up and our guide pointed to me and said: "It's for you". So I got in not having any idea where we were going but hoping. The driver took off up the valley and drove for several miles until he pulled up beside a small concrete building with the one Chinese sign that I had learned to recognize—women's room! And sure enough it was clean, almost unused, with the usual several holes in the floor. What a relief! When my 'chariot' returned me to the group, the other woman asked where I had been, I told her and she said ruefully "I wish I had known". Had I known, I would have told her. It pays to ask!

Silk Factory in Hangzou

After Chengdu, we took a train to Shanghai and then on to Hangzou where we visited a silk factory, probably one of the most fascinating, general interest stops of the whole tour. We saw how they collected the silk worm cocoons and boiled them in huge vats to kill the insect and, I guess, stabilize the silk. Then they unwound the silk on to large reels which was then dyed as desired and woven into fabric. The design and control of the machines for weaving was directed by very large perforated cards that worked on the same basis as the punch cards we used in the early days at Los Alamos. The factory was surrounded by vast rose gardens and the flowers were used to make perfumes but we didn't see the details of this. There were rooms where workers sat and did elaborate embroidery on silk cloth, which took a year for two people to complete a large panel. Gorgeous but boring to me.

Hangzou—Silk Worm Cocoons

In China, Bikes Are Everywhere

Unwinding Cocoons

Winding Silk on Reels

Someplace along the line, during this trip, I had quite a talk with another member of the group which was to have impressive consequences later. While I don't remember details of the conversation, Mark Reinhart did and remembered it so well that later he submitted my name for an award, which will be described in a later Chapter. After everything else, we ended up in Hongkong and were so tired that we spent a couple of days recuperating in a very expensive hotel room before taking off for our trip back across the Pacific Ocean to home.

In January of 1986 a long comprehensive article appeared in Nuclear News about the trip by Bernard J. Verna, who was on the trip although I never talked to him directly. Reading it over 20 years later, it is amazingly perceptive of the future of energy in China. He foresaw exactly what has happened since. He predicted that while they are working hard on Nuclear energy and doing amazing things, it will really be a small part of the mix. Coal and hydro power are becoming the main sources of energy for them. One thing they have not solved is the problem of air pollution. We thought Los Angeles was bad but Beijing is orders of magnitude worse. The column "On line with Verna" was also much better than I am about the detail of the places we visited and who talked to us but not as good at the type of human details which interested me more.

Summary of Other Activities between China and Retirement

That Fall, in October of 1985, while visiting some of our children at school in Las Cruces, we decided that it might to be a good place to retire. We found and bought a lot in a special neighborhood, Mesilla Park, not very far from the University, NMSU. We took detailed measurements of the lot and identified directions in which to orient a hypothetical house. On returning to Los Alamos, I took a pad of engineer's paper and started to sketch and design my dream house. When I would get something that I liked, I would take it to Larry and he would make suggestions and corrections to please him and I would go back to the drawing board and modify it. This kind of interchange went on until we found a plan that suited us both and we thought would fit the lot.

In that December, I had my first Cataract removed from my left eye and this introduced a problem which I had not expected. At the time experience with implanted lenses was still somewhat limited, so the Eye Surgeon did not want to implant a lens. As a result the Doctor said that it wasn't possible to give me glasses that would adjust my eyes to the huge difference between my regular eye and the one without a lens, so I had to learn to wear contact lenses. And was that a problem! I had never worn contacts and it takes a lot of learning to put them in your eyes. Young people may be able to learn easily but it was not easy for me. Furthermore, at first one can only wear them for short periods. But gradually I got used to them and even learned to like them very much for a number of years. I had always hated eyeglasses so was glad in a way to do away with them. But the transition might have been easier if I had been forewarned and it hadn't been quite so abrupt.

The end of that December, Larry decided to retire although he continued to consult for a while. However, now he became eager for me also to retire and began to push me. The following April of 1986, I finally decided that he was right. It was time for me also to call it quits. At about the same time, he was informed that he was to receive the Seaborg Actinide Award for the year. At a formal ceremony and dinner, in April 1986, he was formally presented with the award which is still hanging on the wall in our study.

I also continued to consult with my group for a while until finally, I became so detached that we mutually decided that I wasn't doing much and really didn't want to so called it quits. In May, just before we moved to Las Cruces, I had a Parathyroid Adenoma removed from my neck and Larry had a Hernia repaired. With some of those details out of the way, in July we found a small apartment in Las Cruces where we could live for six months and keep an eye on the house which was being built for us on our lot. That Fall, when we had just about decided finally to sell our Los Alamos house and move everything to Las Cruces, we got a call from our daughter Betty. She and her Husband had jobs with a new startup company which was moving to Los Alamos, Los Alamos Diagnostics (LAD), and would be moving there soon, could they buy our house? Well, of course, we were delighted to cooperate, took it off the market and agreed to rent it to them until they were settled in and had sold their house back in Indianapolis.

Chapter 20

Spread of Family, Marriages and Anniversaries, 1980-95

After the wild seventies and getting most of our kids through college, we could now turn our attention more to ourselves. At the beginning of 1980, the child farthest away was Betty, over in Belfast, Ireland. The closest was Pete nearby in Albuquerque. Barb and Bob were both in Las Cruces. Peggy was in Los Altos with Tom close to her in Mountain View, CA. Finally the youngest, Bill, was up in Boulder CO. Pete, Betty and Bob were all apparently, securely married and it wasn't long until Peggy was also married. I say 'apparently' about marriages advisedly because who knows these days. I guess the Williams girls are more old fashioned, because all Williams marriages have lasted a lifetime and have only been broken by death but that isn't completely true of the younger generation. To compare the Williams marriages to the marriages of my children, I will start with some background on the Williams weddings.

Williams Marriages

One of the things that has changed over the years is the locales and format of weddings. In the Williams family, it was assumed that you were to be married in church unless you married a non Catholic like Dot, Lyd and I did. My wedding to a non-Catholic was described in Chapter 9. Kitty's wedding (in 1946) was a 'proper' marriage because Bob Kallal was a Catholic and they were married in our parish church, St. Ambrose. Kitty wore a beautiful long white dress with a veil. Our Mother's siblings, Isabelle, Arthur and Jack all came for it and this was the last time our grandmother, Gaga. had her whole family together before she died shortly thereafter. I heard that Uncle Arthur played the piano and entertained everyone with his usual magic tricks. Uncle Arthur's playing then made such an impression on my sister Dottie, that later she was convinced that he even played at my wedding. This was not true since he didn't even come for that occasion because it was still during the War. How I wish that I could have been there for Kit's wedding but it was too expensive for the impoverished graduate students that we were, to say nothing of the two day train trip required from Berkeley, CA. It is so easy now to fly across the country that we forget how difficult it was then to go from San Francisco to St. Louis.

About my sister Dottie's wedding (in 1947), I know next to nothing since it was still too far away (California to Illinois) for poor students. But I have heard that, since Bob Carter also was not a Catholic, it was a very simple wedding. It was held in Urbana, IL, with practically no members of the family present. I'm particularly sorry about missing this wedding because Bob and I have so much in common. He worked with Enrico Fermi during WW2 on the research reactor, Omega West, at Los Alamos (on which I also did an experiment many years later). He and Dot, after they were married, returned to Los Alamos in 1947, for quite a few years, In the late sixties, they moved to the Washington DC area where he worked for the Nuclear Regulatory Commission (NRC). They stayed there until she died in December 2000 and Bob still lives. Bob and I both belong to the American Nuclear Society (ANS) and have met at meetings a time or two over the years.

There were no more family weddings for a number of years, until my sister Sally's wedding (on 1953). Her husband, Al Lemker, was a Catholic from Cincinnati, Ohio. Their wedding, as was customary, was held in the bride's church in Maplewood, near St. Louis, MO. Again, to my deep regret, I was not there and don't know details. The next wedding was Lydia's (In 1955), held in Ann Arbor, Michigan. Harold (called Pete) Chadwick was also not a Catholic so, while I'm sure it was not held in a church, I don't know much else about it. I have a picture of them as Bride and Groom only because I recently attended their 50th Anniversary celebration in California. This was the last of the non-Catholic weddings.

Next came Rose marrying Larry Etzkorn (in 1956) also in Maplewood near St. Louis. Finally transportation had improved, as had our finances, so this time, I was able to be there. In fact, Rose had gotten so fond of our twin girls, when she helped me out with them in Los Alamos before our Bob was born, that she invited them to be flower girls at her wedding. We agreed to come and my Mom made fancy turquoise silk dresses for the girls. Dot, also then in Los Alamos, and I drove to St. Louis with some of our kids. This was not quite as great a distance as from Richmond, CA. Rose was a beautiful bride in a typical, long white dress for a formal Nuptial Mass in the local Catholic Church. Since Larry Etzkorn was also from St. Louis and had a large family there, the whole affair was extremely elaborate. Larry's father had owned a hardware store and Larry had to drop out of college to help in the store so never was able to finish a college degree. I think he always felt a little overwhelmed by all the degrees of his brothers-in-law.

My only brother, Grant and Kathleen Concannon were married (in 1957) in the bride's church in St. Louis. For the first and only time my Dad did not have to escort a daughter down the aisle so apparently some of his sons-in-law had a great time getting him 'happy' drunk before the occasion. Just why I wasn't there for this affair, I don't really know. Maybe it was partly because I had missed so many weddings and only Rose's pushing for the twins got me there for hers and partly because I was so overwhelmed by my own family at that time. I would have been expecting my sixth child.

I did manage to get there for my baby sister, Susie's wedding (in 1958). Norbert Hartenbach was also a Catholic so it also was a church wedding in Maplewood. I have pictures of Sue as a beautiful bride in a long white dress. Norbert also was from St. Louis so had many family members there for the occasion. Norbert had just completed his degree as a dentist at St. Louis University, when they were married. Since the US Air Force had partly paid for his education, he owed them some time in service. So Dr and Mrs. Hartenbach headed out to spend time in the Air Force, in Texas. They now have three children, all doctors: Ellen, a Gynecologist in Wisconsin; Bill, an Anesthesiologist in Tampa, FL, and David, a Pediatrician in St. Louis. At least one of them stayed close by! And this ended the saga of the Williams Weddings. And unusually for the time, all these marriages have lasted a lifetime. Three have so far been broken by death but none by divorce.

Asprey Children's Weddings are Mostly Different

Compare all those church weddings with those of our children. The first one, which was Barb to Jeff Ray (1/2/71) It was the only one held in a Catholic church and in Los Alamos. They had met at school at NMSU. She wore a beautiful white gown with veil both of which she made herself and was much more traditional than the later ones. The reception was held in the famous Los Alamos Lodge still remaining from the prewar days of the Boys Ranch School. It began to snow during the ceremony and afterwards every one had trouble getting anywhere! But this first wedding was not to last.

Pete in Albuquerque

Now for the first wedding at the beginning of the 70's. When Pete came back from the Navy, he went back to school at UNM in Albuquerque and did very well. Guess that his time in the Navy helped him grow up. After meeting at UNM through his sister Peggy, Pete and Cindy, decided that this was it and they were married at the Newman Chapel at UNM where they were both students. Pete and Cindy Cornil, also a Catholic, were married on the 23rd of January (1/ 23/ 71). Cindy also was from a family of seven and was the first of her family to get married. She was a beautiful bride in typical long white dress. This was still rather traditional and both families were there making a pretty large crowd. They soon had their first child, David, in November (11/12/1972). When Pete finished up his BS in Operations Research, they then went out to California. Pete went to graduate school at UC Berkeley and got an MS also in Operations Research. During this time they had their second child, Jennifer (1/17/ 74, better known as Jenna). For a while Pete worked in California for some small companies and then got a job back in Albuquerque working for Sandia Laboratories doing Data Management. After about ten years there, he transferred to Sandia Laboratory, Livermore, in California and has been there ever since until his retirement in 2005.

Betty Gets Married in Indianapolis, 1975

After getting her MS degree in Animal Genetics at UC Davis, Betty found a job in Indianapolis and worked there for some years for a medical equipment company, American Monitor. There she met and married David Strietelmeier, who was working as a mechanical technician. Now we begin to see the difference in marriage customs. Betty planned her own wedding (in 5/ 3/ 75) in a neighborhood meeting house in Indianapolis with a Protestant Minister presiding. She wore a short, colored dress, with no veil, but just a hat. The ceremony was very simple with no music and very simple refreshments. Since David Streitelmeier was an only child, only his parents and a few friends were there in addition to Betty's siblings and parents. Since it was a long way and would be expensive for all of the kids to fly, we rented a camper van and Pete and the kids drove it out while Larry and I flew since we couldn't take that much time off from work. It was the first time any of us had met David so I think we rather overwhelmed him and he didn't quite know what to make of us. He still tells of Barb, Betty's twin, knocking on his door in the evening, and he first thought it was Betty. When he realized it wasn't, he said "My God, there are two of them!". I guess he got used to having a duplicate of his wife around but the twins have never lived close together so it wasn't a serious problem.

Betty and David Move to Los Alamos

After working for a couple of years in Belfast, Northern Ireland, as described in Chapter 18, they returned to Indianapolis where their son Joseph Ryan was born (8/10/83). Just as we retired in 1986 and started to get ready to move to Las Cruces, they called to say that they were changing jobs and the new company was a startup and was moving to Los Alamos. Betty asked had we sold our house yet because they might like to buy it. We were delighted to hear the news and immediately took it off the market and agreed to rent it to them until they had sold their house in Indiana and things seemed stable enough to be able to buy the one in Los Alamos from us.

Much has happened to them since. The startup, Los Alamos Diagnostics, failed after a few years and for a few months they were jobless. In time Betty found a job at LANL for a while as a contractor but in time as a Staff Member in what she calls 'Biogeochemistry'. She worked in much the same locations and with the same people that her Dad had in his last years at LANL. When she visited down here in Las Cruces, she and Larry had great times talking about what she was doing, with whom and where at LANL. She has also been wonderful at helping us keep in touch with people at the lab and, since Larry died, of spreading the word of his death to his friends and former colleagues.

Barb in Las Cruces

While not as far away as Ireland, nor as close as Albuquerque, Las Cruces was close enough for some regular visits. After having her first marriage fail and getting her BS in 1971, Barb stayed on for a while in Las Cruces. She continued going to school and got her MBA in 1976, taught a little, worked for the computer center for a while, worked for the Department of Agriculture for a while and even was married briefly to Art Whatley, a Professor in the Business Department. One Summer (1977), they even went on a canoe trip with us down the Upper Missouri River in Montana, along with one of her stepsons, Percy Whatley.

In the early eighties, after being divorced, Barb went off to Australia with a man (Bruce Wilson) that she had known at NMSU. She continued working there for nearly ten years even after the relationship broke up. Of course, we took advantage of her being over there to visit her several times and do some sightseeing.

At one time she and two other women started a very successful computer advisory company, Solutions Plus. At the time she said that the Australians were somewhat backward about computers which contributed to their success. But later when they sold it, the company to whom they sold it, sent in their own managers who ran it into the ground, refusing to listen to the advice of Barb and her friends. The purchasers then refused to pay the balance due to the three women. Besides not having enough money to pay for lawyers, and since Australia is even more misogynistic than the US, they concluded that their chance of winning in court was pretty low and just gave up the rest of the money that was due them.

While Barb ended the decade still in Australia, at about that time she met an American from Kentucky, David Pettus, in a dance class over there. David had been in Australia about the same length of time that she had and also had about decided that it was time to come back to the US. The difference was that he had been married before with two boys but the marriage had broken up before he and Barbara met. In fact Barb says that she was able to mediate between them and they got along better with her there but not enough to put the marriage back together. Barb and Dave almost immediately fell for each other and very soon Barb got pregnant. They came back to the US to get married in December of 1991 (12/28/91).

Barb Gets Married in 1991

Their wedding was held in our relatively new house in Las Cruces and most of his family came from back East. And of course all of our family were here. Barbara again had made her long white dress but no veil this time. I had a good friend who while not a minister was licensed to perform marriage ceremonies as a Justice of the Peace, and agreed to do it. One of David's sisters had majored in music and had a very nice voice so she sang and I accompanied her on the piano to furnish music for the affair. We had moved our dining room table out of the way to make an open space for the ceremony. Afterward we served refreshments including a traditional cake.

After the wedding, they went back to Australia to settle up some business and Samantha was born while they were back there, as I have described before. This time it sounds like the marriage is going to be successful. After several years in Atlanta, Georgia, they found new jobs near Denver, CO, where they now live up in Evergreen, CO, raising alpacas and have several horses. Not exactly a ranch but a nice place in the country.

Bob Also Marries in Las Cruces, 1978

While still working on his degree, Bob married (1978) a fellow student, Joanne Joyce Raabe better known as Jojo. She has worked as a medical radiology technician. Bob and his bride, Jojo, also planned their own wedding but this time down in Las Cruces. They were living in the rented house on El Paseo that we had purchased as an investment and rented back to them. Since Jojo had lost both her parents by the time she was still in her teens, she was very accustomed to running her own life and thought little of planning the wedding herself. Bob was always obliging and let her do whatever she wanted. The wedding was held in the side yard of their house and the feast was laid out on tables in the front yard. The ceremony was performed by a Justice of the Peace.

After a few years in Las Cruces, Bob found a job in Huntsville, AL. with Brown-Teledyne and she worked in Doctor's offices in that area. On the side Bob and some friends, started a small company which was finally successful enough to go public as CYBEX. Before it finally went public, he gave gifts of stock in it to his parents and all siblings. This was a large bonus for the whole family and very generous and thoughtful of him. So Bob ends the decade in Huntsville, Alabama.

Bob and Joan, 1978
in Las Cruces

The Feast in the Front Yard

Peg Fixes Bobs Flower

The Wedding in Yard on El Paseo

A Garden Wedding for Peggy in Los Alamos, 1981

After meeting Dick Lyon as described in Chapter 16 and deciding to get married we helped her plan a wedding in Los Alamos. Since Dick grew up in El Paso as the third of nine children, this was not too far for them to come. His parents still live there and we see them from time to time. Peg and Dick Lyon's wedding was held in July (7/25/81) in the beautiful rose garden at the historical Lodge in Los Alamos. The ceremony was performed by two of their brothers, one of hers, Tom, and one of his, both of which are part time ministers in addition to being computer programers. All of both families were of course there which made a large crowd since there are nine children in Dick's family in addition to our crowd! A local blue grass band led by Gary Eller, one of Larry's colleagues, played for dancing in the Lodge after the ceremony. Peggy wore a beautiful white dress that she had made with a wide brimmed hat, very appropriate for a garden wedding.

Peg and Dick, 1981
Mom & Dad walk her in

The Wedding in Los Alamos
Rose Garden at the Lodge

The Happy Couple
Walking Away

An Even Bigger Reception in Silicon Valley

Since they had both lived so long in the Silicon Valley area, most of their current friends actually lived out in California which was a long way from Los Alamos. So they wanted to have another reception out there in addition to the one in Los Alamos. As Larry and I wanted to be there, we with our daughter Barb, flew our Cessna 210 out for the occasion. The affair out there was even bigger than the one in Los Alamos. So they were well showered and feted and apparently started off to what seems to be a very successful marriage. Both of their children, Susan (11/24/86) and Erik (9/26/89) have been born during the decade and they have ended up back where they started in Los Altos, CA. Dick had graduated from Cal Tech and still works with Carver Meade and others from there. For many years his principle job was with Apple Computer, but he now works for Google.

Tom in Mountain View

In some ways, Tom was very different from all his brothers, who mostly seemed to have trouble settling down to business and deciding where they wanted to go and what they wanted to do when they went to college. Tom knew what he wanted to do from the beginning. He started off in Electrical Engineering, kept with it and went straight through in four years. All the others started in one direction, changed their minds, fooled around and got there eventually but it took them awhile. After he graduated, Tom drove his little car out to California and stayed for a while with his sister, Peggy. He looked for a job and found one with Hewlett-Packard as a chip designer and has been with them ever since.

One night in his thirties, Tom met a young lady at a party, Carol Fitchette, and they talked and talked and talked. She also worked for Hewlett-Packard but in Colorado and was out in California only temporarily. Later she called her hostess and asked who that was she talked to for so long. She got his e-mail address and they corresponded via the internet until finally they met again and decided this was it. He requested a transfer to Colorado and the company was happy to do it since they were eager to get some of their people out of the bay area. They moved in together and eventually got married.

When Tom first told us he had a girl friend and was in love, we were astonished because he never had girl friends much and we had about concluded that he was a permanent bachelor. But apparently her parents were even more surprised because she didn't date either. Her parents were not too impressed with Tom at first because his hair was thinning and made him look older. They even offered Carol $200,000 not to marry him which she indignantly refused. When she told Tom about it. He laughed and said "why didn't you just take the money and we'll just live together". I'm sure this would have upset them even more. However, he likes to cook and later on made some special feasts for them, which won them over completely and they now regard him as a prince. He even got along better with her Mother than Carol did.

A Wedding on Top of a Mountain, 1990

Carol and Tom, planned their own wedding entirely and there was even some question if her parents were going to be there at all. (They were still not sure they approved of Tom). Well, said I, "the senior Fitchettes could do what they liked, but Tom was my dear son and we had every intention of being there". Furthermore, "we had every intention of putting on a traditional groom's dinner the night before and the entire party was invited, including the brides parents". Well her parents finally decided to come and the dinner was a big success, and I'm sure they were glad they attended.

The wedding itself was held up on top of the mountain on a gorgeous overlook out over the valley which had been a very special spot to Carol in her college days. Tom and Carol had made her dress together. It was pink and calf length with a 'train', a little embroidered 'train' on the hem. In the same spirit of fun Tom wore 'tails'. It consisted of two fox tails tucked into his belt in back.

While the wedding was small it was a most spectacular affair with the Rocky Mountains as a backdrop, not at all like any other. The reception was held at a beautiful house they had bought together in Boulder. It was decorated with many flowers and hanging plants and refreshments were served in the back yard. Tables were set up in the back yard for food and the photographer took pictures of everyone there. I particularly remember Peggy's Erik who was a crawler then loving the grass and crawling under chairs and tables. They have since made many elaborate plantings around the house, including 40 rosebushes and thousands of bulbs. I hope to be up there some Spring to see the show. An unfortunate memory that I have of that wedding is that I developed shingles, an itchy rash along my back. It is apparently a result of the virus from many years ago when as a child I had Chicken Pox. Carol's Mother actually made the suggestion that led to the diagnosis.

Tom and Carol, 1990 on Mountain above Boulder

Wedding Party before Ceremony

Bill Gets Married, 1997

While Bill has had several serious girl friends over the years, the most serious and the one he finally married (in 11/25/97) is Susan Henry. She is from Bloomington, Illinois, but decided in college that she wanted to go someplace different and picked NMSU. What I hope is to be our last wedding took place between Bill and Susan Henry also here in our home in Las Cruces. All of Susan's family came for the wedding except her father who had died recently. We held it on the patio and Bill asked his brother Tom to perform the ceremony. After marriage they were very fortunate to soon have a beautiful little girl (8/11/98), Amelia Marie, who for a while called herself Mimi.

Bill and Sue, 1997 in Las Cruces, cut cake

Bill and Sue with Asprey Family

End of the Eighties

Having started the decade in Belfast, Albuquerque, Las Cruces, Mountain View, and Boulder, our children ended up: in Indianapolis, Indiana (Betty), Livermore & Manteca, CA (Pete), Australia (Barb), Huntsville, AL (Bob), Los Altos, CA (Peggy), Boulder, CO (Tom) and Las Cruces, NM (Bill). They do move around.

Reunions and Anniversaries

While my sisters and I are spread all across the country from Delaware (Kit) to California (Lyd) and Duluth (Sal) to Las Cruces (me), we are still very fond of each other and try to get together as often as possible. We have had several reunions up in Colorado which is a favorite and centrally located spot, in addition to the fact that a number of us have children in Boulder. In view of all this, it's where Larry and I decided to celebrate our 50th Wedding Anniversary and invite as many as possible to join us and many of them did even Kathleen, the widow of my only brother Grant.

Winter Park, where we assembled, is a great place for hiking and fishing as well as having a ski lift for sight seeing from the top of a mountain. The ski lodges are quite reasonable during the Summer being out of season for skiing. All-in-all a great place for being together as well as having a vacation. We gathered for the occasion in a central meeting room and had a catered dinner. And of course there were lots of bridge games, conversation and laughter.

Larry and Marge at 50th Anniversary in Winter Park, Colorado

With Sisters Who Came
Kit, Dot, Sue & Lyd (l-r)

With our Seven Children Who Helped us Celebrate

At 50th Anniversary noticed All Daughters-in-Law are Blondes

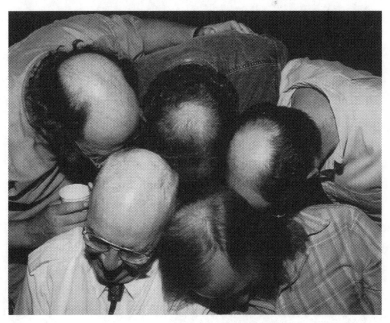

Boys Get into Act and Show of Bald Spots

Chapter 21

Early Retirement.
Building our Dream House
1986-1995

As the middle years came to an end (1986), it was time for us to retire. As I noted above, I had not been happy with my last position at Los Alamos, working for the 'alphabet soup' out of Washington. They told you what you could and couldn't do. They knew little about science and yet were making scientific decisions which always seemed inappropriate to me. I also really missed the computer programming which I had done over so many years. The one part that I did like was giving a week long seminar for new recruits from Washington organizations such as the CIA and the State Department. We gave lectures in an attempt to teach groups of 20 or so a little about nuclear weapons, how they were made, and what materials to look for. We took them on tours of the various sites to see how it had all been done in the early years in Los Alamos when the first bombs were put together. This might not be too different from what beginners in third world countries would do. We only did this a few times a year however, and the rest of the time, we read interminable documents that they sent us and wrote reports. And there was the constant search for financial support from the various agencies. So when Larry decided that he was ready to retire, I decided that it was probably a good idea. While I missed working after I retired and had not wanted to stop, it was with a sense of relief.

To sum up the final working years, they turned out to be very good for both of us. Larry had accepted my education and working efforts very well. Our marriage, despite an occasional rocky part, seemed as solid as ever. He was almost always a wonderful husband and father. At times, I know that he would much rather have had me stay at home with the kids, just like most men would I guess. But I think he realized that I wouldn't have been a very happy person if he had tried to force me. He said once, while there were still many children a home, that in a way, my going to school and working was a kind of insurance in case anything happened to him. I would be able to take better care of the family with an educated and working background. Also, over time my extra salary helped pay for college for the kids. I never made enough to send so many in luxury but we could give them a strong start. We expected them to take it from there and they did, very well. The extra salary has also helped make our retirement income more generous.

Achievements

Comparing my child dreams to achievements, I can say that most have been fulfilled. First, Marriage and children, was certainly fulfilled completely with Larry and seven children. Second. My education and scientific work on technical projects fulfilled that dream. While I hadn't quite made it to the PhD, I had come close and, if younger, or had gotten enough support, really believe that I could have achieved it. Certainly I did do some technical work in the fields of Computers and Nuclear Engineering. Third. My dream of flying my own plane was certainly achieved with our Cessna 210, and could have continued but my eyes failed me at the end. Fourth. The year in Germany at KfK, certainly fulfilled the dream of living abroad. Many other trips, Africa, Australia, China and others, have fulfilled my dreams of traveling. Fifth. I thought that it would be fun to design and build our own house. We had remodeled and added on to several houses but then we were always changing something somebody else had designed and there were so many constraints. For once, it would be nice to start from scratch and do every thing our way. So that was the thing that we decided would keep us busy in early retirement.

Choosing Las Cruces for Retirement

As to where to retire, we wanted a warmer climate than Los Alamos. When we first moved to Los Alamos, the climate seemed delightful after Iowa and Chicago and we loved it. But now we were older and our joints seemed to need more heat. On many of the trips that we took over the years, we looked at many places such as Mexico, Florida, California and the Bahamas as possible places for retirement. None of them had appealed to us and having lived for so many years in New Mexico (since 1949). we decided that we really would be more at home staying in the state Our oldest son, Pete was located in Albuquerque at that time and thought that we should consider Albuquerque so he would be closer in case we needed help. But Albuquerque seemed like too big a city for us, so we rejected that idea. Furthermore, if living close to him had been one of our goals, a few years later he moved back to California, so we would have been left behind. Five of our children had gone to school at NMSU in Las Cruces in southern New Mexico, and most liked it so well that they didn't want to leave. One of my main requirements, as well as a warmer climate, was a University town so Las Cruces seemed to fit that requirement, as well as being a relatively small town. One New Years day when we were visiting kids at school there being outside in shirt sleeves, clinched the decision for us. While w were still working in Los Alamos, we firmed up the decision by finding and purchasing a lot in Mesilla Park between Mesilla and the city of Las Cruces, just a mile or two from the University as described in Chapter 19.

Designing our Dream House

And building the house did make a difference in helping us adjust to retirement. It gave us a goal and intense activity to keep us busy, so I didn't even miss working much for a while. We had started the project several years before retirement. After buying the half acre lot, we measured it in detail and tried to design the house to fit as to size and orientation. Or should I say that I designed it and Larry critiqued and made suggestions. We wrapped the house around a courtyard which contains a patio and swimming pool with a retractable cover. The East wing contains the kitchen and a double garage with enough room at the south end for some tools and work tables for Larry. The main wing contains the living-dining area, a study with space for desks and a computer table, a master bath and master bedroom. This is our suite. We had wanted a fairly small house that would be easy to take care of but still have enough room for at least some of our children to visit from time to time. We tried to resolve this by adding a wing on the west which can be shut off when not in use. It contains two guest bedrooms, a bathroom and laundry. The kids call it our 'motel wing'.

Being pretty much amateurs, we turned our original sketch-to-scale of a floor plan over to an architect in Los Alamos for a set of building plans. This wasn't too successful because he didn't understand some of our ideas and spent a lot of time changing our plans and doing things that we didn't want or need.

Building the House

When we were finally ready to start building, Theresa Bozeman, sister of Art Whatley (Barb's ex-husband), was a real estate agent in Las Cruces at the time. She had helped us sell the house on El Paseo that we had rented to the kids and then use the money to find and buy our new lot. Now she helped us find a good contractor, Larry Jeter, to build the house.

The Contractor didn't find the architect's plans very successful and had a draftsman draw up the kind of plans that he was accustomed to and found useful. It was probably what we should have done in the first place since we had so much trouble with the architect who couldn't seem to understand much of what we wanted. The actual building began in July of 1986. On July 1st, we found an apartment to rent for the six months while it was being built, where we could live and keep an eye on the building process. By December the house was essentially complete and we were able to move in for Christmas with many children there to see and admire our new project. The details such as painting and plastering were finished up by Spring. And that Summer we had grass put in and some landscaping done. Larry and I of course continued the landscaping and planting as time went on.

Welcome to Our New House

Courtyard and Pool

In moving down that Fall, we had not only our Cessna, a pickup truck and a Chrysler Le Baron to move down along with all our 'stuff'. We had most of the furniture and big things shipped down and stored in the garage (of the new house), which was complete by that time. Also, both of us were still consulting in finishing up our jobs so were commuting from time to time. Some of the commuting was done by plane but one time when I was driving down by myself in the Le Baron, I had a blowout and I overcorrected and rolled the car. Fortunately, I had my seat belt fastened and after the car rolled it ended back on the wheels and I had only a slight scratch on one arm. Several kind strangers stopped and offered help but all I really needed was someone to call Larry and tell him what had happened, for him to come get me in his pickup, and then have the car towed. A very nice policeman came and took care of all the above. So all's well that ends well aside from the expense of replacing the car beyond what insurance covered.

Like all amateurs we made a few mistakes in design, but on the whole, it has been very successful and we think it's about 95% of what we wanted. We have been told many times that it is a beautiful house. We find it very comfortable and not too expensive or difficult to maintain. It is warm in winter partly using solar heat from a large sun room backed by a Trombe Wall, which is a massive wall which soaks up solar heat and releases it gradually. In addition we have gas heaters for backup when the sun doesn't shine. It stays comfortably cool in summer when the sun is high by the use of overhangs, opening windows at night when the desert cools down, and the use of several swamp coolers at other times. The children do like to visit, which is very important to us. And in particular, all children and grandchildren enjoy the pool very much.

Retirement Job for Me

After settling into our new house for a few months, I was lucky enough, in September of 1987, to find a job in the NMSU Computer Center for nearly a year. My daughter Barbara introduced me to Joe Denk, one of her former bosses at the NMSU Computer Center. He hired me on the spot for a special project on a parallel processor, a Floating Point System T100. This involved developing and running 'bench marks'. These are standard problems that measure the capabilities of a given machine. We also tried to help staff at the university run their problems on it by giving talks on it's operation.

After about ten months, this project unfortunately ended. I could have looked for another job at the university, however, I felt that it was time to take retirement seriously and began to look into other activities. One of the principal ones was to audit classes. Since then I have continued auditing classes of all kinds: Music, was what I started off with at first. Electrical and Mechanical Engineering were other of my early loves. Since then, I have tried Chemistry, Biochemistry, Biology, Linguistics, Entomology, Soils, Math and Computer Science. There are so many fascinating things to learn and never enough time to learn them all. One of the more challenging Electrical Engineering Labs in 1989, that I remember with amusement, was run by a young Jordanian. There were just three students in the class: a Malaysian, Vietnamese and me. Communication was something of a problem but among us we managed to complete the required experiments.

Playing the Piano

One of the first things after getting settled into retirement, I decided that I wanted to go back to playing the piano. As a small child, I had learned from my Grandmother, Gaga, but over the years I had been too busy to play very much. But what you learn in childhood never quite goes away. I had never been able to play music from memory and couldn't understand how people could do it. One day I read an article about a man in his eighties who had a hobby of memorizing the Iliad in the original Greek. He now was starting on the Odyssey. While Greek wasn't something that I wanted very much to learn, it galvanized me into thinking that if he could memorize something as esoteric as that, I should be able to memorize piano music.

So I picked out two small one page pieces that I liked, Finlandia and America the Beautiful and started to play them over several times every day until, surprisingly enough, I actually could play them from memory! So I kept playing them every day so as not to forget and added a couple more. Since then I have learned nearly a hundred pieces of varying length and try to repeat them at least every week. As I get older, I find them slipping away but I try to go back and relearn them when necessary. I keep asking myself how much longer can I play at all? When will be the last time that I play a given piece of music? No way to tell, I guess, so one must keep pushing forward. The only alternative is to give up and that is one thing that for a long time I refused to do.

In May 1993, I ended a course in the structure and history of the piano at NMSU. After listening for a semester, I decided that the sad little piano that I was playing on was pretty poor, so on a trip to Albuquerque, we acquired a new upright Yamaha (a piano not a motorcycle!). It has added greatly to my enjoyment over the years.

T-1 (Theoretical Division) Reunion

In June 1987 I received an invitation to a reunion of the Group that I joined when I was first hired at the laboratory in Los Alamos. The original mission of this group, led by Bengt Carlson, group leader, and To. This is the key to the behavior of atom bombs and nuclear reactors. I've described the complexity of this problem earlier and in time, it led to the development of the big, multipurpose computers. It had thus been the basis for the Computer Division which during the many years that I worked there, furnished computer operations for the entire Los Alamos laboratory.

The reunion was to be held at a Twin Rivers fishing camp, where Tom Jordan, had retired with his daughter Barbara, near Antonito, Colorado. While I did not know all the old timers from the original group, I knew most of them and it was fascinating to hear their stories of the early days in the 40's, 50's and early 60's. They told of running problems that took four or more hours to run on the fastest computer then available. However, the early computer being used was liable to crash about every half hour, on average. So this meant, making a 'dump' or copy on tape of the problem data every 15 minutes so the problem could be restarted whenever the machine crashed, without losing too much time.

It was also interesting to me that most of the group, already retired or getting ready to retire, mostly wanted things like fishing cabins in the wilds. They were surprised to hear that as a recent retiree, I thought a nearby university was a necessity for retirement for classes, lectures, concerts and plays. They hadn't even thought about that but agreed that it might be a good idea.

Trips to Australia, Starting in 1987

During this period of early retirement, our daughter Barbara was fairly permanently situated over in Australia. We thought it a great idea to take advantage of her location to visit her and see something of that part of the world which we had never seen.

New Zealand

The first trip was in February 1987. We went first to New Zealand, rented a Camper-van and spent several weeks driving around the South Island. To go fishing on South Island, New Zealand, had always been a favorite dream of Larry's. To my surprise, it was a rather primitive country with huge mountains and a number of glaciers, that I have seen compared to the European Alps. We took a helicopter trip up to land on one of the glaciers and, on the return flight, they flew at low levels, tipping from one side to the other, so we could see the structure in great detail. Those glaciers were retreating even then.

One time while driving around, we crossed a small one lane bridge with railroad tracks down the middle of that single lane. Fortunately no trains came by but we had to wait for cars from the other side before we could cross. Another amusing thing happened when we stopped at a rest stop. We noticed some Kea Birds, sort of like a parrot, flying around and several were on our camper. At first we didn't think much about it but suddenly noticed that they were pulling strips of insulation out of the joints of the roof of the camper. We decided that we had better take off while it was still in one piece. Guess they were collecting nesting materials but to us it appeared a bit destructive.

One final fun activity on this trip, was a flight we took from the town of Queensland to the sea end of the Milford Sound trail. The plane was a familiar Cessna 172. Because that particular day, the sky was cloud covered, we had to fly over mountains but under the clouds. Since we started at an altitude of about 5000 ft, and the area was surrounded by mountains, to get down to sea level, we had to fly around in circles for a while. We ended up landing right on a Pacific Ocean beach and at the very end of the trail. Then after some sightseeing, the flight had to be repeated in reverse to go back up to Queensland. It was exciting if a bit scary.

Australia for the First Time

After leaving New Zealand and all it's huge fields of sheep, we flew to Sidney, Australia, where we joined Barbara for a few days and the spent a long weekend with her driving around Tasmania. As many people don't know, while part of Australia, Tasmania is a large separate island off the southern coast of the country. Here we visited several sites where some of the early convicts from England spent their first years over there. The cells were made of concrete, mostly windowless, very small and unheated. In a chilly climate, it must have been a very unpleasant experience. One place along the road, we visited a small corral enclosing a group of the nasty marsupial, the Tasmanian Devil. And they are just as nasty looking as described and the name seems to fit them well. More beautiful and pleasant were the big flocks of Black Swans on the rivers in Tasmania. This is truly the end of the world with some very strange jungles.

Back in Australia, we took a trip to a winery at a ranch on the edge of the jungle where grapes were being grown. The rooms where we stayed were in a large old ranch house surrounded on all four sides by verandahs, or what we might call porches, with the room doors opening onto these verandahs. We were also warned to keep the doors to our rooms closed because there were many tame kangaroos around and they thought that human beds were a great place to take a nap and would move in if you left your door open. It would be very strange to come to your room and find a kangaroo on your bed!

March 1989, Second Trip to Australia

This trip started off to be a three week Elder Hostel Trip and we hoped to visit Barb briefly at the end of the trip. The first week was on Heron Island which is the largest island in the Great Barrier Reef. The University of Queensland has an installation there doing research on the Reef and it's inhabitants. There had recently been a typhoon, which in the Pacific, is what they call a storm equivalent to a hurricane in the Atlantic. The sea had been stirred up so was full of suspended sand and not much could be seen underwater which was disappointing. We had looked forward both to snorkeling and to taking a glass bottomed boat out for underwater viewing but it was not to be. However, the weather was pleasant, the food good and the company enjoyable.

Accident on the Great Barrier Reef

The last day that we were there, Larry was walking along a path and fell tearing the quadriceps tendon loose from his knee cap. Someone picked him up and got him into the main building, but he was almost completely unable to walk. He was flown by helicopter to Sidney where he was put in the hospital for surgery to reattach the quadriceps. From my point of view, the worst part was that I had never driven on the left side of the road as they do in England and Australia. I had assumed that if any driving was done, it would be Larry who would do it since he had experience with it. But there was no choice Barbara had a small car and gave me some lessons in driving on the wrong side and then lent me the car to go visit Larry in the hospital. I was amazed that she trusted me.

When at the end of his stay in hospital, I went to pick Larry up, the trip that had taken Barb an hour from her house to the hospital, took me two and a half hours! First of all at best, I was terrified of driving on the wrong side of the road. Next, Sidney traffic is awesome with narrow and winding roads around the various inlets. Since they don't have one large map for the city, but have a book of maps with a page for each section. I kept getting lost and when I would go off the edge of one page, I had to find a side street on which to pull over and find the next page, decide where I was and where to go next. I'm sure Larry breathed a huge sigh of relief when I showed up an hour and a half late. He was in a cast now so I still had to drive but at least he could navigate and follow the maps for me so we made a little better time.

Fortunately, for us during the next two weeks, Barb was staying with a friend named John Allen who had a very nice house in a suburb of Sidney. The one disadvantage was that the house was built on a slope so was on three levels which made it hard for Larry to get up and down on his crutches, but he managed.

A Canceled Trip

The next disaster occurred as a result of the managers of the Elder Hostel trip trying to help us out by canceling the rest of our flights for the trip. Well, this was fine for the flights within Australia. What they didn't realize was that we had made our own reservations for the overseas flights, not they, and we had made a connecting flight in Los Angeles and arranged for pickup in El Paso for the drive to Las Cruces. We had originally planned to stay on with Barb after the trip was over so were still assuming that our overseas flight was as originally planned. Not realizing all this, they had canceled our overseas flight along with everything else. So when, luckily, I called a few days early to confirm our overseas reservations, we didn't have any! And furthermore the flights were full and we would need special accommodations because of Larry's cast. After much complaining and pounding on the table, arrangements were finally made but we had a few black days wondering if we would ever get home at all.

When the original trip ended in Sidney, they held a farewell dinner. We were able to attend this dinner, and say goodbye to the other members of the trip who had gone on for the remaining two weeks of the Elderhostel Trip. One thing that made me feel somewhat better, was that, all the other members agreed that we had seen the best part of the trip on Heron Island. The other sites had not been anywhere near as interesting or the accommodations as pleasant. However they would have been better than a hospital or the terror of driving around Sidney on the wrong side. The return flights were difficult at best but we made it with wheel chairs for Larry in the airports.

Home Again

After returning that Summer of 1989, Tom brought his new fiancee home to meet his parents. And we found her a very charming person. We also were pleased to hear that our daughter Betty, who was then up in Los Alamos, had recently gotten a new job in Larry's old group and would be working with many of his old friends.

In September, daughter Peggy gave birth to Erik William (9/26/89) and we went out to help take care of two year old Susan. The main thing that I remember is trying to soothe Susan who cried and cried. She just couldn't understand why her Mom couldn't be there to tuck her into bed. Somehow Grandma wasn't quite the same, although I tried.

Chapter 22

Other Great Retirement Trips 1987-95

O ver the years we have taken a number of different kinds of trips. I have no desire to take any of them again but they were great fun at the time and I have very strong memories of some in particular. One of the most impressive was to Kenya in Africa.

Trip to Kenya

Close to the beginning of this period in February 1990, we took one of the most memorable trips, a commercial one to Kenya, Africa. While it was advertised as sponsored by the American Chemical Society, since there was only one other Chemist and one Physicist, I guess they filled out with lawyers, military, business men and what have you. At first we were to go via Frankfurt so we considered a side trip to Karlsruhe in Germany to visit some of our friends from the year in Germany. But the stopover was changed to Rome so that didn't work out. After our flight to Rome and spent a night in a hotel there, in the morning we took off for Nairobi, the capital of Kenya. After another night in a hotel in Nairobi, we were bussed to a park in the southern part of Kenya where the Mountain

Kilimanjaro was looming just across the border. There for the first time, we saw hippos, elephants. giraffes, and so forth wandering around freely. Somehow that's what you expect in a zoo and not out in the open. Surprisingly enough, the animals didn't seem to pay much attention to us. All the vegetation was of course equally strange to us. Amazing how even the trees grow differently over there.

After a few days, we moved on to the most interesting park of all. Here we were taken to see a Masai village nearby, a really primitive place where people were actually still living. The village was completely surrounded by about a 20 foot wide swath of dead thorn branches except for one opening about 10 feet across which was obviously closed up at night. When you entered through this opening there was a large open center of dried and compressed dirt. We were told that this was where they kept their cattle at night to keep them safe from predators and from wandering off and getting lost. A number of blankets had been spread in the center with necklaces, bracelets and so forth made of beads, seeds, pieces of wood and other bits of stuff. They were of course ready for us as tourists, the children sang songs for us, and encouraged us to consider their wares.

Entrance to Masai Village

Kitchen in Masai House

Views of The Masai Village in Kenya

One of the things that really impressed me was that all the children had flies walking around on their faces and arms and seemed completely oblivious of them and made no attempt to brush them off. I had seen this before on TV shows but those were mostly very sick children so I had thought they were just too feeble to brush them off. These kids, however, were quite healthy and just didn't bother to brush them off. Somewhere I heard that the flies were regarded as possibly being souls of dead relatives so you don't want to hurt them, much less kill them.

Since I don't wear jewelry, I ignored the blankets and instead looked around at the mud huts which lined the inside of the surrounding mounds of dead branches. In one hut, a woman stood in the door smiling at us and waved to me to come in, which being curious, I did. She was very obviously pregnant and didn't speak a word of English beyond 'come'. The furnishings of the hut consisted of a pile of what looked like straw in one corner where they apparently slept. In another corner was a pile of a few pots, apparently their kitchen, next to a hard packed pad of dirt. By sign language I tried to ask when her baby was due but I couldn't get that across. I also tried to ask where the baby would come and she pointed to that hard packed dirt. Sounded terrifying to me but she seemed unperturbed. I guess you're comfortable with what you know.

Another Life

Having seen the village made the incident the next day even more impressive. In the morning the tour group was being taken very early to a special place where it was possible to see many hippos up close. Not being too interested in hippos and by now being a bit tired, I decided to sleep in the next morning instead. Our accommodations consisted of little huts, each including just a small bedroom with attached bath with shower and out front a tiny porch with just one chair on it. The cabin was on the gentle slope of a hill which led down to the Serengeti Plains in the distance. The sun was shining so I decided to settle on the porch with a book and enjoy the scenery for a while. While I sat there, along came a nice looking young man and asked if he could make up our room. I of course agreed, if I wouldn't bother him sitting on the porch, which he agreed I wouldn't. A few minutes later, along the little rock path in front of the cabin a few feet away, came another young man, this time in native dress, wearing a loin cloth with another cloth around his shoulders and fastened at the waist, and with a crude hoe over his shoulder. I smiled at him and said, "Good Morning". He looked fussed, said nothing and kept on walking. Behind me the young man working in the room said

"He is Masai. He does not speak English".

I said "Oh, but what about you, Aren't you Masai too?"

He said "Yes I am, but the missionaries 'took' me when I was small and taught me English. I also speak French and Italian.". This last was said very proudly.

I said "Do you still live in the village then?" And he said "No, I cannot go back."

(He didn't say why but seemed to assume that it was obvious.)

I said "Well then where do you live?"

He continued to tell me that he has a wife and children in Nairobi whom he sees periodically. They can't be with him where he works. I asked more questions like what group of missionaries had 'taken him' and he didn't know. He thought they might be from Italy but wasn't sure. I asked if he ever saw his parents and he said yes but he reiterated that he couldn't go back and live there. It was a fascinating glimpse into what their lives are like in living between two worlds.

While this conversation was going on, the second young man in native clothes had walked on about 20 feet and then started to hoe weeds around a number of little trees or bushes that had been planted across from the huts. As he worked he started to sing one of the most beautiful and unusual songs that I have ever heard, singing two separate notes at the same time and in harmony! It was really spectacular and I asked the first young man to tell him that I thought his song beautiful. They exchanged a few words and that was essentially the end of the incident as the cleaner took off shortly thereafter and I went back to my book, just enjoying the singing.

Balloons over the Serengeti

Another very enjoyable experience was a morning balloon ride over the Serengeti. We were taken to the launch site at about 6:00 AM. The baskets were on their side on the ground. There was room in each basket with a divider down the center for about six passengers and a pilot Several of us crawled into one side and several in the other, The pilot ignited the heater which furnished hot air to the balloon. The bag began to expand and rise up eventually tipping the basket up so we were standing erect instead of lying on our sides as before. As he continued to feed heat to the balloon, eventually it began to rise up and we were off and out over the plains. It was not the best time to go since the huge herds that you see pictured were not there at that time. From time to time however, we would see small groups of elephants, giraffes or other animals, but we were pretty high up to see much detail. Furthermore, they told us that they couldn't go any closer since the balloons frightened the animals and that was against the rules. But it was still a spectacular view, partly because it was just at sunrise with a glorious sky.

After about an hour or so of flying, the balloon was headed for a field where several vehicles were parked and down we came to be served an elegant breakfast laid out on blankets over tall grass. While I'm not much for champagne breakfasts under most circumstances, it was unusual to be served out on the Serengeti plain. Particularly if you happen to like Champagne, which I don't.

Larry by Balloon ready
to Soar over Serengeti

Animal Rescue
Park Friend

Balloon
Ready
to Board

Another interesting place that we visited was an animal rescue park that was maintained by Kenya for animals that had been hurt and had been rescued but couldn't live independently. One shown in a picture was a huge tortoise with me seated on his back. When I first saw the tortoise, the keeper was seated on him and they seemed to be having a 'chat'. He waved me over to try it out so I did and the animal seemed very friendly when I patted him and didn't seem to have minded being sat on.

The trip continued in this fashion through several other camps which had originally served as bases for big game hunting, largely by British, Europeans, and Americans. In our more ecologically oriented times hunting has now been discontinued and the camps serve only for camera safaris like ours. One park was particularly set up for viewing at night when animals came to drink at a nearby stream. Another had several big peacocks on the lawn who seemed to enjoy spreading their fantastic tails for the peahens and making ungodly noises. Finally they flew us back to Rome and on home.

Amboselli Park
Accommodations

Bouganvillia
at Mt Kenya Park

ACS Meeting in Washington DC

In August of that year (1990), we went to an American Chemical Society (ACS) meeting in Washington DC to commemorate the 50th anniversary of the Manhattan Project. Many old friends were also there and we enjoyed visiting with them. Glenn Seaborg, the

Nobel Prize winner for his discovery of Plutonium, and Richard Rhodes, who had written the History of the the Atom Bomb Project, both gave talks about the old days. We also visited my sister Dottie and her husband Bob Carter who lived near by in Bethesda, MD. After the meeting was over, we drove on up the Atlantic coast to visit my sister Kitty and her husband Bob Kallal on the shore near Wilmington, DE and then on up to Poughkeepsie, NY to visit Larry's sister Tim Asprey who was a professor of Mathematics and Computer Science at Vassar College.

After a few weeks back home, in October, we went out to San Diego to spend some time with our daughter Peggy on the Pacific Beach and to enjoy the grandchildren, Susan and Erik. We think it very important to visit grandchildren often so they don't forget us. Besides it's fun!

Finishing Up our 1946 Side Tracked Trip to California, 1991

Bill and Sue had a 'new' (to them) house in Magdalena, NM, and Tom and Carol had planted thousands of bulbs and many Rose Bushes up in Boulder,CO. In April 1991, we just had to go see all the excitement in both establishments along the way. After both visits and leaving Boulder we turned west and set out to finish that trip through the Rocky Mountains that we had missed so long ago in the Spring of 1946 (Chapter 10) when our car broke down. The rebuilt motor that had been put in to the car in Colorado couldn't take the steep hills. I'm sure many things have changed in the intervening years but it is still a spectacular trip driving through the Rocky Mountains. We visited Pete and Cindy in Manteca, CA, to see what they had been doing to their house and then went on to Los Altos to visit Peggy and her family. Finally we rounded out the trip by driving down the California coast on Highway One, which we had never done before. It's a slow trip on a narrow, winding road, so not one to take in a hurry. But it is beautiful with the ocean in view most of the way and wild hills on the left. After getting somewhat lost at the end, we found UC Santa Barbara for a brief visit with our grandson David Asprey who was finishing his first year of college. Then we went on down to Highway 10 and back east to Las Cruces.

Self Massage

One of the things that, as I remember, I discovered on this trip and expanded later, was the benefits of "self massage". My left hip had been hurting badly and I didn't know why. One night, lying in bed, I thought to myself, 'if I took a felt tip pen I could draw a circle around the area that hurts. Maybe then I could show it to a Doctor and he could tell me what is wrong.' So I started to poke around the edges of the area to try to outline the edge. I rubbed and rubbed around the edges but it was hard to find the edge because it seemed to move around somewhat. I soon fell asleep.

The next night I tried to find the edges again and realized that the area hurting was somewhat smaller so I rubbed some more. The next night the area hurting was even smaller so this time I massaged it all and it hurt less and less. The next night to my surprise, I could hardly find any sore spots at all! So I started on my right hip and found there was also a small sore area there which was small enough that I hadn't even recognized it as sore. As I massaged, it also began to feel better. I continued like this and worked on massaging my lower legs which also felt better after the treatment. Just what was happening, I don't know. Maybe the rubbing just stimulates the blood flow to the area or helps loosen up the lymph nodes which I have read, are all over the body, but have no mechanism for pumping like the blood vessels do. They just have one-way valves which trap the fluid and only let it flow up. And as we get older these valves tend to leak. So maybe that's the answer. I only know that my legs felt much better after a good massage. And I've found since that it works on my face, arms, and the rest of my body. I like to do it in the morning before I get out of bed. After massaging for a while I couldn't find any sore spots at all no matter how I searched. Later on these sore spots do come back but are easily dispelled with more massage. Don't know why no one ever told me about this. Maybe my readers can find it useful.

Call to Duty

In December 1991, just before Christmas I received a call to Jury Duty. I was excused temporarily for a long planned family reunion in January with my six living sisters in San Destin, FL, near Pensacola which is described below. Afterwards I was to be on call for four months. During the time that I was on call, the judges seemed more rational and considerate than I had expected. It was a first for me. Larry had been called four times and I was beginning to think they were discriminating against me as a woman. It turned out that I only ended up sitting on one rather boring case about injury on a job. They had picked 13 jurors, including an alternate in case someone got sick. Well I turned out to be the alternate so was dismissed early. In a way it was a strange feeling, almost like someone taking a book away before I got to the end.

A lady from the defendant's table followed me out and asked if she could ask me some questions, which of course I could do now that I was off the case. Earlier we couldn't talk to anyone about it but now she was interested in what I thought about the case and if I had suggestions of how to make the presentations better. Of course I did have ideas and gave her my opinions. Mainly I thought that they could do a better job by giving the jury a general overview of what the case was all about at the very beginning. At first we hardly knew what they were talking about. Despite a general dislike of lawyers, I was impressed both with her attitude and the defendant's lawyers in general. I had no more calls or they were dismissed so that was the full extent of my jury duty.

San Destin Family Reunion in January 1992

This was one of our better family reunions. It was right on the beach of the Gulf of Mexico. We even went sailing in the Gulf when Sal and Al rented a sail boat and took us out on the Gulf one afternoon. As usual, there was bridge and lots of happy talking.

One of the unusual activities this time, each sister had been assigned in advance to write up her memories of different periods in the family history. As the oldest, I was assigned the 1920's; Kit was assigned the first half of the 1930's and Dot the last half. Lydia was assigned the first half of the 1940's and Sally the last half. Finally Rose was assigned the first half of the 1950's and Sue the last half. Not everyone actually wrote up her assignment but those who did, read the results. Those who hadn't just talked generally off the top of their heads of what they remembered of the assigned period. In addition, each sister was to write up the story of how she and her husband met and married. Kitty's husband, Bob Kallal, recorded all this on tape and actually had the courage to transcribe all of it. He says that we all talk at once and it was often hard to tell who was saying what. It still made a pretty good story when he got through with it and sent us each a copy of the transcript. And, of course, we all got copies of what had actually been written up by some sisters. So it's quite a record of the family history and I have used much of it in writing this book. Thanks to all for the help. It was great fun seeing what each one remembered out of our joint past and also how much some had forgotten. It will be interesting to see how many have corrections, additions and suggestions for this book when they get around to reading it if they ever do. It would be fun to have a reunion to talk about that but since Dottie died and it's harder to travel since we are older, it probably won't happen.

Barbara in Australia

After Barb and David Pettus were married in our home in Las Cruces in January 1992, they went back to Australia to finish up some business. They also wanted to take advantage of the health insurance they had there to have the baby which was coming soon. I offered to come over to help out, when Barb was going to have the baby in Australia, Larry had been over often enough that he didn't really want to go. So I went by myself and it was quite an adventure. Not only is it a long trip to Sidney (about 17 air hours), but there is an additional hour flight from Sidney to Adelaide. When I arrived and David picked me up at the airport in Adelaide, after nearly 24 hours traveling, he told me that Barb was already in the hospital and the baby was on the way. We immediately went to the hospital and Samantha arrived promptly on May 24, 1992 in Adelaide! A nurse-midwife very successfully delivered the baby. A doctor came in briefly to take a few stitches where Mom tore, but that was all she had to do. I was very impressed with the care she received. Hope Sammy is as prompt all her life!

The couple came back to the US (about August 1) after the birth to look for jobs in this country. We enjoyed having them stay with us for about five months while job hunting by long distance. It gave us a chance to get acquainted with their lovely little baby girl, Sammy. Up to this point, I thought that I was the prime bridge addict in the family. But when they stayed with us for those five months I found that David Pettus can beat me in enthusiasm for bridge, even if he didn't always win at the table not that anyone always wins. In January, not having found jobs while staying in Las Cruces, they decided that they would do better on the spot and moved to Atlanta, GA, where very soon both were employed.

Some More Activities

In September 1991, I was asked to volunteer to teach something about Nuclear Engineering to beginning engineering students. The Professor, Eldon Steelman, who taught an orientation class for all beginning engineering students, first gave them information about use of the library, where to get help with problems in classes and things like that. Then he divided them up into groups of about eight to ten. To each group he assigned a volunteer like me to conduct a six week problem course in the volunteer's specialty. There were about ten of these volunteers and during the six weeks, we were to have the students pick a problem in our field and find a possible solution. Then the students were to make a presentation of the problem solution to the rest of the whole original group. Not that any of them were very serious entries.

Because Nuclear Engineering is so complex and not too generally known, I had insisted that I be given students who had at least some background in Chemistry or they wouldn't be able to understand at all what I was talking about. At the beginning, I spent several periods giving them a general introduction to what Nuclear Engineering is all about. Most years, the students proposed to design a space nuclear reactor, although nothing that would really work of course. One year the group was more interested in medical applications so we went more into isotopes and radioactivity I enjoyed the time with the students and hope they learned a little something too. One year after the first meeting, one of the girls came up to me after class and asked "who is Pete Asprey to you?" and I said, "My son, why?" Her response was a real surprise, "He's my Uncle." It seems that her name was Tara Davenport and she was the daughter of one of Cindy's sisters and was majoring in Civil Engineering. What a surprise for both of us.

At about this same time, Larry, who was also taking courses, began to get interested in Biochemistry and through some of his courses, he started working with Champa Gopalan in the Plant Genetics Engineering Laboratory (PGEL) at the University. How useful he was I don't know, but they seemed to enjoy having him there as a volunteer. They called him the 'Oldest Post dock' ever. Champa and her husband Amahdu Gopalan, who was over in the Chemistry Department, became good friends to us.

Cruise to Alaska

In July 1992, we took a cruise through the Inland Passage along the coast of Canada up to Juneau, Alaska. We drove up to Vancouver from where the cruise was to depart and did some visiting with friends on the way up. This would all have been very pleasant, except that Larry got an infected knee, diagnosed as an impacted hematoma, on the way up. As a result he couldn't walk much and, since he was on antibiotics, which upset his stomach, couldn't eat much either. So it was disappointing in a way although I did some sightseeing on my own including a small plane trip to land on a glacier. It rather spoils the fun of a cruise if you can neither walk nor eat.

Trip to Belize

In March 1993, we went with Bob and Jojo to Lands End, Belize, to see what they had been up to there and what that part of Central America is like. It was a part of the world that we had never visited before. Larry did some of the most spectacular fishing that he ever did in all his life. It was nothing to eat because they were all thrown back but it was just the fun and excitement of catching them. I understand that it was called 'bone fishing'. Since at the time, it was still associated with Great Britain, some British Military were doing some sea rescue training from helicopters off our beach which to me was great fun to watch. Later when they finished their training exercises, some of the men came into the bar for drinks where I was playing the local piano. That also made some fun for me.

Gardening, Compost Queen

Another activity that for a long time kept me busy several mornings a week is our half acre yard and garden. Since it's getting more difficult for me now to do the heavy work, I am trying to hire as much help as I can. For a long time I had a student, Erik Weaver, from NMSU who did an excellent job of helping me. He seemed to enjoy it too and we had fun working together, battling the weeds, bugs and so forth. Two years ago, he and his wife Lindsey and baby Esau went back to Indiana where their parents live and now have jobs. I miss them but have been fortunate to have found an excellent replacement. Jesus Carrasco is in his late forties and after having had a brain aneurysm, cant work full time. He is on partial disability but still needs some work to survive. In many ways he is as good as Erik but in different ways. I also enjoy working with him.

Several years ago, Larry made some chemical tests of our soils and as expected in the Western part of the US, it has a very high pH, but even worse than expected. This may explain some of our trouble growing things. Plants can be picky about soil and pH is one of the most important conditions. We keep adding sulfur to lower the pH and make and use as much compost as we can. In fact, composting everything in sight has been one of my main approaches, including all weeds, all trimmings and scraps from the kitchen and as many leaves as I can collect. For a long time, I was taking all the leaves from neighbors on two sides and adding them to my piles. One year Larry gave me a shredding machine for my birthday and I shred and compost all sticks, branches and pine cones that we collect. One of my friends, Helga Delisle, when I was showing off my composting system laughed at me and called me the "Compost Queen".

In September 1994, we had a new irrigation well drilled on our property. Since we are not too far from the Rio Grande, we only had to go down about 30 feet to reach water. It was getting hard to maintain our large garden using house water, so we decided that this would be a good investment, which it has indeed turned out to be. The 30 feet to find water for the well as compared to the house water which is from 600 feet. This helps keep the garden growing and is probably better for the environment to use the slightly subsurface water than from the deep aquifer.

Chapter 23

Rest of Retirement, 1995-07

W hile many good things happened in this period, unfortunately many bad things also happened as they did to the country as a whole. For example the Stock market disaster of March 2000 caused much pain and loss to many people including some of our children. And no one will ever forget the attack on 9/11 when the twin towers in New York fell and a jet plane crashed into the Pentagon near Washington, DC. All this was done by and bragged about by Islamic radicals from Saudi Arabia via Afghanistan. I find this far more upsetting than either Pearl Harbor or dropping Atom Bombs on Japan, bad as they were. At least the Japanese were trying to take over a large part of the world and we were trying to stop them, which at least seems rather rational. However I don't believe that any war really solves anything in the long run. In the case of the Jihadists, they seem crazed by their religious ideas and just seem to want to kill everyone who doesn't agree with them. We will live with the results of this disaster for many years. One of the worst results now is the ongoing Iraq War. Surely they can end it soon. For Larry and me, despite these disasters, our life went on fairly calmly although our children suffered some personal disasters.

In 2002 when my 81st birthday came, my five year old granddaughter, Mimi, asked me how old I was going to be on my birthday. I started to say 81 and then laughed and said that I was going to be one and start over again. Her eyes grew big and she shook her head and said "You can't do that Gramma". We all laughed. How I wish that there was a way to do it but I'm afraid that she is right, and I will have to settle for what time I have left.

The Good Things First

In July of 1995, the CYBEX Company, which was started by our son Bob and several of his friends, including Remigius Shattus, went public. Since Bob had given everyone in the family some stock before it did go public, that was a boost to the whole family because the value increased immensely when it was sold on the Stock Market. We were very proud of our Bob's accomplishment.

In the Fall of 1997, we were pleased to have our granddaughter, Jenna Asprey, come to stay with us for a year while she attended NMSU to obtain her Master's Degree in Business Administration. To us the most amazing thing that she did while she was here was to study for her classes while she roller bladed down the street in front of our house! She also found a place for her horse, Pistol, to stay, over in Mesilla where she could visit and ride him. He seemed a rather unusual pet for a young girl like her.

In September 1998, we enjoyed a great trip with Pete and Cindy up to Canada where we rode the railroad starting at Vancouver and then across the Canadian Rockies. We went on the train as far as Calgary where we rented a van and explored further up the Canadian Rockies on our own. That part of the Rockies is really spectacular and one that I had always wanted to see. It was a great and memorable trip.

Playing Games

It's very interesting how much children born of the same parents and raised in the same family can have such different tastes. As an example, most of our children like to play board and card games but a few don't much. Some of our children-in-law like such games and some don't. It really surprises me how variable it is and how very determined they are with what they like and what they don't. Sometimes it can be changed but more often not. One success we had was with our middle son Bob. He never liked to play contract bridge, which Larry and I have always loved, and he didn't even particularly want to learn. His wife, Jojo, had played a little and enjoyed it but wanted to learn more.

Solar Eclipse Cruise

One time I read an article about what fun a cruise to observe a Solar Eclipse at sea could be. One day when Bob and Jo were around, I said that I would love to go on one and had found one that was just right. However, I didn't think Larry and I could go alone. They thought it was a great idea, agreed to go with us and even agreed to spend some time playing contract bridge with us and Bob would agree to learn the basics. The cruise was to depart from Miami, go through the Panama Canal and then out over the Pacific Ocean to find the best spot for totality of the eclipse. There were nearly 100 professional and amateur astronomers on board and many gave lectures on related topics. In particular around 80 were from Germany so the shipboard announcements were all made in German as well as English. There were even meteorologists who helped to pick the right spot for observing where the weather would be the best and the sun wouldn't be obscured by clouds.

On the actual day of the eclipse, there were dozens of telescopes all over the deck waiting for the big moment. It was indeed spectacular and we were much impressed even if we didn't have a telescope. And we didn't, as the article which started us on the trip had said, see any Dolphins doing back flips. However, I'm sure that such intelligent animals were very relieved when the sun came back. It must be really shocking for them to have the sun disappear in the middle of the day without any warning. We were also surprised by the number of eclipse 'addicts there were on the ship. Some said that they hadn't missed one at sea in years.

After the eclipse, we came up the west coast of Mexico ending at Los Angeles. It was a very memorable trip and Bob and Jojo became almost as avid bridge players as we were. So whenever they could find time, we then had partners for a bridge game. Both Larry and I were always ready for a game. In addition, when I can find someone who likes to play, I enjoy playing 'Upwords', a 3-dimensional game similar to 'Scrabble' but I think is much more fun and only needs two or three players. Jo and I had played on the cruise and were watched by many curious observers who had never seen the game before.

Political Activities

A few years after retiring, in 1992, I became very upset about what was going on politically and became active in the local Democratic Party. I was even elected Treasurer for two years. Later I decided that I didn't feel capable of driving at night so couldn't attend the Executive Committee meetings as was required of the Treasurer. Instead I continued to help the Treasurers elected later, by keeping books, paying bills, filing reports and answering the phone for one morning a week at the Headquarters as my contribution. I did this for four years in addition to attending many local meetings and thus meeting many candidates in person. After watching how difficult running for office is, I have come to have a lot of respect for those who do. These candidates work very hard, with the best of intentions, and then may end up half the time, enduring the pain of losing. At least I got to know many of the local politicians and believe that I know something about the people that I vote for. Contrary to most people's opinion of all politicians being crooked, I find that most of the locals are good and honorable people. This may not be so true at the upper levels but it seems to be locally here. We ask a lot of them to run our government. The fact is that Democracy is a great idea but not an easy one to implement.

Started Writing

In the Fall of 2003, along with a great course in biochemistry, I took a course in 'Writing Your Life Story' from Dee Davis, at the local Branch College. I got started writing this book and found writing to be kind of fun. For a while after the course ended, three or four people from the class met weekly and read and critiqued what we had recently written. This lasted for about a year but I have continued by myself since then resulting in this book.

60th Wedding Anniversary

In 2004, close to end of this period, Larry and I celebrated our 60th Wedding Anniversary. In addition to a private celebration in May, when we had actually been married for 60 years, we celebrated more formally over the 4th of July so that many of our family members could come. Even three of my sisters, Sal, Rose and Sue, who had actually been there for our wedding, were able to come. Somehow, I thought at the time that we would be celebrating many more such anniversaries but it was not to be. When I get depressed about the present, I think about that wonderful celebration.

Currently (in 2007) I'm still writing but am also taking a course called "Crime, Justice and Society". and have learned so many things that I had not known about the police, courts and prisons. So much to learn and so little time to learn it. But along with the course and my writing, in addition I'm working my way thru a text reviewing BioChemistry. I still manage to satisfy two of my passions, learning and writing. Whenever he calls me, Pete comes over and plays his guitar with me playing the piano. So I satisfy this other passion.

My Sister Dottie Dies

Finally a Williams family tragedy occurred in December of 2000 when my sister Dottie (Dorothy Carter) died. About a year earlier, she suddenly had a violent nose bleed. After X-rays and other tests, it was found that she had a brain tumor but in a location where they couldn't operate. Her husband Bob Carter was very wonderful with her but things were very difficult for both of them during the year before she died. Kitty and I had gone to visit them the previous May during that year. It was obvious then that she was in pretty bad shape and had to be helped to the bathroom and given baths, which we tried to help with. We even took her out to dinner in her wheelchair one time but she couldn't even feed herself much less talk much. She lived for the rest of the year, but finally died on Christmas Day.

I went back to Bethesda, MD, for her funeral which was very beautiful if sad. Being the week after Christmas, the church was still decorated with banks of Christmas Poinsettias. The readings were given by several of her eleven children. Some of he Carter children claimed that she was so organized that she would have planned it that way. To die right at Christmas when many of her children would have planned to come for Christmas anyway just seemed like something she would do. Over the years she certainly must have been well organized to raise eleven children and work part of the time teaching high school Physics. She has certainly left her Husband a large legacy with all those successful and attentive children.

Pete retires from Sandia

Pete retired from Sandia, Livermore, in January 2005, and, they have sold the new house they had put together after the flood. They then bought an RV which they drove to Las Cruces in time to be here for Larry's last few months and during the period when he died so were a big help to me. The following Summer, they drove up to Alaska to see how they liked living in that part of the world over the winter. I went up with my son Tom and his wife Carol to visit them for a few days around March 1, 2006 to see what that part of the world looks like. After visiting Pete and Cindy, Tom, Carol and I went with a tour group to view the Northern Lights. They were interesting to see but unfortunately not very spectacular while we were there. Pete and Cindy have since come to Las Cruces to live for a while. Their children, David and Jenna, bought a rental house for them and they have settled down for the time being. It has been wonderful having them here. It was also fortunate for them that they did settle in because since then Pete has had a heart attack which resulted in bypass surgery from which he is still recovering. They first tried to put in a stent but the blockage was too severe. Had this happened while they were still on the road in the RV it would have been an even worse disaster.

Chapter 24

Losing My Friend and Center, March 6, 2005

On March 1, 2005 the telephone rang and Larry was calling from Mountainview Hospital. He said, "Marge, come here right now. I need you. It's very important." Well I didn't know how important it was, but if he wanted me, I would as always go as soon as possible. He has been the center of my life for 61 years and as long as he needs me I'll be there if I'm able.

The End After 61 Years

This was the beginning of the end of what had apparently started about a year earlier. Along in the Spring of 2004, Larry began to lose weight—not intentionally—it just seemed to go off without limit. Actually, I think he was happy to lose some weight at first. For some years he had seemed to get weaker but not in any specific way that we could identify. His legs didn't have much sensation and walking became more difficult. The doctors didn't seem too worried about his weight loss but I was, not that I had any idea what to do about it. He had always seemed better during the Summer because then he could spend some time exercising in our pool which he dearly loved.

The rest of the year he didn't do much in the way of exercise. In May 2004, we had celebrated our 60th wedding anniversary and over the following 4th of July the family gathered, including a couple of my sisters, for a belated celebration with us as described in Chapter 23. It was a wonderful day and one that I will remember as long as I have memory. That Summer Larry had seemed more energetic.

That September Larry also began to get worried about his weight loss and finally his regular doctor began to suspect that his kidneys were failing and sent him to a kidney specialist. She agreed with this diagnosis, officially 'Autosomal Renal Attack'. Her suggestion was that they try strong doses of a steroid, prednisone, starting on 15 November, to shut down his immune system, which was damaging his kidneys. The hope was that when the prednisone doses were gradually decreased, the kidneys would gradually return to functioning. She said the second or third week would probably be the worst.

So we celebrated Thanksgiving with as many children as were here. At dinner one night about a week before the holiday, Larry had said something about 'did we have to have turkey' which he really didn't like very much. I said 'what would you like, dear?'. He said that he would much prefer leg of lamb which was his favorite. So we voted and almost everyone there agreed that they too liked leg of lamb better than turkey. So we had a rather unique Thanksgiving Day dinner in his honor at which a large roast leg of lamb was the star attraction. Being perennial optimists, we rather thought when Larry started on prednisone it would just be a matter of weeks and he would be back to himself.

The Disaster Begins

The last week that November, we had agreed to rent a guest bedroom in our house, as of the first of December, to a young Canadian, Steven Vanstone (better known to us as Van or Vanner), who at the time was working at the airport but staying with our son Bob and his wife Jojo. There was a mixup at the airport about fuel and Van lost his job on the last day of November but as planned he moved in with us on December 1st. That very evening, Larry had a fall and dislocated his shoulder. Vanner was there to pick him up (I couldn't have) and took him to the emergency room at the hospital to get his shoulder back in it's socket. By this time Larry had begun to realize that he needed more help than I was able to give him, so hired Van on the spot as a live in aid. And were we lucky in the coming months to have him!

Things were bad enough by now that in the first week of December, I sent an e-mail letter to all our children to warn them that this Christmas was not going to be like others. We had always welcomed any and all children along with their families to come for all holidays. We loved to have them all stay as long as possible even if they had to sleep in sleeping bags on the floor. But this time it would be different. A copy of the e-mail is in the footnote[15]. Bob

---

[15] Dear Kids: With xmas bearing down on us so fast, I need to bring you up to date on the situation here. As you know Dad has autoimmune kidney disease with the threat of kidney failure and dialysis hanging over him. The medication that they are giving him is heavy doses of prednisone to knock out his immune system temporarily. And then gradually, in a few months, decrease the dose, let the immune system come back up in hope his kidneys will no longer be attacked. He started the medication on November 11 so is now into his 4th week. The doctors say the 2nd week is the worst and it was pretty bad. Furthermore it doesn't seem to be getting any better. To add to our miseries, the week before Thanksgiving, I developed a bad attack of tendonitis in my left wrist which, while better, is still pretty useless. Then on the 1st of December, Dad had a fall which dislocated his left shoulder. A trip to the emergency room got the bone back into it's socket and into a support splint but he can't use the arm and needs help with everything. The only wonderful bonus is that Steve Vonstone (Vanner), our new helper had just moved in so was here to pick him up and take him to the hospital. Along with Larry's worries about unexpected infections, while his immune system is inactive, he's afraid to have people around, particularly children and dogs,

and Jojo agreed to host the family gift exchange in their house on the west mesa, to which I would come but Larry would not be able to. Despite everything, the holiday was fairly successful with most of the kids coming for short visits and staying in motels, despite my discouraging letter.

In January the decrease in prednisone began but it was soon fairly obvious that Larry's kidneys were not recovering and furthermore his shoulder was not getting better either.

However things rocked on and we kept hoping against hope. We were fortunate that Pete and Cindy had come in January in their RV and settled into a nearby campground so were there to help out with Larry's ongoing problems. We tried to do everything that we could to help Larry function as best that he could. In the morning I would help him get dressed, including putting on his shirt because he couldn't use his arm and putting on the shoes and socks that he couldn't reach. Then he would stand up by grabbing hold of one of his dresser drawers with his good arm and walk in to breakfast using his wheeled walker.

After one disaster at 1:00 AM when everything fell off of the top of the dresser when he tried to standup, we decided something needed to be done. I had to crawl around on the floor in the cold, collecting odds and ends before it was safe for him to walk to the bathroom. To solve that problem, our son Tom fastened the dresser

---

because the noise and confusion bothers him so much and he is so afraid of falling again.

So I guess the bottom line is that, at best xmas isn't going to be much fun here this year. Everyone is definitely going to have to stay in motels. And fortunately we have plenty of good restaurants. Visits to the house will have to be limited and we will have to keep Dad isolated as much as possible. Subject to all these restrictions, we will understand anyone who decides not to come at this time. In fact it might be better to cancel completely and have you come later in small groups. But we do love all of you and still hope we can get together, now or later, if only for a little while. Mom

to the wall so things wouldn't go sailing in the future when Larry used a dresser drawer as help in standing up before moving to his wheeled walker.

In early February, Larry decided that he wanted another opinion about what was wrong with him. He had heard good things from our son Bill about an environmental doctor up in Santa Fe so called to make an appointment. Before she would see him, she wanted a lot of information about him including copies of all the records from the doctors that he had been seeing. She also wanted a biography for him and to know everything that he had worked on over the years. An excellent idea and probably should have been done much sooner.

Chemical Research

His approach to this last question was very unusual. He dug out a chemistry book and found an appropriate copy of the familiar Periodic Chart of the Elements, and asked me to make a copy of the Chart. On this he proceeded to mark those elements that he worked on most with an A; those he put considerable work on, he marked with a B; occasional effort was marked with a C; and just a little effort with a D. When he finished, there were only about a dozen elements out of a hundred marked with a D or not marked at all. While I realized that he had spent 40 years working in Chemistry Labs, I had not realized that his efforts were spread over such a large part of the Periodic Table. It included almost all of the heavy metals and many of the radioactive elements. He also spent a lot of time on Fluorine, one of the more poisonous gases of all. Belatedly, when I saw this chart, I began to wonder if this could have anything to do with his failing kidneys. An article that I read recently stated that 70% of kidney failure in the US resulted from lead poisoning and this is only one heavy metal! He worked on dozens! By the time I realized this however, it was probably too late to do anything about it.

Well after we collected all the required information, he made an appointment in Santa Fe, but never got there. On 14 February I came down with double pneumonia which was cleared up pretty well by antibiotics. Three days later, Larry also came down with pneumonia. After two days of antibiotics, they were clearly not doing the job for him, so it was back to the hospital. After a week he was better but still pretty weak and the doctor wanted to release him to a 'rehab center' but made the mistake of calling it a 'nursing home'. On hearing this Larry went through the ceiling and would have none of it. He just wanted to go home not caring what happened. We didn't even know about this misunderstanding until later. There was more miscommunication when they told Larry what they were going to do and what he needed to do when he went home. He apparently seemed so rational and still mentally alert that he managed to fool them into thinking he understood their instructions. Either he didn't understand or didn't remember to pass on the doctor's instructions to us. So we didn't understand what was going on and when he came home on Friday, we were completely unprepared for his weakness and unable to handle his needs.

Disaster Back Home

They had him on Oxygen, which helped some, but the weekend was a complete disaster. He had several falls and since he wasn't able to help at all, it took three men to pick him up. Fortunately we had several sons around in addition to Vanner. On Monday, we had made an appointment with our regular doctor, so we didn't take him to the emergency room on Sunday night. When he was doing so poorly we probably should have taken him in that night to the emergency room. By Monday morning he was so badly off that it took three men to get him into the car and he couldn't even get out when he got to the doctor's office so the nurses immediately sent him on to the emergency room at the hospital without him even seeing the Doctor. His blood Oxygen at that point was down to 40% and he was barely breathing. Just looking at him, our oldest son Pete, who was with me at the time, and I, thought that he was dying right then.

With full Oxygen and a blood transfusion, they pulled him back from the brink but his kidneys were down to about 10% operation and his lungs were filling up from the fluid not filtered by them. In addition to the fluid, his pneumonia had now become chronic so his lungs just didn't have a chance. The only remaining solution was a feeding tube and dialysis[16] until his kidneys could do their job again, if ever. So for a week he had dialysis every other day and was put on a renal failure diet which he did not like at all so he just didn't eat anything. It was supposed to be easier on his kidneys but not eating at all certainly didn't help him recover. Among other things, he had become so weak that he couldn't even hold up a book to read which was for him a complete disaster.

Rejecting Dialysis and Coming Home to Die

So this was the situation when I received the fateful call described at the beginning of this chapter. When Pete and I went over that morning at 8:30 AM, he told us that he had spent much time during the night thinking about these procedures (which he had tried for a week) and he had decided that he didn't want them any more. He had said as much on the disastrous weekend that he had spent at home when he said, "Why can't I just die and get it over with?" We had said then, "Oh no don't give up yet. Let's try for a

---

[16] dialysis is the procedure that cleans the blood in place of nonfunctional kidneys by drawing out all of the blood; removing waste material and re-injecting the blood. For complete kidney failure, it takes 3 to 4 hours a day for 3 to 4 days a week.

while yet." Now it was different, he was very positive and wanted no more dialysis. He could not stand the special diet which he had not been eating in the hospital. Apparently he had concluded that there was nothing in life to look forward to without food and reading. He had a living will and we had had many conversations about it. He was not religious and did not want to be kept alive by extreme measures. At one point I tried to tell the doctor, 'He's an agnostic'. But he interrupted and said 'No I am an Atheist'. We all cried together and the Doctor said that she would arrange for Hospice care and he would be home by that evening. When he came home that evening, we all knew very well what that meant. He had come home to die. It was really the end.

When I came home that morning of March 1st. knowing that it meant the end, I couldn't stop crying. And of course, I had to tell the rest of his children that he was about to die so I sat down and wrote them the following e-mail:

Dear Family

This is the saddest letter that I have ever had to write but I did want all of you to know what's going on as soon and as efficiently as possible.

As all of you know Larry's kidneys have been failing ever since last September. They've tried drugs which have not worked. Finally a couple of weeks ago, first I, and then a few days later, Larry got pneumonia. Well I recovered but he didn't and ended up in the hospital for a week. Partly as a result of miscommunication he was released to home over the Doctor's objections but on oxygen. But it was not a good idea and after a number of falls and his blood oxygen through the floor he was back in the hospital. His kidney function was down to 10%. With his agreement, it was decided to put him on dialysis in the hospital with the goal of afterward going to a rehab center for a couple of weeks to get him back on his feet.

After a few days of dialysis and the appropriate diet, Larry has decided that he does not want to live like this. While for our own selfish reasons we don't like it, we recognize that he is fully aware and that it's a sensible decision under the circumstances and will try to do our best for him as long as he lasts. The doctor and hospital have to arrange for his release and contact Hospice for us but as soon as possible, late today or possibly tomorrow, he will be here at home.

So if you want to say goodbye you should probably plan to come in the next week or so because according to what the doctor says, while he might last for several weeks or more, later he will be in pain and probably largely out of touch.

If you want to call him directly he can be reached in the hospital at 505-556-7409. He is very weak and has trouble holding the phone so should not talk long, but you can try. Also I'm sure you all know about special airline arrangements for bereavement flights. Good luck.

Finally, Pete and I plan to call everyone soon after sending this but wanted to be sure everyone got all the same information at the same time in case we can't get through right away or forget to tell everyone everything.

Love you all,
Mom

While I felt somewhat better after writing the letter, I still couldn't stop crying. Van and I looked the house over to find where the best place would be to put his bed. We wanted it to be in the center so that everyone could visit him and yet be possible to isolate him and give him some privacy when needed. The only place that seemed to come close to fitting the conditions was the study. But it was hard to see how without rearranging the computer table and desks to make enough room to fit in a hospital bed. Moving out everything that we could and rearranging the things we couldn't, we managed to fix it so that when the hospital bed arrived about 5:00 PM that evening, we were ready and it fitted in better than I could have hoped.

When the ambulance brought him that evening he was installed as comfortably as possible at the center of everything. And over the next two days, all his children and most of his grandchildren arrived. And in case you think Larry was too far gone to know or care, not so! He kept asking who was here and who else was coming and when. At the children's insistence, someone stayed up with him all through the succeeding nights. They took turns in two hour shifts being with him. We all tried to do everything we could think of to make him more comfortable. I remember giving him a hug and a kiss. At first he didn't respond and then he realized that it was me and a strong response came which I will always carry with me. Most of the time he seemed to be asleep or at least dozing. We had set the bed up so he could see the TV if he wanted to watch it and a few times he did seem to enjoy a favorite program or two.

On Friday evening his great friend Champa Gopalan from PGEL (Plant Genetics Engineering Laboratory) at the University,. with her chemist husband, Amadhu, had heard how sick he was and insisted on coming to say good-bye to him. Amadhu tried to tease him and told him he was going to give him a test. But I'm not sure there was enough of Larry left to understand and respond. But it was so kind of them to come and to try.

On the last evening before he died, Bob, Tom and Bill, his three younger sons, with whom he had been working on a project were sitting with him. They started talking and thinking about the project, which they had called, 'Air Hydro'. Whether Larry could hear them or not, whether he was paying any attention, I don't know, but they thought he was. And maybe he was, as his last contribution to the project.

The Mesilla Project

In the evening of the last day of Larry's life, his son Tom started listening to his brothers Bill and Bob working on the chemical coolant project they had been working on with Larry for several years. Tom decided that as a practicing engineer he was going to "ground" them and help/force them to build a prototype so the three of them went to work. The Manhattan Project being much in everyone's conversation around that time, Peggy dubbed their new efforts "The Las Cruces Project" and took a few photos to document what could well be an important moment if their efforts proved fruitful. Later one of them suggested that "The Mesilla Project" was a better name and everyone agreed.

Never Mind

At the end it got harder and harder for Larry to express himself as he lay in the hospital bed in the study so everyone was constantly asking him "What? What do you want Dad/Larry?" Once when they had asked him to repeat himself several times, and he was clearly getting frustrated, son Tom declared that he would translate for him and what he was saying was "Never mind!". Everyone looked at Larry who nodded emphatically. Everyone laughed.

Best Dad

Towards the end of the process as Larry lay somewhat comatose, Peggy leaned over and gave him a kiss saying "You were the best Dad we could ever have had," and Larry grumbled a terse "Oh, I don't know about that!" and smiled his well-known corner smile. So Tom countered "OK, maybe you were in the top 1% of Dads", Bill chimed in "or even the top 10%". Everyone laughed. Bob topped them all with his "Well, you were definitely the ONLY Dad we ever had!" Larry smiled again and went back to sleep.

On this last night as the family had agreed that they would watch over their Dad in shifts, so the three brothers took theirs together and worked feverishly on their plans as Larry lay drifting in and out of a vague awareness. I got up around 1:40 AM to go to the bathroom and heard their voices so went in to see what was going on and they were hard at work on it. They overran their shift by a couple of hours (Peggy and Susan got to sleep on) but they arrived at a plan for a prototype and for once didn't get Larry's usual joking "It'll never work" but his breathing pattern changed and became relaxed for the first time in days as though to say "It's about time!" It was only an hour or so later that he was gone, so they figured that they must be on to something if he was willing to trust them with it and take his leave.

My Dearest Larry
As He Lives in My Memory

He Breathes His Last

At around 5:30 in the morning of Sunday, March 6, our daughter Peggy was with him and noted that he had stopped breathing so came to wake me and tell me that she thought he was gone and she was right, he was. As we had been told to do, we called the Hospice nurse and she was there within the hour. I have nothing but the highest praise for the Hospice people. It is really a remarkable program and deserves all the support we can give them. It took only four and a half days for him to die but they made it so much easier for all of us and, I think, for him too. It was the way he wanted it and the way he chose to go, at home surrounded by all his loving family, so much better than in a hospital among strangers. Fortunately for him I saw no sign that he was in pain most of the time so he didn't have to request any of the carefully monitored pain medication that had been given to us for him.

His Final Departure

After the ambulance came to remove his body which was to be sent to the medical school at the University of New Mexico, in Albuquerque and after almost continuous crying by everyone, a group of the children, sat down to write an obituary. After they roughed it out, they gave it to me to edit and add anything else that I thought of. And of course, I did think of many other things. A copy of the final result is attached at the end of the chapter.

The very next day, two of his closest friends, Bob Ryan and Gary Eller, came from where they had retired in the Pacific Northwest to say goodbye. Unfortunately they were just a day too late to see him before he died, but all of the family who was still here took them out to dinner, where we heard a lot of stories about Larry's days in the lab. And since then we have received via the internet and mail many other stories about the great and funny things that he did over the years.

Final Farewell

Our final farewell's were said two weeks later, on what would have been Dad's 86th birthday, March 19th. All children, some spouses and grandchildren, three of my sisters, neighbors and friends from Los Alamos came for a memorial of sorts. It was nothing formal or religious but it was our final goodbye to a great and wonderful person, husband and father, who was much beloved and will be missed a great deal by all. He has been the center of my life since March 6, 61 years ago when we went to my parents to tell them we were planning to be married on May 3, 1944. While they have been wonderful years, they have gone by much too fast and were certainly no where near long enough. I still can't believe that he's gone.

Somehow I always thought that he would be around as long as I was. Not a rational idea but somehow I couldn't imagine life without him. And I'm having trouble living it.

The Obituary

Dr. LARNED (Larry) BROWN ASPREY died two weeks before his 86th birthday at home in Mesilla Park, NM, early Sunday morning, March 6, 2005, surrounded by his loving wife of 60 years, Margaret (Marge) Asprey, his seven children and spouses; Pete Asprey of Livermore, Calif., Betty Asprey Strietelmeier of Los Alamos, Barbara Asprey Pettus of Conifer, Colo., Bob Asprey of Las Cruces and Huntsville, Ala., Peggy Asprey Lyon of Los Altos, Calif., Tom Asprey of Boulder, Colo., and Bill Asprey of Alamogordo and numerous grandchildren. He is also survived by a sister, Winifred Asprey of Vassar at Poughkeepsie, N.Y., and a brother Robert B. Asprey of Sarasota, Fla. Like everything else in his life, Larry did it his way. He was one of the best dads, grandpas and husbands ever.

He was born on March 19, 1919, in Sioux City, Iowa. His distinguished career began in Chicago with the Army on the Manhattan Project which developed the Atom Bomb, ending World War II. He then earned his Doctorate in chemistry at Berkeley and spent the next 35 years as a research chemist at Los Alamos National Laboratory.

There he worked on Actinide, Fluoride and Rare Earth, among many other elements. In 1981-82 he was a visiting scientist with the European Community, in Karlsruhe, Germany.

After retiring from LANL, he volunteered as an adjunct professor at New Mexico State University. Ever the scientist, he has donated his body to the University of New Mexico Medical School.

Per his request, in lieu of flowers or a memorial service, donations may be sent to the Larry Asprey Scholarship Fund at New Mexico State University, checks made out to "NMSU Foundation" and sent to: The NMSU Foundation, in memory of Larry Asprey, PO Box 3590, Las Cruces, NM 88003. The family will gather in Las Cruces later this month on what would have been his 86th birthday to remember and celebrate the life of a wonderful person.

Going on Without Him is Hard

So the major part of my life has come to an end. And for a long time after he died, I was not able to see any future for me and wanted only to die myself. But after three years, I have finally decided that whatever time is left, I will try to spend doing things for my children and grandchildren. On thinking about my grandmothers, I realize that both of them lived around thirty years after each of their husbands died in their fifties, one of cancer and one of stroke. So I should be able to go on for at least a few years. At least I will try as long as I can be of use to my children and not too much trouble. But I sincerely hope that they recognize that I feel like Larry did and do not want to cling to life when I cannot do anything.

Chapter 25

Surprising Award from ANS, June 6, 2005

The Surprise

One of the biggest surprises of my life came in early January 2005 while Larry was still alive, when I received a call from a man named Mark Reinhart. He asked "Is this the Marge Asprey who was on the American Nuclear Society (ANS) person-to-person trip to China in the mid eighties?" When I said that I was indeed. He told me that he had also been on the trip and some things that I had told him about my life during the trip had made an impression on him. He believed that I deserved an award for my work over the years. He would like to submit my name to the ANS for the Walter H Zinn award and said "Would you have any objection to that?" Well of course I had no objection. Then he told me that I would have to send him a brief biography (bio) of myself which he would then modify if necessary to satisfy their requirements, and submit it with his nomination. I had to agree that I would be at the 2005 ANS Annual meeting in June in San Diego, CA, and would be expected to give an approximately 20 minute acceptance speech. I of course agreed to all of this.

Then he told me that the award was in honor of Walter H. Zinn and had been awarded by the ANS since the mid 1950's. And he told me where to send my bio and he would send me more information later. Very excited, I told Larry about it and he was very pleased for me and agreed that we would do our best to be there. I prepared and sent my bio as instructed and then waited. Mark sent me back his slightly modified version for my approval and then submitted my name for consideration by the Operations and Power Division Committee for approval.

From late January I heard nothing more about it. Being curious, of course, I looked up Walter Zinn on the web. I had heard of him but couldn't remember much about him. Well it seemed that he and I were both at the University of Chicago in the same period on the Manhattan Project. He was a Canadian and of course was a "medium big shot" and I was just a "little shot" but we worked only a block apart. He was in charge of building the first nuclear reactor under the West Stands at the University of Chicago, with Enrico Fermi while I, at the time, was just a Chemistry Student in Kent Hall. Later I became a technician working in the Chemistry Building, Kent Hall, and still later in New Chemistry, the building built later for the Manhattan Project. So our paths had essentially crossed then. Later he was the director of the Argonne National Lab and first President of the American Nuclear Society (ANS) which I joined in the early 1970's. The award was in his honor as that first President. He was also responsible for building the first successfully operating Fast Breeder Reactor in Idaho in the early sixties. While small and only experimental, this reactor furnished all the electricity for a nearby small town for a number of years. Anyone who thinks Breeder Reactors don't work just doesn't know the facts. To say nothing about the fact that much of France's electricity comes from nuclear reactors, some of them breeders.

For my part, I worked for several years on the safety analysis of nuclear weapons and later on analysis of the Clinch River Breeder

Reactor which was planned to be built at Oak Ridge in Tennessee. It was to be a demonstration level plant, but unfortunately was later canceled during the Carter Administration. So you could say our paths had in many ways been parallel for most of our lives. The other thing that I found was that if I won, I would be only the second woman to have received this particular award, the first being Dixie Lee Ray, former head of the Department of Energy and Governor of Washington State. Rather distinguished company for little old me.

Of course, unfortunately, Larry died in early March before he had a chance to hear that I had won the award and he was no longer alive to go to San Diego, CA, with me in June. I was notified that I had won it about three weeks after Larry's death. And I suppose that it was a blessing for me in my time of loss, because it gave me something to think about and look forward to which helped to assuage my grief over my loss of Larry. Also, of course, I had to turn to and prepare my speech, which I did. Over the years, I have learned that work is the best anodyne for pain that there is.

When our children and my siblings heard about my big achievement, all children and several of my sisters, wanted very much to come to San Diego for the affair. And come they did! The meeting was held at the Town and Country Hotel, a gorgeous setting. I don't think that I have ever seen so many beautiful roses, which I love so much, in bloom at one time. It was almost as if they were celebrating with me. The luncheon of the Operations and Power Division of the ANS, which was giving the award, was held there in the Sunset Room. My sponsor, Mark Reinhart, was the Master of Ceremonies and he had brought a lot of slides from the China trip where we met and showed them as an introduction while we ate a very good lunch. My family furnished almost half of the audience but there were still a fair number of professional attendees. I've also heard since that some of my former colleagues would have been there if they had known about it at the time but it was not announced in advance. Two of my sisters, Lydia Chadwick (the engineer from Livermore) and Suzanne Hartenback (the paint chemist from St. Louis), came; along with all seven of my children with three spouses, Cindy, Jojo and Dick, also came; and finally, eight grandchildren came, David, Jenna, Samantha, Joseph, Alyssa, Susan, Erik, and Amelia.

The Luncheon and Award

Mark Reinhart introduced me and told about all the great things that he thought that I had done. My daughter Betty showed the slides for me. Then I gave my speech and it was well received and I was roundly applauded. I'm not at all sure that I deserved all the good things that were said about me, but it was nice to hear them. It's particularly great as you grow old to know that you have not been completely forgotten.

Marge & Award with Amelia & Samantha

After the award luncheon, we had also planned for those who could afford a little more time, to get together to spend the rest of the week on the shore of the Pacific Ocean at the Blue Sea Lodge. Not everyone could come of course but for those who could, we had much fun as we always do when we get together. Some of the children and grandchildren enjoyed surfing and we (even I!) tried out rental 'segways' These are small 'person carriers' that balance themselves as you stand on them (I have read since that some police departments are actually using). They have upright handles on which one pushes to go forward and pulls back to stop. One turns left or right to go in any required direction. It is never too late to try something different, even if it's a little scary!! The kids still love to tease me and Peggy took a picture of me on it and sent it with the following comment to the:

'Fambly' After you all left, Mom, not satisfied with a life time achievement award, decided to try riding a motorcycle. The Harley's were all rented so she tried one of these babies. Whoowee, what a rush!

Peggy

(Peggy takes after her Dad and always
makes things such fun!)

Some Fun After the Award

Chapter 26

Kids as Adults, Being Parents, 1990-2007

Parenthood

While it was generally accepted when I was growing up that mothers of small children did not work, most of the time I enjoyed the about 20 years that I spent not working but raising my children. To me parenthood was never anything that frightened me but only something exhilarating and to be enjoyed. The things that I did fear when they got older were the ordeal of having them learn to drive and the possibility of their experimentation with alcohol and drugs in high school and college. Many of the things that I should have feared I didn't learn about until much later when it was too late to do anything about them. Fortunately they seem not to have made much difference. Our major success seems to be that, over the years, we have always had good relations with all of our children. And most have made reasonable successes of their lives and seem mostly pretty happy. When they come to visit there is always much talk and laughter and we always enjoy having them.

What have they learned from us? I think they have learned many of the same things that we learned from our parents. Family is always very important, Idealism, honor and hard work always matter. Learning and education should be primary and they all seem to agree with this. All our children are excellent readers and have all completed one or more college degrees. As parents, I believe that my husband and I did a better than average job. Certainly over the years there were hard times, but most of the time we had enough money to care for them reasonably well intellectually and physically. We always loved and enjoyed all of our children. We taught them to love and respect nature, the wilderness in particular. We did a lot of camping and backpacking with them both as a family and with scout troops. Both Larry and I were Boy and Girl Scout leaders extending what we did as a family to the wider community.

While Larry and I didn't always agree on discipline, our differences were minor enough that they didn't make much trouble. As I said above, one thing that really frightened me was the possibility of drug and alcohol use and abuse during their high school and college years. I'm sure they did some drinking and playing around, but it seems to have been limited enough or they were able to handle it well enough, that it didn't interfere with their education.

Differences if I Could Take a Fresh Start

The one thing that I would do differently if I could start over again, is to spend more time talking to the kids about marital relations, sex and handling money. Why? Because both the twins seemed to have trouble getting their lives straight. Barb married at 21 and was divorced a year or so later. Too young, I thought. But she was married and divorced again a few years later. Finally when she was older she found a husband in Australia and this seems to be lasting. They have a lovely little girl, Samantha, and this marriage has lasted for over 10 years. Betty managed to get pregnant while in her sophomore year in college. She didn't tell us about it until after the baby was born so we weren't able to make arrangements for him and he was given up for adoption to my great regret. I never even got to see my first grandson. I blamed myself for not talking to her earlier about how strong the sex drive is and being careful. Our family tradition was not to talk about things like that. One of my sisters recently told me that when she began to menstruate, she had been told nothing and thought that she was dying of cancer until she found someone outside the family to explain things.

Others have trouble keeping track of checks and money and some have problems with income tax. As a child, I was never really taught about keeping track of money myself but mostly figured it out on my own, so I guess that I expected them to do the same. Partly, I always waited for the children to ask and they never did. Guess I should have brought things up first and not waited. Somehow the years went by and there was never as much time to do all the things that I wanted to do or should have done but I can't change that now. All of the children have done reasonably well despite my lapses. Most have reasonably steady, stable jobs and apparently good and satisfying, to them, marriages. They are all very good to us and we have excellent relations with all of them. Not that we always agree with or approve of what they do. They seem to enjoy coming to visit and we love to have them along with their spouses, children, and pets, mostly dogs, but even cats at one time.

Our Children

Here I will introduce my children as adults and tell a little about their more recent events. I will start with the oldest, Pete, and continue to the youngest, Bill. The picture of the seven is the one that I used for my award talk. Later are pictures of each with his or her spouse.

Peter (Pete) Larned Asprey

As our first, he is special in many ways and has always been the family leader. He was the only one for the first four and a half years of our marriage. He seems very outgoing and has many friends. His wife Cindy is somewhat quieter, but also very friendly and wonderful about keeping track of things and always knows when appointments and such are.

Pete has become convinced that he has Aspergers Syndrome because he can't remember names and faces which is apparently one of the symptoms. It also seems to go along with being somewhat introverted and technically inclined. A test for it which he took some years ago (taken from a magazine article), gave him a score in that region. When I took the test, my score was also on the edge of that region but Larry's wasn't.

Pete and Cindy Cornil

Barb and Dave Pettus

As described before, several years ago, Pete and Cindy unfortunately lost their house to a flood. They have recovered from that and the disastrous surgery that left Cindy handicapped. Pete seems also to have recovered from his appendicitis and heart attack We felt so very lucky that two of these things happened here where we had plenty of space and while not the kind of visit one wishes for, it was a great chance to see something of both of them and lend them a helping hand when they needed it.

Despite all the troubles they have had, they have two wonderful children. Their son, David Gene has a BA degree in Computer Analysis from UC in Turlock, CA, and has since received an MBA from the prestigious Wharton School of Business. David now works in the Silicon Valley, South of San Francisco, in Information Technology. It was recently announced by Zeus Technology that Dave was appointed Vice President for Technology Strategy. He has recently made Pete and Cindy Grandparents, and me a great-grandmother all for the first time. In June 2007 they took me out to meet Anna Rane who was born on April 30. 2007 to David Gene, and his permanent friend Lana who is a Doctor from Sweden. When they get to it, I am sure they will get married. While there, I even got to meet Lana's mother and stepfather who are also doctors in Sweden.

Pete's daughter, Jenna, has a BA from the University of Wyoming and an MBA from NMSU when she stayed with us. Jenna is married to an Australian, Christopher Keane. They live north of San Francisco where she works on teaching through the internet and live seminars. On the June 2007 visit, I had a chance to see Jenna who was about to start a seminar for hundreds of people on her specialty, Options Trading. All the impressive banners and displays had been generated by her husband, Chris.

While visiting there I stayed with my daughter Peggy and had a chance to visit with her children Susan and Erik. Also Bill, Susan and Amelia came down from Washington State to see me and also to visit Susan's mother who has just moved to the bay area from Bloomfield, Illinois. It was quite a great visit.

Barb & Betty, Our Twins

While they are left and right identical twins and were hard to tell apart when they were small, there are surprising difference, despite having the same genetic inheritances, which have become even more apparent since they are older. The differences in their degrees and jobs is typical. Betty with an MS in Animal Genetics worked in the lab at Los Alamos and later at the Physical Science Labs at NMSU, while Barb, with an MBA, works for Loveland, CO, keeping their municipal computer records.

A recent TV show on how great the differences between identical twins can be, concluded that it was a result of epigenetics. An example they gave, had one twin being completely outgoing and planning for college while the other was completely autistic and unable to learn. This is much more extreme than the differences between ours.

Elizabeth (Betty) Asprey Streitelmeier

As the first of our twin daughters and the left handed one, Betty has been successful as a microbiologist first in the drug industry in Indianapolis, IN, and later at the Los Alamos National Laboratory (LANL). After the MS degree, in Animal Genetics from University of California, Davis she started a job in Indianapolis, IN, at American Monitor. At this time, she married David Strietelmeier a fellow worker who had a daughter, Jody, from a previous marriage. They worked on starting a plant in Belfast, Northern Ireland for a couple of years. After they returned, when the company failed, she worked at several jobs in Indianapolis, one of which, Los Alamos Diagnostics (LAD), transferred them to Los Alamos. In the early

80's, before they moved to Los Alamos, they had a son, Joseph (Joey) Ryan.

They came to Los Alamos (LAD) just at the time that we had already put our house on the market and were planning the move to Las Cruces. They wanted to buy our house so we took it off the market and rented to them for a while until they were established enough to actually buy it. They spent quite a bit of time and money rebuilding and remodeling the house they bought from us. It still seems strange to see the house we lived in so long changed completely. During the time in Los Alamos, David's daughter Jody had a child back in Indianapolis (Alyssa) and when she ended up in foster care, David and Betty decided to take custody and raise her. They had always planned to adopt her officially but never got to it. Betty has now decided to actually adopt her officially. Jody has since married and had three more children but is not well enough off to take Alyssa back.

When LAD failed through mismanagement, Betty found employment first as a contractor and later as a Staff Member at LANL where she was very successful. An example of how well she did is the Distinguished Performance Award she received in 1993. They said such nice things as "She has superb laboratory skills, ingenuity and creativity, and she continually improves her skills and knowledge through course work and an awareness of current literature . . . . Her dedication and laboratory skills were crucial in establishing and extending the national role in soil and surface decontamination of the Laboratory's chelator design and application programs" They talk about her "magic hands" in the laboratory and end with "Her contributions to Los Alamos programs and her dedication and creativity in science are truly outstanding". She seems to have inherited her Dad's skills in the laboratory. To say the least, we are very proud of her.

A year ago, in February, 2006, her husband David died suddenly. Since she was also not happy with how things were now going for her at LANL, she decided the following May, to take early retirement and move to Las Cruces and share my house. She and her step daughter, Alyssa, now live with me and for most of the past year she has worked at the Physical Sciences Laboratory at NMSU. She is continuing to work on her doctorate in Microbiology which she still hopes to get someday soon.

Her son Joey, after graduating from Los Alamos High School, attended Denver Automotive and Diesel College in Denver. He now has a very good job as an auto mechanic in the Denver area. Recently when I was in Colorado, we visited his workplace and his employer seems very pleased with him. He is thinking of going to Colorado School of Mines later on but meanwhile is well established and self-supporting.

Barbara (Barb) Alice Asprey

Barb is the second born of our twin daughters. With her BS in Mathematics and MBA from NMSU, she spent many years in Australia. Before that she was married twice for brief periods, and had worked for a while for the Department of Agriculture in Las Cruces and for a while for Sandia National Laboratory in Albuquerque. She even worked for a while with her brother Pete there. They apparently argued so much that many of their coworkers thought that they hated each other. Not so, they are just both strong minded with their own ideas and not backward about expressing them. Pete says that Barb was such a great programmer that many of the things she wrote are still used today, many years later. After her years in Australia and her marriage to David Pettus as described before, they worked in Atlanta, GA, for a while.

They then both got jobs near Denver, CO, where they have been ever since. They have bought a "farm" in the hills west of Denver and while still working, on the side, are raising alpacas and each has their own horse. along with a colt. They have bought some property near Pagosa Springs, CO, and hope to retire there eventually and build their dream house. Their daughter Samantha is starting her Sophomore year in high school and is doing very well. She is also principal flautist in the school band.

Robert (Bob) Russell Asprey

Bob has always been one of my most adventurous and irreverent children. After starting at NMSU in Mechanical Engineering and then shifting to Electrical Engineering, he spent some years working in the Computer Center. After marriage to Joan Joyce (also known as Jojo) Raabe, who had a son (Clint) from a previous marriage and spending some years in Las Cruces, they both found jobs in Huntsville, AL, Bob with Brown-Teledyne and Jo working for local Doctors as a radiology technician. The company, CYBEX, that he and friends started on the side, making special long distance connectors for computers, was finally successful enough to go public. Before it did, we invested in some of it's stock and Bob gave gifts of stock in it to his parents and all siblings. Since it increased in value very rapidly, this was a large bonus for the whole family and very generous and thoughtful of him. A few years ago CYBEX merged with another company and they became AVOCENT.

Bob and Jojo were quite affluent for a while but they have had reverses partly as a result of mistreatment by the FAA (Federal Aviation Administration). An inspector there decided he didn't like the CEO of SunPacific, a small aviation company that Bob was involved with, so refused to give them a license despite a spotless safety record. According to Bob, he was also the same inspector who looked into one of the Saudi Arabians who was acting suspiciously when taking flying lessons in Tucson before 9/11 but gave him a pass. Had the inspector been more alert perhaps 9/11 might not have happened. Besides losing lots of money, Bob was very frustrated at the arrogance and incompetence of bureaucracy, both the FAA and IRS.

Bob and Joan J (Jojo) Raabe

Peggy and Richard (Dick) Lyon

For some years after Bob and Jo moved to Las Cruces and bought a house, Bob continued his dream of being an inventor and entrepreneur. He spent half his time here in Las Cruces and half in Huntsville where they still owned a small house in which they had lived during their early years in Huntsville. When Jojo went back with him one time, she said there was not even a place to sit down as the whole house had been turned into a research lab. This might be Bob's idea of fun but not hers! She insisted that the bedroom should be exempt and not part of the lab.

Jojo started an FBO (Fixed Base Operation, selling gas and food to passing aviators) at the Las Cruces airport called Adventure Aviation. While not too successful, it continues on. In 2002 Bob and

Jojo were both given honorary PhDs by their Alma Mater, NMSU. At graduation a film was shown about their background and history and all that they have done. We were very impressed and proud of both of them.

Margaret (Peggy) Asprey (Lyon)

As described before, Peggy, our third daughter, started college at UNM in Albuquerque. Then when her big sister Betty went out to UC Davis to go to graduate school, she decided to go with her. There she received her BS in Mathematics and Computer Science. She liked the general area so well, she found a job in Mountain View, CA. While there she has worked for several companies. At one time she worked for Ames Research and worked on a satellite that was to orbit Venus. She was also involved in a startup, DAVID Systems. This last was not as successful as it should have been and failed, probably as a result of bad management. I have heard recently that much of the programming that she worked on there was good enough that it's alive and still running in routers for the internet.

During this period, she met and married a very nice young man, Richard (Dick) Lyon, who is third of nine children from our neighboring city, El Paso, TX. He has an EE degree from Cal Tech and after working for Apple Computer for many years, worked for a while as a researcher for a start up company called FOVEON started with Carver Meade. They use Artificial Intelligence (AI) to make a control which does for a camera something like what the fovea in our eyes do. Recently he has started to work for GOOGLE as a researcher.

After being married for a few years, Peg & Dick, produced a lovely little girl, Susan Margaret, and two years later, a nice little boy, Erik William. Peg has put her successful career on hold like I did, to raise her lovely children. And these children are doing very well. Susan spent her Junior year in High school, as an exchange student in France. All her classes were in French and she seems to have done very well. What a great experience that must have been. Last year she was a sophomore at Princeton in New Jersey which she seems to like very much.

This Summer (2007) during my visit to Los Altos, I was fortunate to visit with Susan before she went off to Vietnam for a six week seminar run by Princeton. It seems strange that she would voluntarily go to Vietnam which has so many bad memories from the sixties. But I guess that it is no more strange than that I spent a year in Germany and worked with the Japanese, after my feelings during World War II.

Also there, recovering from surgery on a bone in his foot, was my grandson Erik who will be a high school senior next year. He is also in the throes of deciding on which college to consider for the following year. When Susan was making that fateful decision two years ago, Peggy called me asking my advice on where she should go. I suggested she flip a coin, which may sound frivolous for such an important decision. But actually it's not, as it changes the 'playing field' a surprising amount. It forces you to act as if you had made the decision one way.

One may not follow up on the coin flip but deciding arbitrarily helps you find out what you really want.

Thomas (Tom) Arthur Asprey

As described in Chapter 16, Tom also attended NMSU but unlike his other brothers Bob and Bill, who changed courses in midstream, he went straight through to get his Electrical Engineering degree. After finding a job in silicon valley as a chip designer with Hewlett-Packard, he has worked for them ever since, but later in Colorado Springs, CO. Some time ago in Colorado, he and his group were transferred to Intel, although in the same location as before.

As described in Chapter 20, he met Carol Fitchette, moved to Colorado, bought a house and eventually got married. They have had no children because they have decided that it's not for them for a number of reasons. One is that both have very demanding jobs, both at Hewlett-Packard. They have continued to work full time and spent a lot of time and money remodeling the house they bought in Boulder, CO. During the remodeling, they bought a cabin in the mountains where they lived while still continuing to work full time. Tom retired over a year ago and has been a tremendous help to me during my time of grief. For a while he came down to Las Cruces every few months to check on me and do anything he could for me. Then in Spring, 2007, Carol also finally decided to retire.

Tom and Carol Fitchette

Bill and Susan Henry

Since then they have been spending time traveling and taking some fabulous trips. The first was up to Alaska with me to see the northern lights in Feb. and Mar of 2006. Next was to New Zealand and the Fiji Islands. Last was to Patagonia and southern South America. This Fall, they along with Pete took another trip down the Grand Canyon of the Colorado River on dories. They did this a few years ago and enjoyed it so much that they did it again and took Tom's brother Pete and Carol's brother David from France along with a friend of Pete's from Albuquerque.

William (Bill) John Asprey

As our youngest surviving child, Bill is just about as different from Tom as he possibly could be which is undoubtedly a source of many of their fights. As described before, after graduating from Los Alamos High School, they went off to NMSU together. Bill decided first to major in Mechanical Engineering and then changed to Physics. After his first year, he signed up for a co-op program where he would take alternate semesters working at various jobs. His first job was with the county sewage plant of Arlington, TX, between Fort Worth and Dallas. He didn't think too much of that but stuck it out. That of course is part of the co-op idea to find out what you do and don't like. His next job was on an oil survey ship in the North Sea off the north coast of Scotland. He survived that and was interested enough to major in oil geophysics. With time off for co-op jobs, he took a lot longer to finish up but he finally did, even getting an MS in Geophysics.

Chapter 27

Times of Disaster
(2006-2007)

Cardioversion

Back in December of 2004 when I was having a routine colonoscopy, one of those unpleasant things one undergoes hoping to head off even more unpleasant things like colon cancer, it was discovered that I had Atrial Heart Fibrillation. The colonoscopy procedure was stopped immediately and I was sent at once to a Cardiologist and put on appropriate drugs. They didn't seem to make much difference to me, however, since the fibrillation was not causing me any pain or difficulty. I would not even know that I had it except that it showed up on the electrocardiogram.

In early December of 2005, Dr Main, my heart doctor at the time, finally convinced me to let him try what he called a cardioversion because the fibrillation causes the blood to pool momentarily and can possibly form clots leading to a stroke. Because stroke is what killed both of my parents, it's something I don't like to take chances with. The procedure involves stopping your heart momentarily and immediately restarting it. He claimed that over 90% of the time when it restarts, the fibrillation goes away.

He also said that he had done hundreds with something like 95% success rate. We agreed on a date of January 3rd after Christmas. I checked with my son Bob to be sure that he would be in town because I did not want to be put under anesthesia and have my heart stopped, unless my executor and health representative was here, in case something went wrong. Since this would be the first Christmas without my Larry and so particularly painful, I decided to go visit my daughter Peggy in California from December 22 to 29th, 2005 In retrospect, I wish that I hadn't gone but it's so hard to know what's ahead.

On the 3rd of January 2006, Bob and Jojo checked me into the hospital for the procedure. As far as I could tell things went smoothly. Afterwards they took me home to recover. The next morning Bob took off on his regular periodic trip to Huntsville promising to be back a week from the following Friday. How I wish that I had asked him not to go because I needed him! He actually might have listened and stayed. But I said nothing but 'good-bye' and wished him a good trip. I didn't want him to go and he had no idea of what was to come.

Heart attack

Two days later I began having intense chest pains. Fortunately my daughter Betty was still here and took me to the Emergency Room at the Hospital. Apparently I was having congestive heart failure, partly because, I thought, that for several days before and after the procedure, I had not taken my usual diuretics which I have taken for unidentified water retention for nearly forty years. The Doctor didn't agree and insisted that he had never had anything like this happen. He thought it was probably because I was unusually sensitive to the drugs that he had given me after the cardioversion and he cut the dosages way back as well as giving me a strong intravenous diuretic with Magnesium. After about five days in the hospital, they sent me home and I seemed to be recovering OK.

A week later on a Monday evening, Bob called me from Huntsville to see how I was doing after my heart attack. We talked for nearly an hour about this and that. One thing he said that I remember particularly vividly, was that he still wasn't feeling too well and if he wasn't better in the morning he was going to see a Doctor. Oh, how I wish that I had a recording of that conversation but didn't realize that it was to be our last. We hadn't seen much of him over Christmas partly because I was out in California, and partly because he had not been feeling too well and spent much of the time in bed. Again, in hindsight, he should have gone to the doctor then. But that was not enough to keep him from his periodic trip to Huntsville to continue his beloved inventing.

Most Painful Surprise

The very next evening after that last conversation, Jojo came bursting into the house with the awful news. "Bob is Dead". My response was "He can't be. I just talked to him last night and he was fine then". But no, it seems it was real. His close friend Remigius Shattus to whom he talked almost every day had been unable to get a response from him that morning of January 17, so came by the Huntsville house but couldn't get in. The neighbor, Debbie, who watched the house when Bob was in Las Cruces, saw the stranger trying to get in, and also got worried. She had a key so came over and found him dead on the bathroom floor. The sheriff was called and the body was taken away. The sheriff didn't realize that an autopsy was to be performed so didn't refrigerate the body immediately. So by the time the autopsy was performed, they could not even determine how long he had been dead or the immediate cause of death.

To my deep regret, we will never really know how or why he died. His son Clint and friend Remigius both think he might have been murdered because of some of his inventions. But apparently there wasn't enough obvious evidence of a crime for the police to follow up. Jojo told me that there wasn't even a police report of the incident. Remigius says there are many things that to him don't add up and Clint says that Bob had been carrying a gun for sometime for self protection but doesn't know why And it's true that the previous fall when Bill and I were towing the helicopter for him, he had warned Bill to keep an eye out for anyone following us. But I brushed that aside as fantasy. My personal conclusion is that it was most probably a stroke because both my parents and one grandfather, also in his fifties, died of stroke. Bob was also very bad about taking care of himself as evidenced by the time a few years ago when he had an almost ruptured, badly infected gallbladder. He seldom went to a Doctor unless pushed by his wife. He also, like his older brother Pete is not very aware of pain. And certainly it was his choice to be by himself doing the inventing he loved when he died so no one was there to help him. All I do know is that one of the most important people in my life was gone very suddenly and unexpectedly. In many ways he had begun to substitute for Larry for me as someone to talk things over with. I was still recovering from the loss of my beloved husband Larry, to say nothing of the recent congestive heart failure, and this shock really overwhelmed me. The world had lost an original and imaginative person who had so much to contribute.

Bob Asprey
Such a Loss to All of Us

Holding on to the Happy Memories

Now I must try to hold on to every happy memory that I can. One of them was an impressive bit of fame which came for Bob in 2001 when he and Jojo were both given honorary PhDs by their alma mater, NMSU, in recognition of all the things that they had done over the years. A film about them was presented to the graduates to encourage them to go forth in the world and do likewise, in particular bring fame and fortune to the university.

One of my happiest memories of Bob are of the times he played the guitar for singing during some of our trips. He was almost completely self taught but had a good natural talent. Anything that we could think of to sing he could make a usually successful attempt to play. A few times he even joined Pete, also on the guitar, and me on the piano for a trio. One particular time shortly before he died we had a particularly memorable and enjoyable session. Some kind person even took a picture of the three of us playing. At the time I thought that we would have many more such sessions but it was not to be. I will have to continue to play with only Pete for company.

A Last Time Playing
With Pete and Bob

We are still trying to follow up on a patent for an invention he made of a Magnetic Thrust Engine that might be very useful for satellite maneuvering. He had submitted it with my name on it the October before he died and I had named it a MATHEN for Magnetic Thrust Engine, which name he seemed to like. He often talked with me about it at length and I checked all his mathematics to be sure he hadn't made any obvious mistakes there. But when it came to the mechanics of building things Larry had been more help. One thing I remember very vividly about Bob was that any time I had a problem with anything mechanical or electrical around the house, I just had to mention it and he was like a trout after a fly. For him a problem was just an entertaining puzzle to be solved.

Some Memories of Larry That Bob Wrote

Shortly after Larry had died the year before, Bob had written up some of his memories of his Dad and of his youth and I found this write-up in a folder with the patent shortly after Bob died, so his brother Tom transcribed it as best he could. Bob's handwriting was so bad that it's amazing he did as well with it as he did. From that huge list here are a few incidents that describe a bit of the kind of original person Bob was. And of course reading it over has brought back some memories to me.

He of course remembered building the swimming pool and screened porch as well as building our own canoe during Espanola days. We had help with these from a young Priest, Father Sierra, from the local parish. He and Larry had become good friends and even tried to quit smoking together one day when they were driving somewhere to a meeting. They made an agreement that if either ever smoked again, they had to put $20.00 in the church poor box. They said that they were both so tight that the thought of the cash would keep them from smoking. It worked for Larry but unfortunately not Father Sierra. We heard later that he had fallen for the addiction and I like to assume put the money in the poor box.

Bob particularly remembered the parties we held in Espanola for Larry's work group at LASL. They were really wild with usually a keg of beer, swimming, singing, barbecues and lots of jokes and games of various kinds. To the children they must have been quite exciting as there were always many young graduate students there, some of whom recalled these parties when they heard about Larry dying. Bob also recalled smuggling a pint of wine into the Espanola hospital when Larry was in for surgery one time Don't know what the doctor would have thought of that had he known. Bob and Larry always enjoyed sharing drinks. He remembered visitors day at the lab where he had a chance to see a little of what his parents worked on. He remembered packing, hunting and fishing trips as well as gardening in the spring. By summer I guess it was too hot to be much fun but they did a lot of it especially irrigating the large garden.

Bob remembered canoe trips, especially one on the Snake River. Tom, who was along on that one, tells of Bob jumping out one time to stabilize the canoe when the one he shared with Larry almost tipped over. Ellen Wilkerson (a friend from Colorado who taught canoeing) and was with Tom in the other canoe, called to ask if they were all right, and across the water, they heard from Bob, "Damn! I got water in my beer". Tom said sardonically "Yeah, they're all right"

Bob was always good at telling jokes. One time on a backpack trip, his brother Pete tells of trying to learn from Bob one of his favorites. Pete was having trouble catching on when he suddenly realized it was different each time. Bob was just making it up as he went along. No wonder it was hard to memorize!

This is a quote from the list, probably edited by Tom when he transcribed it. "Tom and Pete were having trouble removing an old water heater from Pete's RV, getting sweaty, tired and bloody. Bob walks up and smiles and says to Pete "Where's your scrap pile?" Bob hooks odd pieces of metal together to make an instant tool, breaks the water heater loose and walks away. Leaving both of his brothers standing there in awe.

In college, Bob owned a dark olive-green, 5 speed, Fiat 124 coupe. Since it was an Italian made car, he affectionately called it the 'spaghetti machine'. Bob was always "adjusting", fixing and just tinkering with it. He told me of one time when he had the transmission all apart and he just sat back and admired the complexity of such a machine. And of course he got it all back together again successfully.

Here's another quote from the list. "Bob had many "El Corral" stories. El Corral was a redneck cowboy bar in Las Cruces that was in business during Bob's college years. Just going in there looking like Bob would get you in a fight. One time he and Bill went in to "entice" some "entertainment". They escaped on the RUN and drove off in the spaghetti machine. Bob would go in wearing sandals and a holey T-shirt with "very dirty T-shirt" written on it". Bob loved beer, theories and bicycling. He worked out that if he rode his bicycle to a bar, he could drink a pitcher of beer before riding back with minimal weight increase.

Bob was an eager inventor, usually with whatever was at hand. He built an igniter unit for Bill's motorcycle from a lamp dimmer. He also built a wheel cutter for a toy car project Pete was working on. Pete had mentioned the problem one day. Some time later a package with a device to solve the problem arrived in the mail from Bob. He also built an automatic transmission like that for a car, but for a bicycle. Unfortunately he was not so good with marketing and business skills. So most of his inventions never made it to market.

In Las Cruces and Alabama, Bob had a huge but gentle St. Bernard-Labrador cross named Daisy. Betty remembered going for a walk with them followed by a line of 'Daisies' kitties. Jojo and Bob had so fallen in love with New Mexico chili that they grew large amounts of it back in Alabama. Everyone had told them it wouldn't grow there but it turned out to do very well.

In the days when Bob had his own plane, he flew Pete and his son David up to Alaska for some sightseeing and fishing. Apparently a very successful and enjoyable trip for all of them. Along the way Bob decided to play a joke on his brother Pete. Bob gradually tilted the plane slightly by slowly lowering the angle of attack. This made the mountain in the plane's path look very high and Pete to doubt his navigation, not to mention getting an adrenaline rush. Bob got a good laugh before restoring the trim of the plane and flying easily over the high mountain.

Bob, Pete and Son David on Alaska Trip

Another Disaster in February

Less than a month later on February 15th, Betty called to tell us the sad news that her husband, David Strietelemeier, had also died suddenly of heart problems. Jojo decided to have her pilot fly her up to be with Betty and asked if I wanted to go and of course I did. So we flew up to Santa Fe, rented a car and drove up to Los Alamos to spend two days with Betty so she wouldn't be so alone in her time of sadness right after his death. His funeral was to be about ten days later but since Tom, Carol and I had signed up for a trip to Alaska partly to visit Pete and partly to see the Northern Lights, we were unable to attend because it was too late to cancel. Barbara and Peggy came to represent the Asprey family, while his daughter Jody and his son Joey were also there. David had many friends around Los Alamos as did Betty so there was a huge crowd there for the funeral without us.

Before David died Betty had been talking about the possibility of moving down to Las Cruces and had even been looking at houses because there would not be room for all three of them, Betty, David and Alyssa, to live with me. However with David dead and Larry gone, there was room for Betty and Alyssa to live with just me. So when Betty was able to find a job with the Physical Sciences Laboratory at NMSU, our local university, she made her decision to retire early on May 1st and start work down here in Las Cruces.

Life Continues On

Although after the triple tragedy, life continued on, I was still overwhelmingly sad. In fact my grief was so intense over the loss of my husband and then my son that I had trouble getting up in the mornings or making myself do anything at all. One particular morning in April when Betty was here getting ready to move down, I felt a dizziness and numbness in my left arm. I had an appointment that morning with the doctor so went over with Betty who was down getting ready for the move. When the Doctor examined me and heard my story, he decided that with my history, I was probably having a small stroke or TIA (Transient Ischemic Attack) and called 911 to take me to the hospital where I stayed for five days. Because I have had no more trouble, I think that it was a false alarm.

The first week in May, Betty did retire from the Los Alamos Laboratory and she and Alyssa moved down to stay in the house and help look after me. At first, the job with the Physical Sciences Laboratory at the local university, NMSU, seemed successful. She also hoped that she would be able to continue with work on her PhD on the side.

Then in June, Pete and Cindy came down from Alaska and decided that they wanted to stay here for a while and since there wasn't room in my house, their children, Jenna and David, decided to buy a rental house for them where they could stay for the time being and not have to spend all the time in their RV. The house they found is a couple of miles away but close enough that it takes only about five or ten minutes to get back and forth. We have seen a great deal of them for a while over the past year although they have been taking trips from time to time. That Summer, I also decided that at 84, it wasn't very smart for me to keep driving with my dizziness, failing vision and depression. Pete and Cindy were talking about buying a small car so they didn't need to drive their huge truck all the time, which uses so much gas, so I lent them my RAV-4. The understanding was they would take me places whenever I needed to go and this has worked out well. I have driven very little since then.

In that July, Pete spent several weeks gold mining and fishing up in Alaska with his friend Bob Bikerstaff from Albuquerque. Pete seems to have developed quite a passion for Alaska. I think he would live there except for the fact that it is so far away from his family, especially his children and now grandchild. Cindy stayed with us for at least part of the time while he was away that Summer. so she wouldn't be all by herself. But oh were we all glad to have Pete back on his return.

Another Disaster

Along in August, Pete, Cindy and I talked about going up to Washington State in September to visit my youngest son Bill and his family who had just moved up there that Summer. Suddenly in mid September, in the middle of the night Pete had a heart attack and Cindy took him to the hospital emergency room. After a day or two of tests, the doctors decided he had two blocked arteries and they would need to put in stents. This is a device which is pushed through the blockage of an artery and then is 'opened' up to hold the artery open and allow the blood to flow through. However when the Surgeon tried to do this, he couldn't even get through the blockage so had to do a double bypass instead to keep him alive at all. Pete felt so terrible when he came out of the anesthetic that he wished that he had died instead. However, we are all so glad that he didn't. We have lost enough family for one while.

The hospital has a very impressive rehab (rehabilitation) center with a nurse available who monitors the patient regularly to be sure he's pushing hard enough but not too hard Since the surgery, Pete has been taking full advantage of this rehab center, where he exercises several times a week. The nurses wish that others would take advantage of it because they know that otherwise the patients will be back in the hospital again soon. Pete is very determined that this won't happen to him. This support has made a huge difference and he seems to be recovering very well even if he is not quite the same as he was before. At least he no longer wishes that he had died and seems to be enjoying life again. And was it lucky that they decided to settle into the house in Las Cruces before the heart attack happened and were not still wandering around the country in the RV.

Trip to Northwest

While Pete was still in the hospital, I found out that Jojo's sister Ginnie was going in September up to Portland to visit her daughter Ginger there and since I couldn't go by myself, she was kind enough to let me tag along with her to make the visit that Pete and I had talked about earlier but now he was unable to make. I am so happy to see that Bill, Sue and my beloved little Amelia have made a happy transition to the area. Bill seems to be much better at sea level and Sue seems very content with her new teaching job up there. They found a nice small house not too far from the ocean in Hoquiam, WA, and Amelia has made many new friends and is doing very well in school. Susan is even able to ride a bike to her teaching job. Bill has a garage large enough to continue his experiments which he is vigorously pursuing. But I very much miss having them close enough for the occasional visits from Alamagordo. that we enjoyed so much for so long.

Serious Problem with C Diff

The winter of 2006-2007 passed fairly peacefully but I still was not feeling very well. The previous Summer, I had begun to have continuing mouth sores that would not go away. Then in October I began to have unidentified stomach pains which again were ongoing. Then in February, I developed an ear infection for which they gave me a version of Penicillin and this brought on drastic problems. Looking back, I can see that the previous problems were probably the onset of this new problem. I began to have constant diarrhea and couldn't eat much. I eventually lost over 20 lb. It finally got bad enough that in March they put me in the hospital and after calling in a specialist, it was found that I had Clostridium Difficile (or C Diff)!

This is one of the worst bacteria that kills three times as many people each year as MRSA that are spread in hospitals as spores and have become resistant to most antibiotics. What happened in my case was that the variety of normal bacteria in my gut had been holding the C Diff at bay but the ordinary ones had been killed off by the penicillin leaving the deadly one free range to attack me The one antibiotic exception is Vancomycin, and it took two complete prescriptions of this along with stomach bacteria pills which C Diff apparently doesn't like, Culterelle, to get me over it. Apparently, I was lucky to survive since a high percentage of the patients who get it die from it and at my age it was pretty severe. It was nearly two months before I began to feel anything like myself.

Finally by June, when Betty was to be gone for several weeks and Pete & Cindy were going out to California also for several weeks so that I would be left alone. I decided to go out to Los Altos with Pete to visit my daughter Peggy and her family and also see my new Great Grand Daughter, Anna Rane, who had been born that Spring. As an added bonus, Bill, Sue and Mimi came down to visit for a few days so I got to see them too. It was a fabulous visit. Then in July, when again my supporters were all going to be gone for a while, I decided to go along with some of them up to Colorado to visit my other children, Barb and Tom. I spent several days with Barbara and her family. Barb, Betty and I went to see the opera, Cinderella. Then Clint and I went up to Boulder for a few days with Tom and Carol. It was so great to again feel like myself after that terrible time in Spring.

Chapter 28

Successes and The Final Journey, 2007-2012

Sunset and evening star
And one clear call for me
And may there be no moaning of the bar
When I put out to sea.

. . .

Twilight and evening bell
And after that the dark
And may there be no sadness of farewell
When I embark.

. . .

The World and Travel

These words of Alfred, Lord Tennyson from "Crossing the Bar" say very well how I feel at 85 as I am finishing up this story. Obviously since I'm still writing, I'm still here but I know too well that it can't be for very long. I've chosen 2012 as the closing date of this chapter, because recent information about the Maya calendar in early Mexico, told about their three cycles, solar, lunar and 'great' cycle of the cosmos. It intrigues me that the cycles are calculated to coincide on my birthday December 21, 2012. They believed that the world would come to an end then. So I have made it my goal to live to see what happens on that particular date. Perhaps they believed that at least MY world would end. If I don't make it, I'm certainly ready to take my final journey into the hereafter sooner.

It's strange how different my feelings about life have evolved. I guess the flame of life is burning a bit low. For so long I was wildly eager to travel and see different parts of the world. For so long I couldn't wait to try different activities and to learn new ideas and do experiments. To me everything was an adventure. But now, of the places that I wanted to visit, I have checked off more than enough to satisfy me. Surprisingly most of the places that I've visited, while enjoyable, never quite lived up to my expectations. Canada, Europe, China, Australia, Tasmania, Africa, Alaska, Mexico and the Mediterranean Area, while fascinating, were none of them as wonderful as I expected. While there are some places to which I would vaguely like to return—Germany and Spain.—none seem to me important enough to be worth the increasing difficulty required of me to actually go there. And the places that remain on my 'still would like to visit list'—Vienna, Switzerland, India, Finland, Russia, South America, South Africa—don't seem worth the physical effort to undertake. The only journey that I really look forward to is the final one into the hereafter.

Not that I'm in pain but the remainder of life just doesn't have much appeal for me. I have no fear of dying but I want so much to be with my dear Larry again. Since I'm strongly Agnostic (not like Larry, Atheistic), I don't really have much hope of seeing him again. But if it's at all possible, I don't need to stop hoping. If there really is a Supreme Being of some sort, who brought the Universe into existence, and has another form of life to send us to, I'll be happy to go.

Larry's death is still confusing for me. I keep expecting to see him in the familiar places, like his chair and our bed. And then comes the sharp realization, 'no he's gone forever' and I remember our last kiss and his body being carried out. I keep thinking about what it must be like to die. Whatever it is that we call "spirit", must leave behind all sources of energy and all sources of input such as seeing, hearing, touching, tasting, and smelling. As far as we can tell all memories, knowledge and feelings seem to be stored in the brain so must also be left behind. And I wonder how I would know Larry's spirit without his physical presence and how would he know me without mine. I guess that I will only find that out when or if it happens. One time long ago, I had a dream of dying and after many years, it's still very vivid. I was lying on a bed and all my family was standing around crying. Gradually I turned over and I started to rise up but was watching the family standing around my body but they apparently couldn't see me going up. I went up and up and was just about to turn over again to see what was coming above when to my great disgust, I woke up!

My Successes

First, let me say that I am writing this for my family and friends and anyone else who might be interested in knowing about my life and experiences. In addition I'm writing it because I get the pleasure even at this late date of reliving some of the happier times of my life. Personally the most important thing that I have done is to make a success of my sixty-one year long marriage. Fairly unusual these days when half of all marriages end in divorce long before 61 years. My husband, Larry, from the night we met has been and always will be the most important person in existence to me. When we met in Chicago in February there was snow everywhere but to me after that night, no matter the weather, the world was warm and rose-colored. The sound of his voice sent shivers down my spine. Even after over 60 years no one else ever mattered so much, and both my husband and I felt very lucky to have found each other and were still deeply in love when he died two years ago at almost 86. And of course that successful marriage has, I believe, partly led to the success and happiness of our seven children, our most important joint production. And once my children were all in school, I found that I could have my professional dream sequentially after the first.

From being a scared little girl and the usual lost teenager, many exciting things have happened to me or at which I felt successful. While it is sad that the Atom Bombs that we worked on had to be dropped on civilians, under the circumstances, I believe it was forced on us by the Japanese Military. Actually as many were killed earlier in one night in the fire-bombing of Tokyo as were killed at Hiroshima. When Pearl Harbor was bombed without provocation, Japan opened the door to anything that happened later. From the way they treated the Chinese, Koreans, and Filipinos, perhaps they had to be stopped. It was almost as if they were in competition with Hitler for who could behave the worst at treating innocent bystanders. And I am not ashamed to have made a contribution to that historical development.

My husband's brother, Bob (Robert B) Asprey, who was with the Marines who took over after the surrender of Japan, told us of what he saw on Japanese beaches. They had prepared an awful reception for our troops. He and I believe that many more lives, both American and Japanese, were probably saved by ending W.W.II so abruptly than were lost by the atom bombs. Additionally, it seems to me that warfare never really solves anything. When it's all over, the whole world only has to rebuild everything and we just have less in total for everyone on the planet. Many people have suffered and died and for what? But I guess that when there are monsters like Hitler, Stalin and Osama bin Laden, loose in the world, war seems to be unavoidable.

Apparently my 'second life' after College Graduation was worthy of recognition. As described earlier, my graduation was picked up by the national news and was announced on the radio. I received dozens of congratulatory letters including one from the Governor of New Mexico. Graduation was probably one of the high points of my life after meeting Larry and having my children.

I spent two years teaching Mathematics to teenagers at the Junior High level. I learned to use the biggest computers of the time and became very proficient with them at the Los Alamos National Laboratory. I worked on the biggest and, at the time, most important codes for the design of Nuclear Weapons. I then worked on codes for calculating the possibility of Nuclear Reactor Accidents, in particular Breeder Reactors. My skills allowed me to work as a visiting scientist at the KfK lab at Karlsruhe in Germany for a year. I was able to give a seminar at a national meeting of the American Nuclear Society; and to take part in a scientific exchange in China under the People-to-People Program. This last eventually led to the national ANS award described in Chapter 25. All of this gave me a lot more self-confidence than I had ever had when I was home with the kids. I relished those early years taking care of and watching our kids grow up, but I also enjoyed my second technical life.

Finally all my other less important dreams have also been realized: 1) Fly my own plane, which my husband and I did for about ten years; 2) Live abroad for a year, which Larry and I did for eleven months; 3) Design and build our own house, which Larry and I did after retiring; 4) Play piano music from memory, which I have done over the past ten years although I now find my memory failing and things don't stick too well anymore.

Who Am I?

At the beginning of this story, I asked "Where did I come from?" Now I ask "Who and what have I become?" Physically, there isn't much question that I am of the female gender. (Incidentally, I feel very sorry for the poor souls who are not quite sure which gender they are. And it makes me very angry to see these people punished and treated badly for something that, I strongly believe, is not in their control.) While I am larger than average (even though I've shrunk over the years from 5' 9" to 5' 7.5"), most of my build is clearly female. And I have a very strong 'mothering' gene. Yes, research has shown that such a thing actually exists in rats and from personal experience I'm sure that it's true in humans too. I've known some women who say frankly that they have no interest in or even like babies. From my earliest memories, I've always loved and desired babies. On the other hand, I do not share the interests of most women in things such as fashion, clothes, makeup, art and jewelry. Sometimes I think that with my passions for mathematics, science and engineering, I got an unusually large dose of testosterone from someplace probably my mother, the chess player or my dad, the engineer who liked to read encyclopedias.

Partly as a result of my hectic life of so many years, I'm restless, don't like standing around and don't sit still very often except when reading, playing the piano or writing. Usually, I'm a cheerful, optimistic, and affectionate person. I generally like people, all kinds of people, one-on-one or in small groups, although I am generally not a 'party person' and don't like large groups and purely hate crowds, particularly those at organized sports or concerts. I am an avid reader and like very much to be by myself with a magazine or a good book. While some of my passions, like travel, have diminished or disappeared, I continue to have a passion for learning more and more. There seems to be so much to learn and so little time left to learn it. As I finished this book, I was reading four books at once; two for my class on 'Crime, Justice and Society', during the day; one, a review of Biochemistry when I eat lunch; and finally one at night before I go to sleep about Schizophrenia. While editing this, I've gone on to a class in advanced Biochemistry and am reading 'Power to Save the World' by Gwyneth Cravens. It is a fabulous book! So I haven't given up yet!

My Philosophy of Life, Religion

While I was raised a Catholic and attended faithfully for many years, the services always bored me although I tried not to admit it. I don't believe in doing things halfway, so as long as I believed I tried to be very faithful, to be the best Catholic that I could and attended services regularly. Since I have left the Church, I admit that I do not miss it at all and have trouble understanding why I ever believed at all. Undoubtedly much of my Philosophy is a result of that early Catholic teaching despite having left the Church. I believe strongly in being honest and truthful. I believe that one should always be as fair and respectful as possible to everyone around you. While I don't believe in the Bible any more, I think the ten commandments codify most of the things that should order behavior. I believe that we should always take care of our own family first and then reach out to others. We used to accuse our mother of not preparing us properly for the world outside the family! If she promised us something she would do it, no matter what and always tried to treat us all fairly and evenly, which the world doesn't always do. In particular, if I come on an accident or a person in trouble, If I'm the first person there, my belief is that, like the good samaritan of the Bible, I should stop and offer any help that I am able to give.

My General Philosophy

It is not easy to reject what you were taught as a small child. For a long time I thought that I was born a Catholic and therefore I had to be one. One morning I realized that acting on my conscience is what counts and that judgment should be passed on conscience based activity. Many of the things that had always bothered me about the Church became to me obviously wrong. The treatment of Gallileo and other so-called heretics by the Catholic Church was always intolerable to me. If there is a God, which there may or may not be, I have come to believe that no human being can officially speak for Him. Nor can I believe that any book written in the past can have all the answers whether Torah, Bible or Koran. To say that one man, such as the Pope or Mohammed, can be so inspired by God that he can dictate what we can know and believe just makes no sense to me. The patriarchal attitudes and the treatment of women, divorce, abortion and birth control increasingly make no sense to me. The world simply cannot continue to accept the many people that continue to be generated by following the principal religions of the world. I have had no regrets about detaching from religion. I'm glad I don't have to explain or apologize for the pedophile priests.

One of the things that particularly bothers me about the Islamic and some other religions is the tolerance and encouragement of polygamy. It is degrading to women to expect them to be second, third or fourth wives as the Koran permits and some even encourage. Since male and female babies are born in about equal numbers, if one man has more than one wife, there will be men with no wives. So these extra men do not have the moderating influence of a woman and can have no hope of raising their own families. Often their only life choice is that of the warrior. Not having a family future, perhaps it's not surprising that they do not object to being suicide bombers.

My Personal Beliefs

Finally, I believe that everyone should contribute something to make the world a better place. One of my political projects, in addition to voting myself, has been to help out for many years at local Democratic headquarters once a week, to help elect better candidates and encourage other people to vote. Some people claim that all politicians are the same but I don't agree. I see major differences between the Democrats and Republicans. While I don't deny that they don't always live up to their ideals, the Democrats that I have met or listened to, worry about and try to do things for everyone particularly the poor and the lower classes. On the other hand, the Republicans seem to worry mostly about the wealthy and big businesses. Capitalism, which is not equivalent to Democracy, can lead to independence and innovation but also to greed and gross differences between the wealthiest and poorest. Here's where the government has to step in. It seems to me that while Communism originally tried to use the ideals which work so well in a family or very small group cannot work on a community wide scale. When it is applied to large groups such as countries, it usually ends up in Dictatorship as it did in Russia, Cuba and China. On the other hand Democracy can lead to incompetence and bureaucracy but still seems to be the best system that has been worked out yet. I've seen up close from my work with the Democratic Party how difficult it is to run for office and then lose, resulting in much money and time spent for nothing. We are very fortunate to have as many good people as we do, who will do it as hard as it is. But I don't see any other system that is likely to work any better since it gives us the freedom to change when things get too bad. Although at the moment our government has become so corrupt and inefficient that perhaps what Thomas Jefferson said needs to be considered. He thought we needed a revolution every 20 years. Maybe we do but I hope it can be bloodless.

When I first retired, I tried to help improve the world by tutoring students in math and science. I contribute financially to causes that I think are important for the well being of the world. Some of my favorites are Amnesty International (to aid people imprisoned unjustly); Planned Parenthood (to help limit the overpopulation of the world, which I think is the major cause of many wars and of Global Warming); CARE (to send aid to the children of the world); various environmental groups (to help limit damage to the environment on which we all depend) and many educational groups of all kinds, PBS (Public Broadcasting System), NPR (National Public Radio), NMSU (New Mexico State University), UNM (University of New Mexico) and CSF (College of Santa Fe). The last three have furthered my own education.

While I support the environmental groups and believe that we do need to protect the environment, I believe that they have gone off base in rejecting Nuclear Energy. They fight anything that will support and encourage it and try to insist that we don't need it. But I think with the world population growing so fast, we need all available forms of energy. I've read one suggestion that if Nuclear Energy is prevented, Nuclear Bombs will also be prevented. However, I think they are completely wrong and have it backwards. If Nuclear Energy is expanded, there is a place to put surplus Nuclear Bombs where they can't be stolen, namely in reactors as fuel!

Why am I Here?

"Why am I here and where did I come from?". Since my Husband died I seem to be asking myself this all the time. Out of the depths of my brain comes the answer perhaps out of the Catechism studied at an early age. "God made me to know Him, to love Him, and to serve Him in this world and to be happy with Him forever in the next world". It's a simple straightforward answer but it depends on a couple of basic assumptions: There is a God and He made me, neither of which I can any longer accept. When I left the Catholic Church, I agreed with James Joyce when asked if he would then become a Protestant, "I said that I had lost my faith not my mind. If I can't accept a logical reasoned faith, like Catholicism, I certainly can't accept such varieties of unreason". This is probably not an exact quote but it expresses well my reasons as best as I can remember it.

To Sum up, What do I Believe

From my overall view of the world and religion, love of Science is probably my substitute for religion. To me, it is the best way we have of knowing anything. Astronomy was my first fascination as a teenager and that has now branched out into interests in Cosmology, Physics, Chemistry, (especially Biochemistry), Mathematics, and Engineering.

So what do I believe about where I did come from and why I am here? I guess the answer to the first is 'I came by Evolution from the same process which brought all life that we know into being'. But why am I 'me', this particular person? Well for better or worse, I came from all my ancestors back through Europe and back to Africa and directly from my parents' relationship and ultimately as a result of evolutionary chance. As to the second, why I'm here, I believe that my purpose in life is to use what I am and what I have to make the world as fine a place as I can. In particular to help and support my children, my direct descendants, as best I can. At the very least tI try to leave the world better than I found it without using up any more of it's resources than I really need. And finally my own personal reason for existing is to use my brain to learn and understand all that I possibly can about life and the universe, in the place that I find myself and in the time that I have. The thing that I "know" in my innermost being is that experimentally tested Science is the best way we have of knowing anything.

Is This the Twilight of the Enlightenment?

A recent editorial by Donald Kennedy in the magazine, Science, published by AAAS (the American Association for the Advancement of Science), asked that question. Both our Country and Europe have benefitted hugely from skeptics and questioners. Many have believed in Science resulting from experiments, proof and rational thought and not in inherited dogma and simplistic, literal reading of an 'inerrant' Bible as translated by Ministers who claim to speak directly for God. But in our country this skeptical attitude seems to be losing ground. There seems to be a convergence by evangelical, dogmatic Christianity on many fronts. Instead of teaching Evolution and Geology, they are trying to teach "Creationism" in the form of so-called "Intelligent Design". They are setting our research agenda on stem cell research, based on their belief in what is "moral". Pro-life is their idea of what is 'moral' even if others don't agree. They want to teach 'abstinence only' to teen agers and not the science of sex. Is the Age of the Enlightenment coming to an end? I certainly hope not but the results of the last two elections surely seemed to result from that attitude and in the coming election, the country seems almost equally split on the subject.

Personal Ending

One morning in bed recently, I was haunted by a fragment of poetry followed by two of my last experiences with my dead husband, Larry, and son, Bob. These three cycled through and through my brain.

The poetry is from Omar Khayam:

> *"The moving finger writes and having writ moves on.*
> *Nor all your tears, nor piety nor wit*
> *Can call it back to cancel half a line."*

The memory of Larry is when we last brought him home from the hospital under 'hospice' care. As they put him on his bed in the study, an unusual place for him, he looked up at the ceiling and asked me "Why did we buy this house?" Well since we had bought the lot together, designed the house together, had it built and lived in it together for nearly 20 years, this was a strange question. To me it said that a large part of his memory was gone, but I still remember the question vividly myself and can see him ask it.

The memory of Bob is the conversation we had the night before he died. Had he not died the next day, it would probably have slipped into forgetfulness, because we really didn't say much. He promised to bring me the list of companies In which he had invested money for me. He said he would be back in Las Cruces by next Friday. And I said that I would look forward to seeing him. I remember that he said he wasn't feeling too well and if not better in the morning he would see a doctor. Well his tomorrow never came and his death froze the talk in my memory. I only wish that I could have a recording of it. And so the cycle in my brain went on and on and on.

Another recent unbelievable night has made a deep impression on me. It began in the evening when I was reading an article in Scientific American for January 2008 on Microchimerism. According to recent research, a pregnant woman and her fetus exchange cells during gestation. This means that not only do I probably have cells from my Mother but also that I also have cells from my dead son Bob hidden inside me, to say nothing of the rest of my children. I found this idea so overwhelming and exciting that I couldn't go to sleep that night until very late. After getting up to get a snack about midnight, I finally went to sleep and dreamed that my oldest son, Pete, was dead but strangely enough, I was still talking to him as we walked together to his grave. To end the night overwhelmingly, when I woke from the dream and got up to go the bathroom, on returning to bed, the moon was shining directly on my pillow and shining in my face and kept me awake for the rest of the night.

The End

And so I come to the end of my life story. At least the end of all that I'm going to write. I may make it to 100 or into the nineties but

I'm not counting on it. I have been an extremely fortunate person in so many ways. I have known many pleasures and of course a few tragedies. I have been asked, "if you could choose to be any person in the world, who would you choose?". I think that I really would rather be me than anyone else in the world that I have known about. That may be rather self centered but I really think that I've been as fortunate and happy as any person could possibly be. Another question is, if reincarnation is really true (and I really hope it is), what animal would you like to come back as? From my days of dreaming of flying, I guess that I would pick a large bird. Flying free has always appealed to me and, I would love to come back as an Eagle. There's even a song about it ending with:

> "We gotta be free, the possum and ivy,
> the bird in the tree, the bumble bee,
> We gotta be free, the eagle and me".

In my final closing, now that I'm reaching the end, I say with (apologies to) Robert Louis Stevenson:

> Under the wide and starry sky
> Scatter my ashes, and let me lie.
> Glad did I live and gladly die
> And I lay me down with a will.

> And this be the tale you tell for me
> Here she lies where she longed to be.
> Home is the traveler, home from the sea
> And the learner home from the hill.

Epilog

After further reading and thinking about things, I believe I have the answer to the question that I asked at the beginning of this book. I believe that Genetics is the primary answer to why so many of the Williams girls ended up in technical fields. While my Mother had no technical background, she did have a love of logic and complexity as shown by her passion for chess and complicated piano music. And my Father, as noted, had a passion for understanding how things worked, loved to read encyclopedias (a love I share), and could fix anything. Both of these mindsets lead to interest in science and technology so I guess it isn't too surprising that most of us children, even the girls, inherited it. The other part was an environment where reading was our primary means of entertainment and always encouraged. From what I've read about twin studies, about 60% of what a person is comes from their genes with the rest from the environment.

Unfortunately, current scientific studies seem to be principally concentrating on defective genes that cause disease rather on the promising genes that may lead to the future thinkers and inventors such as Ben Franklin, Thomas Edison, Bertrand Russell and Albert Einstein who may change our world for the better. About ten years ago when I took a course in Genetics, I thought seriously about trying to collect genetic samples from all the members of my family and doing such a study. However I really didn't have the ability or tools to actually do it so gave up. I wish someone someplace with such an ability and tools would take up the challenge. Perhaps one of my readers will consider it since it's too late for me.

Appendix A

Fan Chart of Ancestors

Here is a copy of a chart that I made some years ago to keep easy track of what records that we have of our ancestors. Much of what I have has come from my Mother, as she was quite good at digging out such things. Some she got from my Grandmother Williams and Cousin John Soule. As time passed I have added to it any information that anyone has produced. My sister Rose has given me some details that she had collected and I hope others will come up with more. I don't have anything equivalent for my Husbands family as they didn't have much in the way of records.

Index

abrv = Abbreviations